Doctor DeMarco Answers Your Questions

First Edition, September, 2000. Includes Index.

ISBN 0-9694766-4-7

Copyright Carolyn DeMarco M.D.

Published by: **Well Women Press**.

Order Line: 1-877-9361.
See Back Page For Prices.

Format, Index and Cover Design by **Douglas Toner.**

Front Cover Photograph: **Douglas Toner.**
Back Cover Photograph: **Carolyn DeMarco.**

Dedication

Victoria Ida DeMarco
And
Anna Marie

Always Remembered
In Our Hearts

Introduction

This is the age of information overload. We are being inundated with health news from newspapers, magazines, TV and the internet. The quality of the information varies from the profound to the ridiculous. In particular, health information from the net seems to be biased in favour of Western medicine and seems to scare people more than help them. With all this influx of information there is a need for guidance in order to separate the truth from the hype.

Dr. DeMarco Answers Your Questions is a book that provides answers and guidance in an easily accessible format. It is divided into three formats: Columns, (where the topic can be covered in greater detail) questions and answers, and summary fact sheets on various topics. This text was based on writings previous done for the Toronto Star, Vancouver Sun, newspapers and Health Naturally Magazine.

The topics chosen were based on those questions most frequently asked as Dr. DeMarco toured throughout the country. She has also included new research on natural remedies and topics that particularly interested her. Such as the relationship between the environment and health and the health effects of genetically modified foods.

Included are everything from natural alternatives for prozac, ritalin, migraines, osteoarthritis, ulcers, cataracts and glaucoma, to remedies for cellulite, eczema, acne and excessive hair growth.

There is a whole section on cancer, and how to find out information about alternative treatments. Another section covers diets, good fats, weight loss, and nutritional supplements. In addition, there is an excellent section on women's health issues like infertility, endometriosis, PMS, fibroids, childbirth and menopause.

As with Dr. DeMarco's first book, Take Charge of Your Body: Women's Health Advisor, this books is extensively indexed. On each page of the book, are kaleidoscopes of different scenes from the mountains surrounding Dr. DeMarco's home in British Columbia.

Dr. DeMarco Answers Your Questions is also cross-referenced with an a leading edge CD-ROM designed by Douglas Toner. This innovative CD-ROM contains the contents of Take Charge of Your Body as well as this book, Dr. DeMarco Answers Your Questions.

The content of this CD-ROM (both text and audio) is fully indexed. You can also click to any article in Dr. DeMarco Answers Your Questions book, and a voice will come on and read the article, with or without background music (your choice) against a background of striking scenes from the British Columbia interior. You can also click on any topic in the index and you will go straight to the internet, with the key search words already typed in and the results of the search instantly available. This CD-ROM can be purchased either with this book, or on its own.

About The Photography In This Book

Many times in our lives on planet earth we fail to realize than nature is what sustains us. More often than not we look for solutions that are overcomplicated and driven by our need for scientific complexity. The answer simply surrounds us. The photos you see printed in this book are a walker's view of a unique interior rain forest in British Columbia.

For the last twenty years, Carolyn DeMarco has been taking photographs of her twenty four acre land and the surrounding area in the south eastern corner of British Columbia. She says she is still amazed by the rare beauty of the river, lake and mountains in this area. The scene outside her door is constantly shifting and evolving through the seasons. Every time she looks outside her door at the day to day scenery, she is inspired and awed. New miracles appear before her eyes.

Douglas Toner, inventor and designer, has taken these photographs and incorporated them into Dr. DeMarco's book. He has made a kaleidoscope of each of these photos and used a different photo for each article in the book. The result is beautiful and truly unique. Through Doug's work the spirit of the natural world in this area shines through. The photographs are a natural accompaniment to this book on remedies from the natural world and bear witness to the power of nature to heal by its presence alone.

The West Kootenay area of British Columbia is located in the Rocky mountains of Canada. The river being photographed most often is the Slocan River, which flows from Slocan Lake. The Slocan River is one of the few undamed wild rivers left in southern British Columbia and its water still runs pure. Pure water has become one of the rarest commodities on this planet. The water quality of this area is currently being threatened by proposed logging activities in community watersheds.

For over twenty-five years, Dr. DeMarco has been championing the cause of alternative medicine. She was among the first to advocate the pro-active take charge approach to health care that is now accepted as a mainstream approach.

She obtained her medical degree from the **University of Toronto** in 1972. She has worked as a consultant in alternative medicine in both the city of **Toronto** and in rural **British Columbia**. She has been a pioneer in natural childbirth and been involved in training lay midwives. She has also lectured and given workshops across Canada and the United States.

Dr. DeMarco takes her message to the media through her many television, radio and newspaper interviews and her nationally syndicated newspaper columns. She has also lectured to both public and professional audiences across Canada and the United States on both women's health and complementary medicine.

Dr. Carolyn DeMarco is one of only a dozen medical doctors in the United States and Canada that write regularly for the lay public. For four years, she was one of four doctors writing columns for **Lifelines** in the **Toronto Star**, the largest newspaper in Canada. The column was syndicated in major newspapers across Canada, with an estimated readership of over two million. For two years, she had her own column, entitled Second Opinion, in the **Vancouver Sun**, the second largest newspaper in Canada. She was a medical advisor and major contributor to **Health Naturally**, a Canadian health magazine and **Health Counselor** an American self-help magazine with a readership of one million.

For eight years, she wrote the **For Women Only** column for **Today's Health**, a magazine distributed inside 350,000 copies of **The Globe and Mail**, with an estimated readership of over one million. She was also the medical advisor and a major contributor to **Wellness MD** a magazine focusing on complementary medicine and distributed to every Canadian doctor.

Her article, **Medical Malepractice**, is a chapter in the book **Misdiagnosis: Woman As A Disease**, published by the **People's Medical Society**. Her article on menopause is a chapter in the book **On Women Healthsharing**.

She is also featured in the **National Film Board's** documentary **Born at Home**, a film about natural childbirth.

Her media work includes the **CBC** television programs **The Journal, Prime Time News, Marketplace, Midday, Alive** and **The Best Years**. In addition she taped thirteen segments for **CBC TV's** morning series **What On Earth** which is now re-broadcast on the **LIFE** channel and twenty six segments as the weekly health columnist for the **Women's Television Network.**

Currently, she is a regular guest on **Marilyn Dennis**'s live **CITYLINE** show on **CITY-TV** broadcast nationally which introduces the concepts of alternative medicine to the public. She was featured on Dini Petty's show on alternative medicine in 1998. She took part in two programmes of the twelve part series **Uncommon Touch**, hosted by Tom Harpur on **Vision TV**.

Her book, **Take Charge of Your Body: Women's Health Advisor** has been widely acclaimed by women's groups across the continent. It provides a gold standard for women's health information. It is one of the best selling book on women's health in Canada. She has recently completed a second book called **Dr. DeMarco Answers Your Questions**. The book is accompanied by an innovative **CD-ROM**.

Carolyn DeMarco lives with her husband, a designer and innovator, in the southern interior mountains of British Columbia. She and her husband have travelled extensively. She has a organic vegetable and herb garden on their 24 acres which borders a wild river. She also maintains a part time medical office in Toronto. She is the oldest of nine children from an Italian Canadian family.

Combining Scientific & Natural Treatments

I have put together some guidelines for people who want to approach natural medicine, but don't know where to start.

1.   Use your doctor as a resource rather than as an authority.

It is essential to knock the doctor or naturopath or chiropractor off their pedestal and establish an equal relationship. If your doctor doesn't listen or treats you in a patronizing manner, then change doctors or at least get a second opinion.

2.   Educate yourself about the problem. My favourite type of therapy in my practice is bibliotherapy.

Read everything you can get your hands on, ask a lot of questions, find out, listen to tapes, go to courses, talk to as many people as you can, make use of local experts.

Educate your doctor as well. Bring him or her appropriate reading materials, especially articles from the medical literature or newsletters from self-help organizations.

3.   Seek out and create support for yourself.

Solidify your network of family and friends. People with health problems, chronic illness, pain, or disability have to learn how to say no, to delegate tasks to other family members, to know how to communicate their needs and how to ask for help. Most of all, people have to put their own health needs first.

Join a self-help group or form your own branch. Many groups have accumulated more research than most doctors will ever find time to read and offer the invaluable support of other people with the same problem. They also investigate the natural alternatives as well unusual or innovative treatments.

4.   Experiment with safer, cheaper and more sane methods of therapy.

When people turn to alternative therapies, they are using systems of healing that work to stimulate the body's own natural healing abilities. They are working with a system that assumes that normal biological milestones in a person's life are a healthy and even enjoyable part of life. They learn to listen to and trust their bodies. More importantly, they take control of their health and put it into their own hands.

Remember the following when seeking alternative care:

1.   If it works for you and has no side effects then use it.

2.   Trust your own perceptions about natural remedies and whether they are working for you. Trust your perceptions about your alternative practitioner.

3.   Ask you friends. Ask around. Find out who is the best. Consult with health networks, the internet or alternative books and magazines.

4.   Choose your alternative health care practitioner as you would any other service. By quality, experience, reputation and lack of sexism.

5.   Herbs, vitamins, homeopathic remedies rarely have severe side effects. It is possible, but difficult, to overdose on vitamins or herbs. Most vitamins are safe even in high doses. You have to take a large amount of herbs to overdose on them.

6.   Be cautious about the use of vitamins and herbs during pregnancy or breast feeding. Not all herbs can be safely used during pregnancy.

Table Of Contents

Alternative Medicine

Natural Remedies For Common Health Problems

Special Topics

Diet & Supplements

Cancer

Special Interest For Women

Gifts Suggestions

Avoid Getting Ripped Off In The Name Of Natural Medicine

Natural medicine has much to offer as an integrated system of medicine based on the astounding belief that the body has innate healing abilities. It is also a very useful adjunct to conventional health care.

However, consumers of alternative health care must be wary of products which are a panacea for every ailment, and incompetent or poorly trained practitioners. The good news is there are many ways you can ensure that you won't be ripped off in the name of natural, complementary medicine.

First, the cheapest and most effective therapy is bibliotherapy. Save yourself a lot of time and money by making full use of your local library, bookstore and the internet. Invest in some natural health reference books. Read as much as you can about your illness and both western and alternative treatments.

Find out if there are any local self help groups in your area that focus on your particular health problem. Self help groups like the **Endometriosis Association** (1-800-426-2END) have compiled detailed information on both medical and surgical treatments as well as alternative treatments.

Next, find out which practitioners are in your area, which types of natural therapies they use, and how much they charge for their services and their products.

Choose a natural practitioner as you would choose any other service or product. By quality, service, reputation, experience and lack of sexism. Find out if the practitioner has been adequately trained, gone to a reputable school or received a degree.

Training of practitioners may vary from a person taking a six-month course in holistic medicine and calling themselves a holistic practitioner, to the four-year, intensive post graduate course required for chiropractors and naturopaths. There are also some medical doctors who combine Western medicine with natural medicine. Other well-trained practitioners may include acupuncturists, herbalists, homeopaths and other natural therapists, who have been well trained and educated.

Experience is an equally important qualification. If you have a chronic illness, you'd best seek out a practitioner with many years of experience treating patients, preferably ones with the same problem.

Beware of any practitioner who says that you have caused your illness through negative thinking, "bad" lifestyle or "bad" diet. And that if you only mend your ways, you will get better. This is dangerous and simplistic thinking.

Beware of any practitioner who threatens to stop seeing you if you continue to see another doctor or refuses to treat you if you take drugs or have surgery. Or vice versa, beware of a conventional medical doctor who refuses to treat you if you persist in going to that "quack".

Beware of an alternative practitioner who believes his or her method is the only way to treat a problem. Or who has a clearly patronizing attitude and refuses to explain the reasons for treatment.

Finally, natural practitioners may offer people false hope of curing cancer or reversing some other terminal diagnosis (cures at this stage are rare with any method) or deter them from proper diagnosis in the medical system. Good practitioners will know their limits and will get a second opinion or refer to a medical doctor if necessary.

Chronic illness is complex and usually involves many contributing factors. Sometimes the best choice may be to combine a drug or surgery treatment with a natural treatment. Fortunately most natural treatments have only mild side effects that are easily reversible.

While some natural treatments may make you feel worse at the beginning, treatment should be gradual and monitored carefully. Some patients are told that they are in a healing crisis for months at a time, instead of the practitioner admitting that the treatment is not working or has too many side effects.

Make sure you stick to your natural therapies for long enough to give them a chance to work. As a rule of thumb, within three to six months, you should notice significant improvement in your symptoms and/or energy level. A chronic illness will require anywhere from six months to two years to fully deal with.

Don't abandon your common sense and critical mind when you approach non-conventional medicine and you will be able to mine a rich tradition of healing.

Alternative Medicine Based On Solid Evidence

"Echinacea no better than a placebo for common cold", blasted a recent headline in the **Family Practice** newspaper. One researcher was quoted as saying there has never been a study on the effectiveness of echinacea.

In fact, there have been over 300 published papers on the pharmacology and clinical applications of echinacea documenting its anti-viral, immune stimulating and anti-inflammatory properties. However, most of the research was done on injectable preparations, and then it was deduced that the oral capsules or liquids had similar benefits.

Echinacea or purple coneflower, known as the herbal antibiotic, is now the most commonly used herb in North America. The use of echinacea for colds and flus is part of the growing consumer interest in complementary medicine.

An estimated 20 percent of Canadians and 33 percent of Americans use some form of alternative medicine. **Angus Reid** said recently that polls in the United States show the largest group likely to demand access to alternative therapies are educated women in their forties.

Not only patients but their doctors are interested in safe use of alternative medicine. A recent survey published in the **Canadian Family Physician Journal** (June 1995) revealed that 56 percent of general practitioners in Ontario and Alberta believed that alternative medicine had ideas and methods from which conventional medicine could benefit; 54 percent referred to alternative practitioners; and 16 percent practised some form of alternative medicine.

Complementary medicine refers to combining the best of conventional or Western medicine with the best of traditional or alternative medicine. Conventional medicine excels at the management of medical emergencies, trauma care, certain bacterial infections and complex surgical techniques. However, in the prevention of disease and the treatment of chronic illnesses conventional medicine has been much less successful.

The two types of medicine do have some things in common. One is that neither is strictly based on science and both make use of the placebo effect. The placebo effect is the positive effect brought about when both patient and doctor believe that a treatment will work. It is thought to comprise at least 40 percent of any treatment.

The double blind study eliminates the placebo effect by comparing a treated group with an untreated group given an identical appearing treatment that contains no active ingredients.

Most of us believe that modern medicine is based on that kind of research. However, in 1985, the **National Academy of Science** found that 85 to 90 percent of medical practice was NOT based on the gold standard of double blind studies, only 10 to 15 percent was.

According to cancer specialist **Dr. Robert Buckman**, in his book, **Magic or Medicine** (Key Porter, 1993) 85 to 90 percent of medical practice is based on, "accumulated clinical observations, folklore, fad, fashion, prejudice, old wives' tales, institutionalized phobia or prejudice and plain old hokum."

However, in no way does Buckman believe this renders modern medical practice invalid. Clinical observations, clinical experience, and less stringent scientific trials have pointed the way to many valuable treatments for illness. I believe this type of research can prove validity for alternative medicine as well as the stricter more expensive double blind studies.

In fact, several types of alternative medicine have solid evidence behind them in contrast to others which have been poorly studied.

Acupuncture has been rigorously tested and proven to be effective and valid in the treatment of pain. The **World Health Organization** recognizes 104 conditions that acupuncture can treat.

Other major contenders are nutritional medicine, chiropractic medicine, homeopathy, hypnosis and guided imagery, herbology, environmental medicine and chelation therapy.

The evidence behind the use of antioxidant vitamins for the prevention of heart disease and cancer is solid and growing daily.

Two double blind studies showed that chiropractic manipulation produced better relief of low back pain than treatment in a hospital orthopedic department or by a family doctor.

An article published in the **British Medical Journal** reviewed 107 controlled studies on homeopathy (the use of minute quantities of natural substances to boost the immune system). Many compared a homeopathic remedy with a placebo. Of the best designed studies, the authors noted that fifteen trials showed positive results whereas seven trials showed no effect.

Chelation therapy, an intravenous treatment legally performed by medical doctors worldwide, offers a nonsurgical alternative to angioplasty, coronary bypass and limb amputation. Eight million people have received these treatments without serious side effects, and much serious research substantiates its use.

In every state and province in the United States and Canada, there are well trained and experienced chiropractors, naturopathic doctors, herbalists, homeopaths, acupuncturists, and other experienced professionals as well as medical doctors with varying degrees of interest and expertise in natural medicine.

There are also "holistic practitioners" hanging up their shingle after minimal training. **Dr. Zoltan Rona**, author of **Return To The Joy Of Health**, has denounced lay practitioners who have taken a weekend course in nutrition or homeopathy, and then feel qualified to give medical advice.

Both with conventional medicine and alternative medicine, consumer beware, investigate your options, and use common sense. With one proviso, the side effects of natural treatments rarely result in death or hospitalization, and are usually reversible.

Natural Alternatives To Prozac

In August 1996, an editorial in the **British Medical Journal** revealed that German physicians prescribed almost 66 million daily doses of preparations containing **St. John's Wort** (hypericum perforatum) worth over $55 million. In fact, extracts of St. John's Wort are licensed in Germany for the treatment of anxiety, depressive disorders and sleep disorders.

St. John's Wort is an attractive perennial with yellow flowers that smells like turpentine or balsam. If you bruise the flowers, they yield a reddish juice. The plant grows in Europe, Canada and the US.

According to **Rodale's Illustrated Encyclopedia of Herbs**, for centuries it was thought to drive out devils. Later, St. John's Wort was associated with **St. John the Baptist** and said to bleed on his birthday.

Hypericum contains at least 10 groups of components that contribute to its effects. One of them, hypericin, inhibits monamine oxidase, which breaks down neurotransmitters in the brain. Thus hypericin contributes to the antidepressant effect, but other components are involved as well.

The **British Medical Journal** editorial commented on a comprehensive overview of 23 randomized trials on St. John's Wort published in the same issue. The authors concluded that hypericum extracts were more effective than placebo for the treatment of mild to moderately severe depressive disorders. However they cautioned that, "we do not know yet if hypericum is better in treating certain depressive disorders than others."

The researchers also reviewed six studies that compared hypericum to tricyclic antidepressants and tranqilizers, and found it to be equally effective. However, it is worth noting that none of the studies lasted longer than six weeks, and the doses of tricyclic antidepressant drugs used were low normal or less than normal.

Naturopathic physician **Dr. Michael Murray** says in his book, **Natural Alternatives to Prozac** (Morrow 1996), that St. John's Wort is the most thoroughly researched natural antidepressant. He reports that 1,593 patients have been studied in twenty five double-blind studies.

Photosensitivity has been reported in white haired animals taking 30 to 50 times the therapeutic dosage, but otherwise the herb has a good safety profile. A large German study of 3,250 patients showed a 2.4 percent incidence of side effects, minor compared to most antidepressant drugs. Like synthetic antidepressants, hypericum takes two to four weeks to develop its effects.

Other important aspects of a holistic approach to depression include improving the overall diet, eliminating coffee, alcohol, sugar, sugar substitutes, regular exercise, and learning some stress management technique like meditation. Food allergies are important and can be determined through an elimination diet. There are often nutritional factors in depression. Deficiencies of folic acid, vitamin-B-12 vitamin-B-6 and essential fatty acids are very common.

A high quality multi-vitamin and mineral and extra mega-B-vitamins, flax seed oil are recommended for any person with depression, and will not interfere with medication. If you are currently on antidepressant medication, consult with your doctor first before suddenly going off the medication.

A prescription amino acid known as tryptophan has a mild antidepressant effect of its own, is helpful for insomnia and also increases the effect of antidepressant drugs.

Cognitive Therapy (CT) involves observing and altering habitual thought patterns that lead to predictable emotional reactions. CT has been studied in double blind trials and shown to be as effective as antidepressants for mild to moderate depression. In addition, it may have a lower relapse rate than drug therapy. Although it is ideal to have a therapist, cognitive therapy can be learned though books like psychiatrist **David Burn**'s book, **Feeling Good Again Handbook** (Plume 1990).

One thing is clear. Although promising, there is not enough evidence yet to conclude that St. John's Wort can be used alone for the treatment of serious depression. For that kind of depression, drug therapy is still indispensable.

Growth Hormone Can Reverse Aging

At the annual conference of the **Academy of Anti-aging Medicine** (A4M) held in Las Vegas in December 1996, attended by 1,500 doctors and scientists from around the world, the search for the fountain of youth continued and even made progress.

One of the most exciting developments has been the use of growth hormone and growth hormone releasers to reverse aging in older people. Growth hormone is the most abundant hormone made by the pituitary gland in the brain. It hits its peak during the rapid growth phase of adolescence, then steadily declines as we age.

Until recently, HGH was very difficult to obtain and very expensive. It was reserved for the treatment of children who failed to grow to normal height and that was the only indication approved by the **FDA**.

However in the mid 1980's two drug companies were able to produce HGH though recombinant DNA technology, making it widely available for research and treatment. The FDA now allows American doctors to use HGH for anti-aging treatment, and a booming business in rejuvenation clinics is well underway.

Nine European countries have approved the use of HGH for adult growth hormone deficiency. The definition of HGH deficiency is left up to the doctor who may use it for people who have low levels because of aging as well as for people with pituitary disease.

Swedish endocrinologist and leading HGH researcher **Dr. Begnt-Ake Bengtsson** presented the results of his study of 333 patients who had pituitary deficiency caused by pituitary tumours or their treatment. They had received treatment with thyroid, adrenal, and sex steroids but not HGH. When he replaced their HGH, their body composition changed dramatically, and cholesterol levels and blood pressure decreased while cardiac output increased.

In addition, Bengtsson noticed that these patients had "increased energy levels, better mood, greater powers of concentration and improved memory." In fact the effect was so startling in some patients who seemed to be jolted awake, that Bengtsson and his colleagues described it as, "the Lazarus effect."

An estimated one third of men between the ages of 60 to 80 have HGH deficiency according to endocrinologist **Dr. Daniel Rudman**. In July 1990, he and his colleagues published a landmark study in the **New England Journal of Medicine**. Rudman divided a group of twenty one men between the ages of 60 and 80 into two groups. One received HGH injections three times a week for six months and the other no treatment.

The men receiving the HGH all showed a marked improvement in health and appearance. They gained an average of 8.8 percent in muscle mass, lost an average of 14 percent body fat, and increased skin thickness without changing diet or fitness levels.

Rudman commented that these changes were equivalent in magnitude to the changes that occur in 10 to 30 years of aging. As a result of this study, The **National Institute of Aging** has funded nine clinical studies on growth hormone, now in progress.

Dr. Ronald Klatz, founder of the A4M dedicated his book, **Grow Young With HGH** (Harper Collins, 1997) to Rudman and awarded the Academy's highest award to him posthumously for "ideas, vision and daring that opened the door to the future of aging."

Belgian physician **Dr. Thierry Hertoghue** whose father was one of the first doctors to describe the signs of thyroid deficiency discussed "the growth hormone deficiency syndrome." Symptoms included sagging cheeks, deep and large wrinkles, thin hair, lips, jaw, bones and skin, flappy belly, muscle looseness, permanent fatigue, poor resistance to stress, anxiety, lack of self assurance and lowered sociability.

Using minute doses of growth hormone injections combined with oral replacement of other hormones like estrogen, testosterone, progesterone, and DHEA, if necessary, his results have been close to miraculous in reversing the signs of aging.

Dr. Cyril Bowers, professor of medicine at **Tulane University** in New Orleans, presented his work on a new class of growth releasing peptides that stimulate the release of HGH, and can be administered orally or nasally.

Natural ways to boost HGH secretion include caloric restriction, vigorous aerobic exercise and resistance training. Various nutrients such as lysine, arginine, glutamine and niacin also boost HGH. Formulas containing these boosters are currently available.

For aging baby boomers, the conference theme "aging is not inevitable" may soon become a reality.

Natural Ways To Boost Your Growth Hormone

Dr. Ronald Klatz, founder of the **Anti-Aging Academy of Medicine** and author of **Grow Young With HGH** (Harper Collin, 1997) said in a recent interview that growth hormone (HGH) is the first proven anti-aging drug.

Growth hormone is the most abundant hormone made by the pituitary gland in the brain. It peaks during adolescence, then steadily declines as we age.

Nine European Countries and the U.S. FDA have approved the use of HGH for adults with growth hormone deficiency. The definition of HGH deficiency is left up to the doctor who may use it either for pituitary disease or for aging.

Drawbacks include the fact that it has to be injected daily or twice daily and costs about $200 a week depending on the dose given. It also requires close medical supervision and monitoring.

The main side effects are due to overdosing. These include edema, carpal tunnel syndrome and joint pains. They are due to the water retention caused by HGH and disappear when the dose is adjusted downward. However, scientists are divided on whether HGH might increase cancer risk by promoting growth of tumour cells.

Montreal physician **Dr. Roman Rozencwaig**, author of, **The Melatonin and Aging Sourcebook** (Hohm Press, 1997), is concerned that HGH would accelerate cancer in people that had undiagnosed cancer. He is planning to cautiously use small doses of HGH for his frail elderly patients.

In his book, Klatz recommends a well rounded programme emphasizing diet, vigorous exercise and the use of natural growth hormone releasers.

Then if necessary, he suggests low doses HGH replacement 40 to 60 times lower than used in the studies. The aim is to keep the level of insulin-like growth factor one (IGF1) similar to that of a normal 30 to 40 year old.

HGH is converted into growth factors in the liver. The most important of these, IGF1 can be measured in the blood before and during treatment. Klatz also stresses replacing all hormones in a balanced way (preferably using natural hormones) including estrogen, progesterone, testosterone and DHEA.

Plastic surgeon **Dr. Vincent Giampapa**, medical director of the **Longevity Institute** in Montclair, New Jersey, also uses natural growth hormone releasers with good success. He uses an amino acid mixture of 2 grams each of arginine, ornithine, lysine, and glutamine. Giampapa will only use HGH if natural boosters don't work.

The **Health Protection Branch** has taken most amino acids off the market and they are currently being evaluated. However, they can be ordered through US companies like the **Life Extension Foundation** in Hollywood, Florida (1-800-841-5433).

Several oral growth hormone releasers have been developed by the major drug companies but are not yet on the market. These include GHRP-6, hexarelin, and MKO677. These compounds stimulate the pituitary gland to secrete its own HGH.

Meanwhile, **Dr. Edmund Chein**, an expert in rehabilitation medicine and **Dr. Leon Terry**, Chairman of the Department of Neurology at the Medical College of Wisconsin have successfully treated over 900 patients since 1994 with hormone replacement including HGH at their **Palm Springs Life Extension Institute** in Palm Springs California.

Last week, **Biomed Comm Incorporated** of Seattle released the first patented homeopathic growth hormone factors. Researcher **Dr. Barb Brewitt** of the University of Washington did a pilot study on 30 AIDS patients and found that these factors with their infinitesimal amounts of substance produced an increase in T-cell count, a decrease in viral load and weight gain in the treated group. A larger study with 100 patients has just been funded.

Sound too good to be true? Canadians will have to go south to find out or else focus on natural healthy ways of increasing growth hormone through restricting calories, vigorous aerobic or resistance exercises with or without natural HGH boosters.

Treatment For Osteoarthritis Has Wide Safety Margin

Osteoarthritis is the most common form of arthritis. It affects approximately 80 percent of people over age 50. It happens when joint cartilage breaks down leading eventually to bone grinding on bone. A natural product called glucosamine sulphate not only provides pain relief, it may also help rebuild cartilage.

Conventional treatment focuses on pain relief until the joints are bad enough to warrant replacement surgery. The usual pain killers are non-steroidal anti-inflammatory drugs. Some of these drugs may have a deleterious effect on cartilage and should only be used after trying acetaminophen says **Dr. Barry Koehler**, associate professor of rheumatology at the University of British Columbia.

More alarming is the fact that in Canada on average there are 20,000 gastrointestinal bleeds and 1,400 deaths every year due to the side effects of these ant-inflammatory drugs. **Dr. Edward Keystone** of the **Arthritis Society** quoted these astounding statistics to **CTV** reporter **Avis Favaro** during a story on glucosamine aired September 1996.

Glucosamine sulphate, a naturally occurring compound necessary for the formation of proteins that comprise cartilage is one of the cornerstones of the complementary medical treatment of osteoarthritis. Most promising is the fact that it has none of the serious side effects of the anti-inflammatory drugs.

More than a dozen studies in Europe have shown that glucosamine sulphate is helpful in treating arthritic symptoms. In one study, forty patients with osteoarthritis of one knee received either glucosamine sulphate or ibuprofen (motrin, advil, etc) for eight weeks. Pain decreased faster with the ibuprofen in the first two weeks, but by the eighth week glucosamine was significantly more effective than ibuprofen.

Researchers at the University of Pavia in Italy confirmed the value of glucosamine in a double blind study. They also biopsied cartilage from affected joints and examined them under the electron microscope. Patients taking glucosamine showed structural improvement in their cartilage, while those taking placebo did not.

An open trial involving 252 doctors and 1,506 patients in Portugal examined the results of giving 500mg of glucosamine sulphate three time a day for an average time period of 50 days. Doctors found good results in 59 percent of patients and adequate results in a further 36 percent. Painful symptoms improved steadily throughout the treatment period. A significant number of these patients got good results who had not responded to any other medical treatment.

Dr. Joseph Houpt, Chief of Rheumatology at Mount Sinai Hospital in Toronto, became intrigued by patients claiming good pain relief from glucosamine. He set up the first North American double blind trial on glucosamine and its effect on osteoarthritis of the knee.

Since glucosamine in not patentable, Houpt initially had to fund the study out of his own pocket. Eight months later, **Wampole Canada**, a vitamin manufacturer, supplied funding.

Side effects of glucosamine, when they occur, are minimal (light to moderate nausea, indigestion, heartburn, and diarrhea) and are usually eliminated if the supplement is taken with meals.

In a true complementary medical approach to osteoarthritis there is no magic bullet. Besides taking glucosamine, it also involves an elimination diet to determine food allergies, exercise, and a complete nutritional programme including B-vitamins, Vitamin-E, vitamin-C, niacinamide, and herbal remedies. Other essential nutrients include the essential fatty acids both omega-3 (found in flax seed oil and fish oil) and omega-6 (found in evening primrose oil).

Jane Brody said, in a recent article in the **New York Times**, "rebuilding damaged cartilage has long been the holy grail of orthopedics and rheumatology." Whether glucosamine is the holy grail remains to be proven, but a few experts are already saying that glucosamine may safely replace the use of anti-inflammatories in osteoarthritis.

Meanwhile, should you wait for official sanction and deprive yourself of the considerable potential benefits of glucosamine? I think, in view of a large safety margin, an eight week trial of glucosamine should be recommended. Glucosamine capsules are available at any health food store. Since the effect may take four weeks to develop, and doesn't work for everyone, it's best to wean off pain killers slowly.

Chelation Therapy Offers Hope For Heart Problems

Chelation therapy is a well researched, safe and cheap alternative to angioplasty, coronary bypass therapy and limb amputation due to peripheral vascular disease. Most cardiologists and cardiac surgeons are adamantly opposed to it. However with skyrocketing health costs, an aging population and government cutbacks, it's time to take a second look.

Australia and New Zealand already require a trial of chelation therapy before expensive surgery is recommended. Compare $2,000 for 20 chelation treatments versus $5,000 for angioplasty and 30,000 to $40,000 for bypass surgery.

Chelation therapy consists of intravenous injections of a synthetic amino acid whose generic name is ethylene diamine tetracyclic acid or EDTA. This compound removes toxic metals from the blood stream like lead, mercury, and excess iron and calcium deposits. The EDTA grasps the metals with a claw like action and encircles them with a complex ring which is then excreted through the urine. "Chele" comes from the Greek meaning claw of a lobster or crab.

EDTA chelation therapy is officially approved for the treatment of heavy metal poisoning involving lead, mercury and cadmium and for radioactive metal poisoning. Early researchers noted that adults with cardiac disease being treated for lead poisoning improved substantially.

Arterial plaques are made of fibrous tissue, calcium, and cholesterol and their formation is initiated by free radical damage. This free radical damage is accelerated in the presence of toxic metals. The theory is that EDTA or other chelating agents remove the metallic irritants which then allows the leaking and damaged cell walls to heal. In September 1992, Finnish researchers reported on a study that linked heart disease with the build-up of excess iron in the body.

The resistance of the medical profession seems to stem from two reported deaths from chelation therapy reported back in 1953.

The physician in question administered an overdose of EDTA without checking kidney function and caused kidney failure.

There has also never been a satisfactory double blind study comparing chelation therapy with placebo. However, long term studies of the benefits of coronary bypass surgery show no difference in death rate for the surgery compared to those treated with heart medications. And of the 400,000 coronary bypass surgeries performed each year in North America about 20,000 or 5 percent die as a result of the procedure.

Chelation therapy does not work for everyone. However, to date there are 3,539 published articles in lab and clinical journals on EDTA and EDTA chelation. In 1988, **Dr. James Carter** of Tulane University and **Dr. Efrain Olszer** of Brazil collaborated in a retrospective study of 2,870 cases offered chelation therapy. Seventy seven percent of patients with coronary heart disease had marked improvement and 17 percent good improvement. Of patients with hardening of the arteries of the legs, 91 percent had marked improvement and 17 percent good improvement.

In another retrospective study of EDTA chelation done in 1993, 89 percent of patients with serious heart disease were able to avoid surgery after chelation.

Properly performed by trained medical doctors, chelation therapy has a low toxicity. There were no serious side effects in over one million Americans and 8 million in other countries that have been chelated.

Dr. Gary Gordon, a founder of the **American College for the Advancement of Medicine** (ACAM) which trains and examines doctors who practice chelation therapy, points out that chelation therapy has been safe enough to give to toddlers who have been poisoned from lead based paints. Over 200,000 American children have safely been given chelation therapy for lead poisoning.

Reflecting the medical profession's confusion about chelation therapy in Canada, chelation therapy is legal in British Columbia, Saskatchewan, Ontario and Alberta, but illegal in other provinces. In the United States, it is legal for a medical doctor to perform chelation therapy, but the practice is strongly opposed by medical associations.

All patients have a right to safe access to this treatment which is as much conventional as alternative. To obtain a list of qualified medical doctors who practice chelation therapy in Canada and the U.S. call the **American Academy For The Advancement of Medicine** at 1-800-532-3688 or 714-583-7666 or send a stamped self-addressed envelope to Box 3437, Laguna Hills, CA 92654.

Helpful Herbs For Insomnia

In this age of massive noise pollution and increased levels of stress, sleep disorders have become rampant. Insomnia, especially early morning awakening, can also be a symptom of serious depression. Other types of severe sleep disorders deserve a full work up in a specialized sleep lab. However, mild to moderate cases of insomnia can be safely helped with a variety of natural remedies with few side effects and no hang over.

One of the most important of these remedies is a herb known as valerian. Valerian has been known since the time of Galen. Back then it was known as the "Phu plant", an expression of the aversion to the strong odour of its dried roots. More recently that smell has been compared to the odour of smelly socks.

Valerian officinalis, is a perennial plant native to Europe that has been naturalized to North America. The strong smelling root of valerian is very attractive to animals, especially cats and rats. According to **Mrs. Grieve's Modern Herbal**, "it has been suggested that the famous Pied Piper of Hamlin owed his irresistible power over rats to the fact that he secreted Valerian roots about his person."

Fast forwarding to modern times, valerian has been studied in several well designed clinical trials. A placebo controlled study of 128 patients showed that giving 400 to 900mg of valerian root at bedtime resulted in a decrease in sleep latency (time required to fall asleep at night), a reduction in night awakenings as well as in increase in dream recall. All this was accomplished with no hang over effect. The lower dosages of valerian were shown to be as effective as the higher dosages in this study.

A German study found that the combined effect of valerian root and lemon balm on the sleep patterns of 20 volunteers compared favourably with a tranquilizer in the valium family known as triazolam.

Based on this and other research, Seattle naturopathic physician **Dr. Donald Brown** uses valerian root in combination with lemon balm and passion flower for the treatment of insomnia. He also finds valerian root, "a safe and efficacious tool in the early treatment of anxiety, as well as the long-term management of those unable to use or attempting to withdraw from the benzodiazepines (valium and its cousins)."

In fact, Valerian has been called the herbal valium. It normalizes the nervous system. It acts as a sedative in cases of agitation and as a stimulant in cases of extreme fatigue. It also has a minor action of lowering blood pressure, enhancing the flow of bile and relaxing the intestinal muscles. However, its prime pharmacological effect is that of a sedative.

Although considered to be safe during pregnancy and lactation, to be on the safe side its use is not recommended.

Important supplements that help induce a better sleep include niacinamide, inositol and combined calcium magnesium supplements. Tryptophan, a natural amino acid supplement only available by prescription, is also an excellent sleep aid.

Other herbs traditionally combined with valerian root include hops and skullcap. Hops or humulus lupulus is a native British plant well known for its use in making beer. In the herbal world, hops is also used as a sedative and for its sleep inducing effects. Grieves mentions that it was "formerly much given in nervousness and hysteria and at bedtime to induce sleep. In cases of delirium and inflammation being considered to produce a most soothing effect, frequently procuring for the patient sleep after long periods of sleeplessness in overwrought conditions of the brain."

Skullcap or scutellaria lateriflora grows in Europe and North America, and is well known for its beneficial effect on the nervous system. It has a sedative effect on the nervous system and in the past has been used to treat epilepsy.

These days getting a good night's sleep may be greatly aided by making use of a rich repertory of plant medicines that have been safely used for many centuries.

Tryptophan
Safe For Insomnia

L-tryptophan is one of the eight essential amino acids, one of the building blocks of protein. It is precursor to serotonin which is a brain chemical that elevates mood.

It is a little known but useful prescription for insomnia including the sleep disorders of fibromyalgia, chronic fatigue syndrome, grief reactions, PMS and menopause. It can also be used as part of a treatment program for migraines, chronic pain, and even the tremors of Parkinson's disease. In one small French study, of 20 people with severe trembling uncontrolled by the usual drugs, 11 had the tremors controlled by 10 grams of tryptophan daily.

Tryptophan can be used in treating depression, either by itself or in combination with antidepressant drugs like prozac where it counters the insomnia side effect and prevents the need for increasing the dosage.

Dr. Anthony Levitt, Assistant Professor of Psychiatry and Nutritional Sciences at University of Toronto, refers to evidence, including his own research, that shows that 55 to 60 percent of depressed patients who fail to respond to initial treatment with two commonly prescribed types of antidepressants improve with the addition of tryptophan.

"L-tryptophan combines the sleep-inducing activity with a nearly innocuous side effect profile." says Levitt.

Dr. Susan Steinburg, Assistant Professor of Psychiatry at McGill University in Montreal recently completed a controlled double blind study comparing 40 women using 2,000mg of tryptophan three times a day (from day 14 through to the first three days of the period) for PMS compared to 40 who did not take tryptophan. The study, published in **Biological Psychiatry** in 1999, showed that tryptophan provided significant relief of symptoms of depression, irritability and mood swings. Women who were particularly helped by tryptophan were those that at baseline had marital problems, or an increased number of negative life events.

Some doctors are still nervous about prescribing tryptophan. In November 1989, the **FDA** recalled all tryptophan from the health food stores due to a serious illness and fatalities induced by one contaminated batch of tryptophan. The tryptophan was all manufactured by one Japanese company that was using genetically engineered bacteria to produce the tryptophan.

Biologist **Dr. John Fagan** says this is one of the best examples of genetic engineering giving rise to unanticipated allergens and toxins. He cites a 1990 study published in **Science** magazine that confirmed that the tryptophan produced by the bacteria were contaminated by a "novel amino acid" not present in tryptophan produced by other methods.

For unknown reasons L-tryptophan was never allowed back in the market in the United States. Some cynics have suggested that this paved the way for the domination of the depression market by Prozac and its cousins.

Currently in Canada, all prescription tryptophan is manufactured by one company **ICN Canada**, whose product has never been associated with any problem. The cost is about $1.00 per 1,000mg tablet and is covered by some drug plans.

Another very useful sleep aid, melatonin, although recently removed from the Canadian market, is freely available in the United States. Melatonin is a cheap and effective sleep aid in doses of .1mg to 6mg per night. Melatonin also works well for jet lag (taken at bedtime local time), and shift work (taken at the new desired bedtime).

The usual dosage of tryptophan for insomnia ranges from 500mg to 4,000mg taken one hour before bedtime. It is best not to take tryptophan with protein which competes with tryptophan for absorption, but it can be taken with a carbohydrate snack. Vitamin-B-6 and magnesium enhance the effect of tryptophan. Tryptophan can also be combined with the B-vitamin niacinamide for chronic pain or depression.

M.I.T. researcher **Dr. Judith Wurtman**, author of **The Serotonin Solution**, found that a high carbohydrate diet increased the production of serotonin and helped get tryptophan to the brain.

Either tryptophan or melatonin provide yet another safe choice for those suffering from a variety of ills. Increasingly, the ability to get a good night's sleep is becoming an invaluable commodity.

A Unique View Of Schizophrenia

Schizophrenia is a disabling mental illness affecting one percent of the population. It causes enormous suffering to patients and family alike. "The stigma of schizophrenia is still powerful and pervasive" says Victoria psychiatrist **Dr. Abram Hoffer**.

Hoffer, who turned 80 in 1998, is world famous for his outstanding contribution in the area of nutrition and mental illness. He is founder of a branch of psychiatry known as orthomolecular psychiatry. Hoffer has achieved remarkable success in treating both acute and chronic schizophrenics with large doses of vitamins. His landmark work has not been recognized by the psychiatric profession.

"I am very frustrated by the massive inertia of my psychiatric colleagues who are still searching for the Holy Grail: that new tranquilizer which appears every year, which will do for schizophrenia what insulin does for diabetes." says Hoffer, "The number of homeless chronic schizophrenics in the streets of all large American and Canadian cities is evidence of psychiatrists' inability to do more for them than we could in 1950, before we had any tranquilizers."

Hoffer was born on a farm in southern Saskatchewan and later combined an interest in agriculture with biochemistry. In 1944, he received his PHD degree in agricultural chemistry. By this time he was interested in human nutrition and enrolled in medical school, later specializing in psychiatry. From 1950 to 1957, he was the Director of Psychiatric Research, Department of Public Health in the province of Saskatchewan.

In the 1950's half of all mental hospital beds were occupied by schizophrenic patients and one quarter of all hospital beds in Canada. The introduction of potent drugs with serious and disabling side effects, dramatically changed this picture and enabled most hospitalized patients to go home.

But as Hoffer points out, the standard drugs used for schizophrenia do not enable schizophrenics to function normally in society. Not only can schizophrenia be treated nutritionally, Hoffer has found, but such patients can lead useful and productive lives and even pay income tax. In fact, at least twenty schizophrenics treated with Hoffer's regimen have gone on to become medical doctors.

The newer drugs for schizophrenia target specific receptor sites in the brain, thus eliminating the worst side effects. However, these drugs are rarely used in first episodes with schizophrenia but are reserved for cases in which other treatments fail. UBC Professor of Psychiatry, **Dr. Peter Liddle** argues that the newer drugs should be the treatment of choice for the initial treatment since they control symptoms better and have better occupational and social outcomes.

Hoffer and his British colleague, **Dr. Humphry Osmond** postulate that schizophrenia is caused by a biochemical abnormality (excessive oxidation of the neurotransmitter adrenalin into adrenochrome). An excess of this adrenochrome can produce all the symptoms of schizophrenia, including the hallucinations. Treatment with high doses of vitamins, particularly niacinamide, a form of vitamin-B-3, have been shown to prevent excess accumulation of adrenochrome in the brain.

Hoffer and Osmond were the first psychiatrists to conduct double blind trials. They are also credited with the discovery that vitamin-B-3, or niacin, lowers cholesterol. In addition, they developed two innovative diagnostic tools for the early diagnosis of schizophrenia.

Hoffer's early research showed that niacinamide was very helpful in the treatment of acute schizophrenia. Since that time Hoffer has found that his programme is effective for chronic schizophrenics but it takes longer, sometimes as long as seven years.

Hoffer's complete treatment programme for schizophrenia includes vitamin-B-3 as well as vitamin-B-6, zinc, and manganese working in conjunction with a diet free of sugar additives and allergens. Hoffer will also use low doses of drugs, if necessary, to start the process of recovery.

Elizabeth Wade is one of many patients whose life has been transformed by Hoffer's treatments. She had relapsing recurrent schizophrenia which was resistant to both drug treatment and shock treatment. "I almost resigned myself to living as a vegetable propped up with drugs wandering aimlessly through the rest of my days as an outcast from society." wrote Wade.

Fortunately, her mother stumbled across an article on Hoffer, wrote to him and was referred to the nearest clinic in England which used Dr. Hoffer's treatments. Wade eventually made a complete recovery, and is now working as a registered nutritionist.

Hoffer recommends that schizophrenic patients and their families read his book, **Common Questions on Schizophrenia and Their Answers** (Keats, 1987). Readers can also contact The **Canadian Schizophrenia Foundation** (416-733-2117) for further information and an extensive book list.

Light Therapy For Winter Blues

Our exposure to natural sunlight and full spectrum lighting may be as important to health as diet and exercise. These days many of us spend most of our time in florescently lit offices, wear sunglasses and sun blocks when outside, and come home to artificially lit houses.

In addition the lack of sunlight which so many experience in the winter results for some in a "winter depression" known as seasonal affective disorder or SAD. A less serious form of this condition is known as the winter doldrums. Fortunately, both conditions respond dramatically to light therapy within 4 to 7 days.

Light stimulates a tiny gland located in the center of the brain called the pineal gland. The pineal gland regulates the timing of sleep, hormone production, body temperature and many other important biological functions.

The pineal gland secretes melatonin, also known as the "hormone of darkness". Decreased light stimulates the secretion of melatonin, (which causes drowsiness) while bright daylight switches off the secretion of melatonin. Some studies have shown that SAD sufferers have increased levels of melatonin during the daytime hours.

Light promotes the production of serotonin, a neuropeptide that elevates mood. In fact, modern antidepressants like Prozac work by increasing the amount of serotonin in the brain.

SAD usually starts in the late autumn or early winter. An estimated two to five percent of the population are affected. Symptoms of SAD include increased desire to sleep, extreme lethargy, depression, increased appetite, weight gain, desire to withdraw from the world, lowered sex drive and cravings for sweet and starchy foods.

Five times as many people may suffer from the "winter doldrums" with the same symptoms as SAD but not as severe.

SAD usually lasts five months (November through February). The incidence of SAD is still greatest in the North (Alaska, Finland, Norway, Iceland, Yukon and NWT).

In women, light therapy can also be used to as part of a treatment for PMS and to help regulate menstrual cycles. Light therapy can also be useful for shift workers and jet lag. In addition, it can be used to enhance the action of antidepressant drugs.

Natural sunlight and full spectrum light contain the full rainbow of colours from red to green to violet. Cool white florescent lights have a predominance of red and yellow light and a deficiency of blue light. Blue light helps the eye see better detail.

You can increase your exposure to natural lights as part of your daily routine. For example you can sit by an open window for 30 to 60 minutes a day and exercise outside whenever possible. An alternative is buy a portable full spectrum light box.

Both SAD and the winter doldrums are usually treated by using either light boxes, light visors or the newly developed light glasses. The effect usually occurs within days, certainly within the first week.

The mechanism of action is unknown but likely due to psychological as well as physiological effects of light. There may be a placebo effect as well.

Three studies published in the October 1998 **Archives of Psychiatry** have shown convincing evidence of the effectiveness of bright light boxes used in the morning to successfully treat SAD when compared to placebo.

The usual recommendation is to sit close to a specially designed light box ($200 to $400) or desk lamp ($230) with eyes open for 30 to 60 minutes in the morning. The light box consists of 4 to 8 high intensity cool florescent light blubs installed in a box and set up on a table or desk top. Side effects include eyestrain, headache and insomnia.

An inexpensive alternative is to wear a special visor hat ($130) or glasses ($90) for 30 to 60 minutes in the morning. The hat and glasses have a device that gives off dim red light. that seems to produce less eyestrain and other side effects, but is as effective as the white light.

An ordinary bedside lamp may be used to help regulate irregular or long menstrual cycles. Use a lamp with a 100 watt bulb that disperses light on the ceiling for nights 14 to 17 of the cycle.

Light boxes are available from **Northern Light Technologies** at 1-800-263-0066 as well as from many other reputable companies. The light visor hat and glasses are available from **Health Light Inc.** 1-800-265-6020. In Illinois, under the direction of talented author and health consultant, **Linaya Hahn**'s **Light for Health** offers a full selection of full spectrum light boxes and bulbs at 1-800-468-1104 or 847-459-4455 fax 847-459-4492 website:www.lightforhealth.com

Natural Approach To Healing Migraines

Migraine headaches cause disabling pain among the estimated 18 percent of women and 6 percent of men who suffer from them. While pain relieving drugs are invaluable in treating a full blown migraine, natural remedies offer hope for preventing and reducing the frequency and severity of migraines.

While migraine can occur at any age, says a recent article in the American Journal of Natural Medicine (November 1997), 30 percent of migraine sufferers report their first attack before the age of 10, and the condition is most common in adolescents and young adults.

British family physician, **Dr. Mike Whiteside**, author of **Headaches, Finding Relief Without Drugs** (Thorsons, revised 1995), says the first step is to discover your individual triggers. Triggers are different for each person. Whiteside emphasizes triggers such as prolonged or inadequate sleep, bright sunshine or bright lights, strenuous physical exertion, use of computer terminals and food.

Toronto physician **Dr. Zoltan Rona** includes triggers such as air travel, emotional upsets, menstruation, strong odours, weather changes, food additives, spinal misalignments, jaw misalignment (TMJ), underactive thyroid and female hormonal imbalances.

Food is the most common trigger. While a small number of migraine patients react to the tyramine found in aged cheese, wine, yogurt and other foods, the majority suffer from undiagnosed food allergies that can only be discovered on an elimination diet or through specialized testing.

One study looked at 60 patients who had been suffering from frequent migraines for an average of 20 years. They were put on a low risk diet of lamb, pears and spring water. By the fifth day, researchers found that most migraines had disappeared. Patients were then instructed to test one to three foods per day, looking for reactions. Common problem foods were wheat, oranges, eggs, tea, coffee, chocolate, milk, and beef.

Another study found 93 percent of migraine sufferers found relief when allergenic foods were eliminated, often more than one food, and often favourite foods. Sugar and sugar substitutes such as aspartame are often overlooked, but can be significant triggers for headaches.

Feverfew or tanacetum parthenium can reduce the frequency and severity of migraine headaches. Feverfew is a hardy annual with small daisy-like flowers that grows easily in North American gardens.

Canada's **Health Protection Branch** (HPB) has given a drug identification number (DIN) to a British feverfew product known as tanacet based on two British studies conducted in 1985 and 1989.

In the 1985 study, 70 percent of 270 migraine sufferers claimed that the herb decreased the frequency and/or intensity of their attacks. In the 1989 study, 70 percent of feverfew patients showed improvement versus 50 percent of patients on migraine medications.

The HPB recommends a minimum dose of 125mg of feverfew containing .2 percent of parthenolide (one of the active ingredients) daily, but more can be taken. Feverfew can be safely taken over a long period of time. However, its safety has not been proven for pregnant or nursing mothers or children under 2 years.

HPB scientist **Dr. Dennis Awang** stresses that both British trials used encapsulated whole dried feverfew leaf equivalent to chewing two medium sized feverfew leaves daily. Awang says a new Dutch study calls into serious question the assumption that parthenolide is the main active ingredient. However, he points out that the parthenolide content is useful as a marker to confirm the identity of the plant.

Other herbs used for migraines include ginger and ginko biloba. Ginger has anti-nausea and mild pain relieving properties. Ginkgo has shown promise in two small French trials, but more study is needed.

Women with hormonally induced migraines may find it helpful to use natural progesterone cream daily for the two weeks prior to menses, or in severe cases, every fifteen minutes until the pain disappears.

A small double blind study showed that taking fish oil significantly reduced migraine intensity compared with placebo. Other important nutrients include magnesium, niacin, and quercetin, a bioflavonoid.

Chiropractic treatment, relaxation training, biofeedback, or acupuncture can each provide another valuable tool for migraine relief. Whiteside has had great results using hypnosis for migraine.

Taking the natural approach to migraine involves time and commitment, a sense of adventure and a fair bit of detective work. For some dietary change and feverfew is all that they need, while other have to explore many different types of therapies to find what combination works for them.

Alternatives To Ritalin

An astounding number of children in Canada and the United States are prescribed ritalin for the treatment of attention deficit hyperactivity disorder. (ADHD) More than one million children in the U.S. take ritalin regularly, an increase of two and a half times from 1990. In one small Canadian city, more than 10 percent of boys and 4 percent of girls between the ages of 9 and 11 are on ritalin.

There is no specific test for ADHD so the diagnosis is essentially a judgment call. American authorities report that about half of the children diagnosed with ADHD and referred to specialists did not have the disorder.

Psychiatrist **Dr. Peter Breggin**, author of **Talking Back to Ritalin** (Common Courage Press, 1998) says that the criteria for ADHD focus on behaviours that parents find frustrating and disruptive. Conflicts between children and adults are redefined as diseases or disorders within the children. Breggin believes that ritalin suppresses creative, spontaneous and autonomous activity in children, making them more docile and obedient, and more willing to comply with rote, boring tasks such as classroom school work and homework.

"Parents are not informed that they are trading behaviourial control for toxic drug effects." says Breggin, "The label is attached to children who are in reality deprived of appropriate adult attention..."

Not that ritalin cures the problem, at best it is only a short term solution. Little is known about the long term effects of treatment with ritalin and other drug combinations. Follow up studies after ritalin use show no impact on future school achievement, peer relationships or behaviourial problems.

Dr. Ivo Bianchi, an Italian endocrinologist, believes that ritalin overstimulates certain areas of the brain, and changes the immune reactivity of children. American physician **Dr. Mary Ann Block**, author of **No More Ritalin: Treating ADHD Without Drugs** (Kensington, 1996), is concerned about the over-diagnosis of the condition and believes it should only diagnosed after a thorough assessment including history, physical and blood tests to rule out other conditions.

But even given a correct diagnosis, it still makes sense to experiment with natural therapies before resorting to drugs. The natural approach involves a multifactorial attack and may involve a team of alternative practitioners.

Food and environmental allergies are a key part of treatment. The Feingold diet that restricted foods containing additives and salicylates has proven helpful for some, but does not go far enough. A more useful approach has been pioneered by the American pediatrician **Dr. Doris Rapp**.

Rapp says that most kids' behavioral problems are due to delayed allergic reactions to food, dust, pollen, moulds, animal danders or chemicals. She has captured on video the dramatic effects of giving an allergy causing agent to children, and then reversing the effect by giving the appropriate desensitizing shot. The most common problem foods are sugar, milk, wheat, egg, corn, and citrus. Delayed food allergies don't usually show up on traditional allergy tests but can be accurately determined through an elimination diet such as described in Rapp's book, **Is This Your Child?** (Morrow, 1991).

Aside from allergies, too few children are meeting even the minimal requirements of the food rules resulting in widespread nutritional deficiencies. It makes sense for hyperactive children to be on a high quality multi-mineral and vitamin, preferably a liquid, available in health food stores. In addition, green drinks containing sprouts and blue green sea algae like spirulina supply essential trace minerals, antioxidants and other plant nutrients.

Hyperactive kids are commonly deficient in zinc, iron and B vitamins. Holistic physician **Dr. Zoltan Rona**, author of **Return to the Joy of Health** (Alive, 1995), says that the expression, "no zinc, no think" is not without merit. He refers to studies showing that zinc supplementation is helpful for memory, thinking and IQ. As well, cognitive impairment may be associated with low iron blood levels. Rona also points to the accumulation of lead, cadmium or other heavy metals as a cause of ADHD in some children.

Omega-3 fatty acids are essential for the brain's normal functioning and ADHD children have lower levels of them than healthy children. This can be easily remedied through taking flaxseed oil or fish oil daily.

Other important supplements include lecithin which enhances memory, ginkgo biloba which increases blood flow to the brain, and calcium magnesium combined which has a calming effect. A new nutrient called phosphatidyl serine is a key building block for nerve cells and helps normalize brain biochemistry and physiology at every level.

The herbs valerian, passion flower and lemon balm are safe for children and have a calming effect. St. John's Wort helps to improve sleep and lessen anxiety without drowsiness.

Homeopathy may be prove very valuable for children, who often respond to it more rapidly than adults. Naturopathic doctors **Dr. Judith Reichenberg-Ullman** and **Robert Ullman**, author of **Ritalin Free Kids** (Prima, 1996) have treated over 400 ADHD kids with a success rate of 70 percent. An experienced homeopathic doctor is usually needed to determine the right remedies.

Biofeedback can be helpful to teach kids to retrain their brain waves into calmer patterns. Cranial-sacral therapy may help some children especially those who have had traumatic birth experiences. Dr. Block has also found osteopathic manipulation a valuable adjunct for the treatment of ADHD.

Naturopathic doctor, **Dr. Skye Weintraub** has written a comprehensive new book called **Natural Treatments For ADD and Hyperactivity**. (Woodland, 1997) It gives detailed and practical information on nutritional, environmental, and physical therapies to help overcome the behaviourial problems of ADHD.

Many factors contribute to a child exhibiting signs of hyperactivity or inattention, says Breggin, in a letter to the editor of the New York Times (May/20/96) "including a spirited, creative nature that defies conformity, inconsistent discipline or lack of unconditional love, boring and oversized classrooms, an over-stressed teacher, lack of teacher attention to individual educational needs, anxiety due to abuse or neglect at home or elsewhere, conflict and communication problems in the family and misguided educational and behavioral expectations for the child."

With children, the least treatment that does the least harm should be our goal. As psychiatrist **Felix Yaroshevsky** and psychotherapist **David Schatzky** cautioned in a **Globe and Mail** commentary: "People who advocate medication as the first way to make children **behave** without exploring their life situation and real needs might as well treat unhappiness with cocaine."

Natural Solutions For Stomach Ulcers

Peptic ulcers affect 10 to 15 percent of men and 4 to 15 percent of women at least once in their lives. More than four billion dollars are spent each year on anti-ulcer drugs. The conventional treatment includes avoidance of smoking, caffeine, alcohol, eating small frequent meals and taking medications for six to eight weeks.

Three types of drugs are used to treat ulcers. The first are antacids that neutralize acid and the second are drugs that block the secretion of acid like zantac, tagamet and pepsid. The third drug is a complex salt of sucrose containing aluminum and sulfate known as sulcrafate. It forms a protective layer over the ulcer crater, and has the least side effects. However, with any of these drugs, recurrence rates are over 80 percent.

Well known author and nutritional expert **Dr. Alan Gaby** is concerned that while antacids may relieve symptoms, the presence of aluminum in most antacids is cause for concern. "Carefully performed studies have revealed that ingesting aluminum containing antacids increases the level of aluminum in both brain and bone tissue." He also notes that long term use of acid blocking drugs can lead to deficiencies of folic acid and vitamin-B-12.

In 1994, a revolution occurred in the treatment of peptic ulcers when researchers showed that most ulcers were caused by infection by a bacteria known as heliobacter pylori. Ulcers can now be cured in 90 percent of cases by a one week course of two antibiotics plus an acid blocker. The reoccurrence rate is five percent.

However, safe natural remedies offer some advantages for the treatment of ulcers. Licorice root or glycyrrhiza glabra is one of the most extensively investigated herbs. The medicinal uses of licorice in both Western and Eastern cultures dates back several thousand years. Licorice root is very soothing to mucous membranes.

Licorice root extract has been used widely in Europe to promote the healing of peptic ulcers. It works in a different way than other ulcer drugs. According to **Dr. Michael Murray**, co-author of **The Encyclopedia of Natural Medicine**, licorice root extract stimulates the normal defence mechanisms that prevent ulcer formation. The extract increases the number of mucous producing cells, improves the quality of the mucous produced, increases the life span of intestinal cells, and improves blood supply to the intestinal lining.

At least fourteen double blind studies have shown the favourable results of licorice root extract compared to placebo, and even to other anti-ulcer drugs. Some patients on licorice root developed sodium and water retention, low potassium and high blood pressure due to one component of licorice root known as glycyrrhetinic acid. Glycyrrhetinic acid, by the way is 50 to 100 times sweeter than sugar.

A special licorice root extract known as "deglycyrrhinated licorice" (DGL) has been developed to retain all the positive benefits of licorice root without the negative side effects mentioned above.

DGL has another useful effect. A recent study showed that DGL inhibits heliobacter pylori, and its action was similar to that of bismuth. The drawback of antibiotics is that they do not change the conditions that led to the infection in the first place.

DGL must be mixed with saliva in order to be effective. The recommended dosage is two 380mg tablets chewed well twenty minutes before each meal.

An old naturopathic formula known as Robert's formula, although not formally tested, has a long history of use for peptic ulcer. It contains American cranesbill, cabbage, slippery elm, marshmallow and okra (which are all soothing to the mucous membranes) and echinacea and goldenseal (which have anti-bacterial properties).

Traditionally raw cabbage juice has been used for stomach ulcers, and raw potato juice for duodenal ulcers. In the 1950's **Dr. Garnett Cheney** of Stanford's School of Medicine studied 181 patients, and found one litre of raw cabbage juice daily to be highly beneficial. Green cabbages are best, but red cabbages can also be used and it can be mixed 50:50 with carrot and/or celery juice for flavour.

Glutamine is an amino acid found naturally in the body that helps improve the integrity of the stomach and intestinal lining. A small double blind study showed that 1,600mg of glutamine daily resulted in 100 percent healing of peptic ulcers compared to 50 percent in those taking the placebo.

Studies have shown that vitamin-C, vitamin-E and Vitamin-B-6 are low in individuals with peptic ulcers. Vitamin-A is important for the healing of all mucous membranes. Zinc appears to accelerate the healing of ulcers.

Finally, Gaby has seen a number of individuals whose ulcers did not heal properly and whose pain did not subside until they stopped eating foods to which they were allergic.

Kids' Ear Infections Don't Always Need Antibiotics

Chronic ear infections are very common in children and one of the main reasons for repeated courses of antibiotics. Some doctors believe that children are being over-treated or treated too soon. Fortunately natural medicine can provide some useful alternatives or adjuncts to treatment.

The standard 10 day course of antibiotic treatment was chosen arbitrarily, rather than on the basis of research. Recent studies have shown the same results whether a 7, 5, 3 or even 2 day course of antibiotics is given. The studies showed no difference in recurrence rate or hearing loss.

What happens if ear infections aren't treated with antibiotics? This is a scary proposition for North American parents who have come to believe that taking antibiotics is always necessary. But to the European way of thinking, a wait and see approach may be just as safe.

Between 1950 and 1964, more than three thousand children were treated at the ear nose and throat department at a Danish hospital. Later, two doctors examined the records and analyzed the effects of early, late, or no antibiotic treatment. Antibiotics were given usually after the first week and only for threat of complications. The Danish physicians found that 88 percent of the children healed well with no antibiotics. In addition, antibiotics did not shorten the course of the disease, and even if given only when complications were present or threatening, the rate of complications was very low.

In the Netherlands, a double blind study compared children who were treated with antibiotics only, with tubes only, with both antibiotics and tubes, or with neither. According to the authors, "in the groups treated without antibiotics, the ears discharged for slightly longer and the eardrums took a little longer to heal, but these differences were not significant and no complications were seen." **Dr. Van Buchem** and his colleagues recommend using nose drops and pain killers for the initial management of ear infections in children and reserving antibiotics and tubes for complicated cases.

Tympanostomy or insertion of tubes into the ear drum is a surgical procedure under general anesthetic. American naturopathic physician, **Dr. Michael Schmidt**, author of the excellent book, **Healing Childhood Ear Infections: Prevention, Home Care and Alternative Treatment** (North Atlantic, 1996), presents evidence that the procedure is overused, can cause scarring and may not alter the long term course of ear infections. He concludes that tubes may still have a valuable place in well chosen severe cases.

Dr. Michael Schimdt is now a fellow at Functional Medicine Research Center in Gig Harbor, Washington where he is compiling data on the holistic treatment of ear infections.

When it comes to a natural approach, it is important to look at all the factors that could contribute to repeated infections. Important factors include one or both parents smoking, food allergies, deficiencies in essential fatty acids, vitamin-A and zinc, and environmental allergies.

The best way to determine a child's food allergies is through an elimination diet such as the one suggested in pediatrician **Dr. William Crook**'s book, **Detecting Your Hidden Allergies** (Professional Books, 1988).

Some children's recurrent ear infections will stop when they go off dairy. A six week trial off milk and cheese will tell you whether you are going in the right direction. Parents have to become like detectives to track down the hidden food allergies. Other common allergens are sugar, chocolate, peanuts, wheat, soy, citrus and eggs.

Repeated courses of antibiotics can wipe out the friendly bacteria in the gut and cause an overgrowth of yeast which can then cause digestive problems, fatigue and headaches. Treatment involves taking acidophilus capsules and natural anti-yeast remedies like garlic or grapefruit seed extract.

Children's diet these days are often poor, with a high fat and high sugar content resulting in nutritional deficiencies. Children with recurrent ear infections should take a liquid multivitamin and mineral, preferably with no sugar. Extra flaxseed or evening primrose oil can play a role in decreasing inflammation. The herbal antibiotic echinacea can also be taken once daily as a preventative.

During actual infections, whether you choose antibiotics or not, your child can take extra C, A and zinc vitamins. Echinacea drops can also be taken four to six times a day.

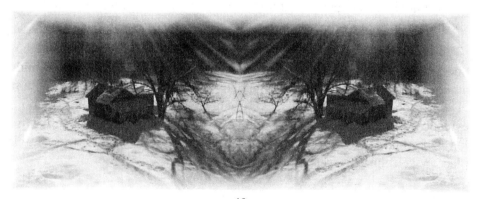

Arnica The Natural Trauma Remedy

Arnica montana is a perennial herb native to Europe. For hundreds of years, arnica has been used externally for falls, sprains and bruises by mountain tribes around the world. In homeopathy, it is considered one of the greatest trauma remedies and indispensable for the homeopathic first aid kit.

The American variety known as arnica chamissonis has the same medicinal qualities as its European cousins. Arnica has bright yellow flowers and looks like a small daisy. It commonly grows on the cool mountain slopes of Europe, the Andes, Northern Asia and Siberia. In Germany it is called "Fallkraut" which means "fall herb". Swiss mountain climbers seek it out to relieve muscular aching after a hard day's climbing.

Homeopathy is the use of extremely minute and diluted quantities of natural substances to stimulate the body's innate healing powers. In England, 42 to 48 percent of British medical doctors refer to homeopathic doctors, and the Royal family has always had a homeopathic physician. These remedies can be used either alone or with more conventional therapies.

While homeopathy is considered more magic than medicine by mainstream physicians in North America, in Europe it is much more accepted by medical doctors. A growing body of evidence is supporting the validity of this branch of natural medicine.

The most recent comprehensive review of homeopathic research was published in the **Lancet** in September 1997. The researchers choose the best designed of 186 studies, and concluded that homeopathic remedies were more effective than placebo.

In homeopathy, arnica is the remedy of choice for falls, sprains, blows, wounds, fractures, and soft tissue injury. It reduces and prevents pain, bleeding, bruising and swelling, and accelerates healing.

Dr. Asa Hershoff, in his excellent book, **Homeopathy For Musculoskeletal Healing**, (North Atlantic, 1996) details the uses of arnica. It is the first remedy for muscular sprains, strains, and bruising. It is excellent for soreness after sleeping on a hard bed or soreness after exercise. It is recommended before and after operations and dental work. After childbirth, it speeds healing of bruised and swollen tissues. It is helpful after eye injuries, head injuries and concussions. It is also used for mental shock after injury, loss or grief.

It is one of the only remedies that can be used for the after effects of trauma that occurred in the remote past, especially if the person has never been well since the injury or fall.

Homeopathic remedies are usually taken as pellets made from lactose or in liquid form. In the case of arnica, it should be taken every ten minutes until the situation stabilizes, then four to six times a day. It is entirely safe for children and infants.

Homoeopathic arnica is available in gels, creams and ointments, but these are best combined with oral forms of the remedy. The herbal tincture (the herb preserved in alcohol) should never be applied to an open wound or taken internally. The diluted homeopathic form of arnica is the safest bet.

A German homeopathic combination remedy known as **Traumeel** applied externally has proven effective for the treatment of sprained ankles. Ten days after the sprain, 24 of 33 patients given Traumeel were pain free versus 13 out of 33 given a placebo. Traumeel is a combination of 14 homeopathic remedies including arnica. Traumeel is also an excellent internal trauma remedy useful for any type of injury or fall.

People who suffer from fibromyalgia often say they wake up in the morning feeling like they've been run over by a truck. This is typical of the condition known as fibromyalgia.

Fibromyalgia, the "**sore all over**" syndrome may be part of chronic fatigue syndrome, with pain being a more prominent symptom than fatigue. In this condition, which affects mainly women in their late 30's and 40's, there is generalized pain and aching throughout the body, morning stiffness, fatigue, disturbed sleep, and multiple tender spots on the body.

Diagnosis is based on the presence of widespread muscle pain, aching or stiffness, (with absence of other conditions that would account for the pain), tenderness when pressing on eleven out of eighteen trigger points, non-refreshing sleep, frequent headaches, numbness, tingling, and chronic pain in the neck and shoulders.

The treatment plan is essentially the same as that used for chronic fatigue. **Dr. Byron Hyde** a leading chronic fatigue researcher defines chronic fatigue syndrome (CFS) as, "a chronic illness of at least six months in duration, that develops after an acute infectious disease, in a well and physically active person. In this disease, the patient develops an unusual form of muscle failure experiencing fatigue, pain, or exhaustion in the exercised muscle."

Other important features of this illness, according to Dr. Hyde, are sleep disturbances, variability and fluctuations of symptoms, serious difficulty processing information (memory loss, lack of concentration, slurred speech, disorientation, loss of coordination) and generalized malaise. Some or all of these symptoms may be present in fibromyalgia.

Treatment of fibromyalgia requires a multi-pronged approach. This involves gentle exercise and massage as well as nutritional and vitamin supplements to stimulate the immune system. A high quality diet with emphasis on fresh fruits and vegetables, whole grains and beans, supplemented with chicken and fish, is essential. It is important to use an elimination diet or specialized testing by a natural practitioner to identify food allergies. Of course, sugar, junk foods and excessive animal protein must be cut out.

Proper rest and balancing of activities with rest is mandatory. This illness also requires a complete change of attitude and lifestyle as well as elimination of all major stresses.

If chronic yeast infection is present, treatment is essential for recovery. **Dr. Carol Jessop**, Assistant Professor of Medicine at The University of California, treated 900 of her chronic fatigue patients with a strong anti-yeast drug known as ketoconazole, and a sugar free diet with 84 percent making a full recovery. 40 hours a week. Dr. Jessop found that 80 percent of her CFS patients gave a history of recurrent antibiotic use and serious sugar addiction.

Evening of primrose oil is usually recommended for fibromyalgia. The usual dosage suggested is four capsules combined with two cod liver oil capsules (containing vitamin-A 1,250 IU and vitamin-D 100 IU) taken with breakfast and lunch but not at bedtime.

Magnesium supplementation is critical to the treatment of fibromyalgia. One study showed that 300 to 600mg of magnesium malate per day had very positive results in decreasing the number and severity of tender points in fibromyalgia. Malic acid (derived from apples) by itself is also helpful in fibromyalgia.

Other important supplements include zinc, vitamin-E, mega-B-50, betacarotene, and vitamin-C. The amino acid phenylalanine 500 to 1,000mg may be helpful in the morning. It is a natural antidepressant and stimulant. Niacinamide 500 to 1,500mg a day is an inexpensive supplement that is helpful for the pain of fibromyalgia.

A six week trial of Co-enzyme-Q-10 in doses of 90 to 200mg daily is recommended by **Dr. Paul Cheney**, particularly for improving fatigue, thought processes, muscular weakness and associated heart problems.

Research has demonstrated low vitamin-B-12 in the cerebrospinal fluid of CFS and fibromyalgia patients. Some doctors have found that daily or bi-weekly injections of vitamin-B-12 are helpful. Most patients can learn to do the injections themselves at home.

For the sleeping problems of fibromyalgia, tryptophan is highly useful. Tryptophan is an amino acid, one of the building blocks of protein and is available only by prescription in Canada. In doses of 2,000 to 4,000mg it helps you to sleep without a hangover effect. In the U.S. and Canada a precursor of tryptophan is available without prescription known as 5-hydroxy-tryptophan (50mg of 5-hydroxy-tryptophan equals 500mg of tryptophan).

Dr. Michael Murray, in the **Encyclopedia of Natural Medicine** recommends a combination of 5-HTP 50 to 100mg; magnesium 150 to 250mg and St. John's Wort extract 300mg (standardized to contain .3 percent of hypericin) all taken three times a day.

For all fibromyalgia patients, it is important to support the adrenal glands, which are often exhausted, through taking extra vitamin-C, pantothenic acid, and adrenal glandulars 2 to 3 times a day.

methylsulfonylmethane or MSM is an exciting new treatment for fibromyalgia, rheumatoid arthritis, allergies, asthma and many other conditions. It is a natural organic form of sulphur with few side effects. Sulphur is concentrated in the skin, bones and muscles and is needed to produce collagen. The usual dosage is 2,000 to 6,000mg in divided doses three times a day with meals day. The dose should be increased until pain relief occurs and must be accompanied by vitamin-C for maximum effect.

S-Adenosylmethionine (SAM) is an important natural supplement formed in the body by combining the amino acid methionine with ATP. SAM is involved in over 40 biochemical reactions and functions closely with folic acid and vitamin-B-12. Three studies have demonstrated that SAM is very helpful for fibromyalgia. The recommended dosage is 200 to 400mg two times a day. SAM is well suited for long term use and it has no side effects.

Acupuncture stimulation of trigger points and tender points by an experienced acupuncturist can be very helpful.

Magnetic therapy often helpful either localized or sleeping on magnetic mattress. Two preliminary studies have been done on fibromyalgia and the use of unidirectional magnetic mattress pads. One was a small pilot study of six patients who had been diagnosed with chronic fatigue syndrome. Many of these patients had symptoms of fibromyalgia. All of the patients showed improvement in their symptoms over the four months. The second study was a placebo controlled study involving 29 patients diagnosed with fibromyalgia. The patients with the real magnetic mattress pad showed 2.4 times the improvement as the placebo group. This mattress has also been found to help many conditions including PMS, arthritis, insomnia and recovery from injuries.

Dr. Dean Bonlie is an experienced researcher in the field of biomagnetism who designed the sleep pad used in these studies. There are several kinds of sleep pads available on the market. Dr. Bonlie's is the only one that provide unidirectional magnetic fields.

Other sleep pads are designed to provide a bipolar magnetic field to the body. According to Dr. Bonlie, this unnatural magnetic field provokes and emergency response which decreases blood and electrical flow to the body. On a short term basis, this is very helpful, but on a long term basis, it uses up the body's reserves. These type of pads should never be used on a continuous basis, but with frequent breaks.

If you suspect you have this condition you may have to educate both yourself and your doctor. Women have tended to be dismissed by their doctors, told their problem was all in their head, or referred to a psychiatrist. Chronic fatigue syndrome and fibromyalgia must be taken seriously by physicians and women alike.

In Pursuit Of The True Aromatherapy

Aromatherapy is a potent and effective branch of natural medicine which is barely recognized in North America. In Europe, medical doctors prescribe the pure oils for a wide variety of medical conditions. The oils are used orally, topically and by inhalation and rectal suppository.

On the other hand, in North America, aromatherapy has a more flaky image because most of the oils are diluted, synthetic or cut with chemicals. In addition, the oils are mainly used in massage or bath oils.

The sensual and pleasurable aspects of the fragrant aromas of essential oils are undoubtably one of the most enjoyable part of using the oils. However, thanks to several outstanding teachers who have trained in Europe, there is a resurgence of interest in the medicinal and scientific applications of aromatherapy.

Dr. Gary Young is one of the leading researchers of aromatherapy in North America. He is also a naturopath, visionary, lecturer and author of two books on aromatherapy. His healing odyssey started at age 24 when a horrible logging accident left him paralyzed for life and in terrible pain.

At one point Young was in so much despair that he decided to stop eating. After a long period of fasting, he started to feel much better. He had accidentally discovered the regenerative power of fasting.

After that, he started his life long search for natural ways to heal his body and eventually became a naturopath. He opened up a cancer clinic in Mexico where he studied degenerative diseases. There he found many herbal preparations to be ineffective due to the lack of potency of the dried herbs. Eventually his path led him to France, Egypt and Arabia to study high quality therapeutic oils.

Young found out that the priests and physicians of ancient Egypt and China used essential oils thousands of years before Christ. The Bible itself contains over a hundred references to essential oils including frankincense, myrrh, hyssop and spikenard.

Young compares the blood of man with essential oils which are the lifeblood of plants. "With increasing pollution we see plants degenerate, the fibre becomes thick and the colour becomes weak." says Dr. Young, "Yet we see in essential oil chemistry the same strong vital life force it had 1,000 years ago. The essential oil still carries the ability to regenerate, protect and sustain life."

Essential oils are very concentrated. It takes 5,000 pounds of rose petals to make one pound of rose oil. One drop of pure peppermint oil is said to be the equivalent of 28 cups of peppermint tea. One pound of jasmine oil requires 1,000 pounds of jasmine or 3.6 million fresh unpacked blossoms. The blossoms must be collected before sunrise, or much of the fragrance will be evaporated. Pure jasmine costs $1,200 to $4,500 US while synthetic jasmine oil costs $3.50 a pound.

Young is now producing some of his own pure essential oils at organic farms in Utah and Idaho. He has 5,500 acres under cultivation and five distilleries. Plants are steam distilled in small batches using a special low-pressure low heat vertical steam technology that was invented by Young.

According to Young "the biggest scam being perpetrated on the North American continent has been the scam of adulterated and synthetic oils being marketed as pure essential oils." Lavender is being replaced with a hybrid named lavendin, grown in China, Russia, and Tasmania. It is then brought to France where it is heated to very high temperature to remove the camphor and synthetic fragrance is added. "That is why pure lavender will heal a burn while lavendin will intensify a burn."

Frankincense oil has been recognized since ancient times as the holy anointing oil, according to Dr. Young. It is another oil that is usually adulterated and sold for as little as $25 per ounce. It costs between $30,000 and 35,000 U.S. per ton. It has to be steam distilled for 12 hours. The cut, synthetic or adulterated frankincense oil can cause rashes, burns and other irritations. And of course this altered oil does not have any of the powerful therapeutic properties of the real frankincense.

Through the sense of smell, the oils act on the limbic system in brain. The limbic system controls heart rate, blood pressure, breathing, memory, stress levels, and hormone balance. Essential oils have a unique fat soluble structure, enabling them to pass through cell membranes of the skin and diffuse into the bloodstream.

The term aromatherapy is misleading, says **Dr. Kurt Schnaubelt**, Director of the **Pacific Institute of Aromatherapy** in Alternative Medicine: the Definitive Guide. (The Burton Goldberg Group, 1995), "In actuality the oils exert much of their therapeutic effect through their pharmacological properties and their small molecular size, making them one of the few therapeutic agents to easily penetrate bodily tissues."

Over 200 types of oils with several thousand chemical constituents have been identified. The eugenol found in cinnamon, clove, and basil is antiseptic, stimulating and acts as a local anesthetic. The ester constituents found in lavender, rose, and geranium are calming and sedating. The phenols found in oregano and thyme are anti-bacterial, anti-fungal, and antiseptic. The sesquiterpenes found in sandalwood, cedarwood and frankincense are soothing to inflamed tissue, immune stimulating, and cross the blood brain barrier to improve brain function

Other actions of essential oils improve adrenal function, balance thyroid function, aid digestive problems, and clear sinus and chest congestion.

An evolving body of scientific literature is showing the concrete benefits of essential oils. Lavender has been shown to be highly effective for burns. Lavender also has a calming effect and induces alpha waves in the brain. Diluted tea tree oil is effective for trichomonas vaginal infections. Peppermint oil was shown to be useful for treating irritable bowel syndrome and in improving cognitive function in classrooms.

One study showed that an oil blend consisting of clove, cinnamon, melissa and lavender was as effective in treating bronchitis as antibiotics. A Russian study showed eucalyptus oil was effective for treating influenza. German studies found that clove, cinnamon and thyme had anti-inflammatory effects useful in treating arthritis.

French medical doctors routinely prescribe aromatherapy, and pharmacies stock essential oils along with conventional drugs. In fact, France, England, New Zealand and Switzerland regulate aromatherapy through licensing.

In England, hospital staff administer essential oil massage to relieve pain and induce sleep. In fact, "English hospitals also use a variety of essential oils (including lemon, lavender and lemongrass) to help combat the transmission of airborne infectious disease" (Alternative Medicine, The Definitive Guide).

In France, according to **Dr. Daniel Penoel**, a world leader in using essential oils as therapeutic medicines, aromatic medicine is recognized as being so important and so effective that it has been established as a medical speciality. Until 1990, all prescriptions were reimbursed under the government health care system. Today, it is left to individual counties in France as to whether they cover the costs.

Many essential oils are strongly anti-bacterial and anti-viral. Thyme oil used to be used as a disinfectant in hospitals and is still the active ingredient in Listerine. As Young says in his book, **Aromatherapy: the Essential Beginning**, researcher **Dr. Jean Lapraz** reported that he couldn't find bacteria or viruses that could live in the presence of the essential oils of cinnamon or oregano. The true future of essential oils may be in combating antibiotic resistant bacteria and other bugs resistant to conventional treatment.

Another important area that essential oils can address is the whole field of emotional health. Young has also been a trail blazer in using the essential oils for emotional healing. Based on his studies of the ancient Egyptians, he has developed essential oil combinations that are highly effective for achieving emotional stability, balance, clearing and inspiration. He also has special oils for healing psychological and emotional trauma, including sexual abuse.

The true scope of essential oils has yet to be fully elucidated. But many more uses for oils are being developed by pioneers such as Penoel and Young.

As Dr. Young says in the preface to his new book, **People's Desk Reference for Essential Oils** "After using them, there is no doubt that essential oils were ordained as the medicine for mankind and will be held as the medicine of our future: the missing link of modern medicine, where allopathic and holistic medicine join together the leap into the 21st century."

The **Young Living Essential Oils** are of the highest quality. Call 1-800-763-9963 and use the live prompt for easier and faster service. Your first order requires the member number of whomever has educated you about the oils (#124899). To become a distributor, (the most economic way to purchase the oils), there is a minimum first order of $50. In addition, you are required to purchase a Policies and Procedure Manual for $5. An excellent way to experience the effectiveness of these oils is to purchase the essential seven kit, containing the oils most important for first aid and household use.

Doctor Flags Dangerous Flaws In Drug Regulation

Dr. Michele Brill-Edwards is a senior physician who spent 15 years with Canada's **Health Protection Branch** (HPB). She resigned after becoming convinced that the HPB was risking thousands of lives by putting the financial interests of drug companies above the protection of the public safety.

At the "heart" of the debate are a class of best selling drugs known as calcium channel blockers. These drugs are used to treat high blood pressure, angina and heart arrhythmias. The problem in recognizing the fatal side effects of these calcium channel blockers, says Brill-Edwards, is that it is difficult for the practising physician to discern between heart attacks due to the drug, and heart attacks due to the disease itself.

Calcium channel blockers were originally approved for the treatment of heart disease, not high blood pressure. The drugs work by interfering with muscle contractions by preventing the movement of calcium across cell membranes.

By the 1990's, these drugs were overtaking the older drugs used for the treatment of high blood pressure. In a **Fifth Estate** expose aired on **CBC-TV** on February 1996, journalist **Trish Wood** put it this way: "these drugs became popular without any solid proof that they either prevented heart attacks or prolonged life, while the older therapies had a good track record."

As early as 1989, **Dr. Salim Yusef**, Head of Clinical Trials at the National Institute of Health and now the Head of Cardiology at the Hamilton General in Ontario was growing concerned about the side effects of these drugs, especially a short acting calcium channel blocker known as nifedipine. He co-authored a paper saying that there was no evidence that these drugs saved lives or prevented a new heart attack. In 1991, Yusef's second paper produced stronger evidence that linked nifedipine to an increased rate of deaths in users. His paper was all but ignored. Dr. Yusef also expressed his serious concerns to the HPB.

Then the issue came into the spotlight in 1995 when three studies were published that showed an increase death rate from the use of nifedipine. In one of these reports, **Dr. Curt Furberg** and his colleagues analyzed data from 16 studies involving more than 8,000 patients. They found that those on moderate to high doses of nifedipine had a death rate almost three times higher than patients not given the drug.

Furberg estimated that tens of thousands of patients had died from taking these drugs for treatment of high blood pressure. Furberg believes that the onus is on the industry to show the safety of the long acting calcium channel blockers which it has not yet done. A large long term study is now underway on the effects of the longer acting drugs, but results won't be in until the year 2000.

Meanwhile, in January 1996, the **Health Protection Branch** prepared a "Dear Doctor" letter to all physicians to warn of the possible dangers of calcium channel blockers, especially nifedipine and cautioned that none of them should be used as a first line of treatment for high blood pressure or angina.

At least two doctors on the expert advisory committee that wrote the letter were closely aligned to the drug companies making these drugs. **Dr. Martin Myers** was one of these. He stated that there was no good proof, only circumstantial evidence, that nifedipine was harmful. He also argued that since there is no good evidence that the longer acting drugs are harmful, it would be a great disservice to take them off the market.

Earlier in 1991, Brill-Edwards had objected to the quick approval of a new migraine drug known as Imitrex or sumatriptan. According to Brill-Edwards, the key problem is the drug can cause spasm in blood vessels leading to heart attack and stroke. Users are advised not to take the drug if they have angina or heart disease.

However, many women prescribed imitrex may be unaware they have heart disease. Imitrex may cause sudden deaths but the connection can't be made because the coroner usually doesn't know that the patient was on imitrex. In the present system, there is no accurate method in place to track these potentially lethal side effects, and this greatly concerns Brill-Edwards.

Brill-Edwards also uncovered fraud within the **Prices Review Board** (which is supposed to be a watchdog on behalf of the public). The committee used inflated prices of drugs as the standard by which to compare prices charged by the drug companies. This board is currently under review by the Auditor General of Canada.

Other senior civil servants, concerned about these serious lapses in the regulatory process have joined with Brill-Edwards to form the **Alliance for Public Accountability**. On their own time and money, over 100 civil servants have committed to working towards a safer system. The public is invited to join in their fight. (see their website, or write mbrilled@uottawa.ca fax 613-523-4244).

The cruel joke, says Brill-Edwards, is that the HPB has lax standards with respect to high risk products like blood and prescription drugs, but high standards with low risk products like herbs and supplements.

However, she notes that "there is a huge difference between a blood transfusion, taking aspirin and taking garlic capsules. The same department which apparently lacks enough personnel to adequately inspect blood centers across Canada can somehow manage to hire an army of inspectors to inspect small Canadian herbal businesses and regulate them out of existence."

Friends Who Have Suffered A Loss Need Loving Support

Anthropologist **Margaret Mead** once said, "When a person is born we celebrate, when they marry, we jubilate, but when they die, we act as if nothing has happened."

A public poll once asked how long it should take to mourn the death of a loved one. Most thought 48 hours to two weeks. According to grief experts it takes at least two to three years.

Grief is a normal and natural reaction to the death of a loved one or to a major loss in your life. Grief is also experienced with divorce, miscarriage, moving from your home, the loss of a major dream, the loss of a limb, the loss of your health, and the loss of a beloved pet.

When a loved one dies, most people are unprepared for the floodgate of emotions that sweeps over them and alters their life irrevocably. They feel devastated, crushed, flattened, disorientated, and confused. They have great difficulty even getting through the ordinary tasks of daily living.

People who have not experienced a major loss can simply not imagine how overwhelming this loss can feel to you.

Friends and relatives sincerely want to help, but they often don't know what to say. They may try to comfort you with empty platitudes and dumb cliches that only make you feel worse.

Loving, patient, and non-judgmental support is the greatest gift you can give people experiencing a major loss in their lives.

On a physical level, the most common symptom you are likely to experience after a major loss is profound fatigue, especially in the first year. Forgetfulness and sleep problems are also very common after a death. Other symptoms include headaches, joint pains, back pain and recurrent infections. You may develop a mysterious ailment for which your doctor can find no answers.

Between three and six months after the loss, when all your friends think you should be over this now, the full and devastating emotional impact of the loss hits you in full force like a tidal wave. It feels like you have been numb before that time.

Commonly a whole year goes by in which you walk about like a zombie, barely able to keep up the pretence of functioning. One day you wake up and know you will recover. But then it will still take another one or two years before you have fully accepted the loss and made it a part of your life.

One of the most important things to remember is that you don't get over your loss, you learn to accept it, work through it, and make peace with it.

If necessary, there are grief support groups available as well as experienced councillors, physicians, ministers and other spiritual advisors. Psychiatrist **Edward Pakes**, director of the Bereavement Clinic at Mount Sinai Hospital in Toronto believes that the guidance and support of families though the grieving process is good preventative medicine.

It's not surprising that most of us don't know how to comfort others or handle our own loss. "Simple first aid gets more attention in our world than death and loss." say **James** and **Cherry**, authors of **The Grief Recovery Handbook** (Harper and Row, 1988): ..."We're taught how to acquire things, not how to lose them... the process of losing something feels wrong, unnatural or broken."

A major pitfall to recovering from grief is feeling pressured to pretend we have recovered. James and Cherry call this the **Academy Award Recovery**. In the end it is much kinder to allow ourselves our grief instead of avoiding it.

Bob Deits, author of **Life After Loss** (Fisher Books, 1988), maintains that grief is an honourable emotion, not something to hide and be embarrassed about. He says that grief is both a testament and a tribute to the one who has died or left.

Deits adds that the only healthy way out of grief is through it because there is no way around it. Grief pushes you to greater depths, understanding and compassion. It gives you a higher level of "bullshit" detector. It makes you aware of what is important in life. It is a difficult and thorny gift whose treasures we only discover with the passage of time.

Ways To Combat The Never Enough Time Syndrome

I don't have enough time is a constant complaint these days. Especially never enough time to exercise, eat the right foods, read, meditate, relax, spend time with family and friends, write, travel, do good things for yourself or do nothing. The good news is that we can learn how to make time stretch out and enjoy more of whatever time we do have available to us right now.

As John Lennon said many years ago, "Life is what happens while you're busy doing other things." Usually the big wake up call to reclaim your life in the present tense comes when you or your loved one comes down with a terminal disease.

Suddenly, says **Stephen Levine**, author of, **A Year To Live**, (Random House, 1997) your whole life comes into sharp focus, dreams unlived, closets full of regrets, unfinished business, tangled and unsatisfying relationships, neglected spiritual growth and lack of authentic joy. Most wish they had more time.

Jean Louis Seran-Schriebner, author of, **The Art of Time**, (Addison Weseley, 1988) put it this way: "Unlike other resources, time cannot be bought or sold, borrowed or stolen, stocked up or saved, manufactured, reproduced or modified. All we can do is make use of it."

Stephen Covey, author of, **First Things First**, (Fireside, 1994) talks about giving top priority to important but non-urgent activities like taking time for spiritual and physical renewal, spending time with family and friends, and planning and crisis prevention at work and at home. Instead we spend most of our time feeling pressured and handling crises, deadlines and problems and deferring what we really want to do.

The solution is not to become more efficient at doing more and more things in less and less time. The solution involves a conscious shift in priorities, focussing on the large and small joys of the present moment and doing a lesser number of things (well chosen) in a longer time. As Stephen Levine says, slowing down and stopping to smell, if not plant, the roses.

"We have forgotten how to rest." says **Stephan Rechtschaffen** in his book, **Time Shifting, Creating More Time to Enjoy Your Live**, (Doubleday, 1996) "I'm not suggesting we discard the skills of efficiency and productivity... What I'm urging is balance, a mindfulness that allows us to bring a different rhythm to our days. When we give it a chance, we'll discover a surprising truth, it's when we slow down that we show up."

Rechtschaffen recommends establishing your own pause button, figuring out your own ways to slow down and focus on the present moment. One easy way is to stop whatever stressful situation you're in, and take three or four slow deep breaths. When the phone rings, let it ring three times, pause and take a slow deep breath and then answer the phone. Pause at least two minutes after you finish one task before beginning another. Arrive ten to fifteen minutes early for work, appointments or important meetings and take the extra time to breathe and think. While in the bathroom, take some deep breaths, become aware of how your body feels and stretch.

One of the worst health habits that seems to affect women more than men is not taking even 30 minutes a day of uninterrupted time strictly for themselves. Women deny themselves even this small amount of time. Not time to catch up on household chores or prepare an assignment for work but time to breathe, meditate, daydream, read, take a hot bath or go for a walk.

Rechtschaffen says he would like to see people using holidays as holidays, not as excuses for shopping sprees. Imagine a Christmas season devoted to meditation. He quotes **Juliet Schor** author of, **The Overworked American** (Basic, 1991). She envisions a time when rest becomes as important as work, and contemplation as important as consumption.

The Power of Words To Harm and To Heal

What we say to our patients, especially at vulnerable times in their lives, may have profound and lasting consequences. As a profession, we no longer believe in the inherent healing abilities of the body. We have put our faith instead in high tech solutions to combat disease, and even death itself.

Even with our new drugs and machines, we have failed to conquer major degenerative diseases like cancer, heart disease, stroke, Alzheimer's and diabetes. So doctors are often in the frustrating position of not having much to offer to their patients. At least we can make what we say to our patients weigh in on the side of healing instead of harm.

In his best selling book, **Spontaneous Healing** (Ballantine, 1995) **Dr. Andrew Weil** coined the term "medical pessimism." He says his patients are often told by their doctors: "There is nothing that we can do for you" and "It will only get worse."

"At its most extreme," Weil says, "this attitude constitutes a kind of medical hexing that I find unconscionable." Weil tries to reverse the impact of this hex by first exposing it, then using humour or hypnosis or whatever it takes to cancel out the hex. In addition, of course, he suggests practical alternative therapies that can alter the course of the disease.

Patients can even hex themselves. There are patients who are firmly convinced that no one can help them, or that they have a disease that no one can diagnose. They have been to a series of specialists to no avail.

On the other hand, the patient may have an undiagnosed psychological condition and/or be suffering from a condition that conventional medicine does not yet recognize. These conditions include chemical and environmental allergies, undiagnosed food allergies, subclinical nutritional deficiencies, low or absent stomach acid, underactive thyroid and adrenal function, candida and parasite infections, and chronic fatigue syndrome.

Negative or derogatory statements said while a patient is under anaesthesia can also have a negative impact. Some patients ask their surgeons and anaesthetists to make positive affirmations for them during surgery in order to speed healing.

Positive prayer can have dramatic effect on medical outcome -whether the person knows they are being prayed for or not. Following the publication of his book, **Healing Words, The Power of Prayer and the Practice of Medicine**, (Harper, 1993) **Dr. Larry Dossey** felt compelled to come back with a second book discussing the negative possibilities of prayer and the power of curses. His second book is called, **Be Careful What You Pray for... You Just Might Get It** (Harper, 1997).

Healing is a mysterious and complex affair and it is never possible to accurately predict the outcome of any disease for any particular patient. Weil recounts hopeful and inspiring stories of ordinary people who have cured themselves from incurable illnesses and chronic pain.

The placebo effect can be defined as the expectations and beliefs of the patient about a certain treatment, which then impacts how effective that treatment will be. The belief and enthusiasm of the doctor in his treatments will greatly influence the patient's expectations.

Weil recommends that, if possible, doctors only recommend treatments that they believe in. Oncologist and author **Dr. Robert Buckman** in his book, **Magic or Medicine** (Key Porter, 1993), advises doctors to use the placebo effect for the benefits of their patients.

When recommending treatments, the doctor should ideally make positive and emphatic statements about potential benefits. And when dealing with chronic or terminal illnesses, it is important to keep hope in the picture.

Dossey wants medical students taught courses about spirituality and the benefits of prayer. Weil has already established a postgraduate integrative medicine course for MD's where doctors are taught the power of words.

Final Gifts From The Dying

In spite of the pioneering work of **Dr. Elizabeth Kubler-Ross** and many others, care for the dying is still uneven and difficult to access. Hospice workers are overworked, and hospices have long waiting lists. Hospital staff may not have the time to adequately address the complex needs of the dying. Care for the dying needs to be made a health care priority. Meanwhile, there is much that family and friends can do to help the dying and to help themselves.

Hospice nurses **Maggie Callahan** and **Patricia Kelley**, authors of **Final Gifts** (Bantam, 1992) have tended the terminally ill for more than ten years. Their valuable book is written for caretakers, the dying and health care workers.

"When someone you love is dying you may not see gifts, but only grief, pain and loss. However, a dying person offers enlightening information and comfort, and in return those close at hand can help bring that person peace and recognition of life's meaning."

The authors go on to give concrete examples about messages the dying give which may seem like confused gibberish or drug-induced hallucinations. Messages about when death will occur, what the person needs to feel at peace, and what or whom is holding them back.

Caregivers should ensure that the will has been updated and if possible discussed with the family. All family members should be notified of the terminal nature of the illness. Finally, you can assist the dying person in taking care of unfinished business. If a person who needs to be forgiven cannot come to the bedside, the dying person can write or have someone write a letter of forgiveness and release.

One of the most important aspects of hospice care is making sure there is adequate pain control, which make take some fine tuning. Too little and the loved one is in agonizing pain; and too much and the dying person feels out of his mind, out of control and helpless in the face of drug induced hallucinations.

Caregivers should support the dying person's spiritual choices. For some, this means arranging prayers and services as well as organizing visits from clergy. **Richard Reoch**, in his book, **To Die Well** (Harper, 1996), compiles practical advice intended for both the dying and their helpers. His book is one of the few that offers information on complementary therapies for the dying from both eastern and western traditions, including herbs, aromatherapy, massage, relaxation techniques, shiatsu and visualization.

Visitors to the dying may feel uncomfortable about what to say or do. **Donald Scanlan** was a death and dying councillor for those dying from AIDS and founder of the **Spiritual Healing Center** in Vancouver. In a 1991 article in **Share Vision**, he advised, "Visitors to the dying need just to sit there, to be there. Unfortunately, many visitors and medical staff chatter away about drinks and bowel movements and such and so miss a last opportunity before death to communicate something real, perhaps even in silence."

Scanlan also used to try to get all the loved ones together to put conversations on tape. While it is preferable to do this sooner, it is never too late, to save precious memories and to take advantage of the wisdom of the dying. As Scanlan said, "when someone dies, a library burns."

What the dying have to offer us is lessons about how to live more fully in the present and what is truly important in our lives. **Marie De Hennezel**, author of **Intimate Death, How The Dying Teach Us How To Live**, (Knopf, 1997) a top selling book in France, says "We hide death as if it were shameful and dirty... It is nevertheless an immense mystery, a great question mark that we carry in our very marrow... Many of the dying in their last moments, send back a poignant message: Don't pass by life, don't pass by love."

In fact, the dying remind us to be fully alive in the present, to align ourselves with our true work and purpose, to fix our unfinished business and to express our love to those around us.

Some Experts Question Value Of Hepatitis-B Vaccine

A universal vaccination campaign is in progress against the virus causing Hepatitis-B infection. At the same time, some doctors are seriously concerned about adverse effects of the vaccine.

Almost 95 percent of adults infected with the Hepatitis-B virus (HBV) will completely recover. Two in a thousand infected will die from serious liver complications. Anywhere from one to five percent of adults will become "healthy carriers" having no symptoms, but capable of spreading the virus. Twenty five percent of these carriers will develop life threatening liver disease later in life.

However, Hepatitis-B virus is almost always acquired through infected blood, through an infected mother or through sexual contact. Until recently, the vaccine was only targeted to persons at high risk, such as IV drug users, persons with HIV/AIDS, women and men with multiple sexual partners, and medical personnel.

Now not only children and teenagers have been targeted but infants as well. Infants born in New Brunswick, Northwest Territories and Vancouver are now receiving the vaccine. In the United States, infant vaccination is now officially recommended and in 36 states, children cannot attend school without the vaccine.

Eighty countries have now followed the advice of the World Health Organization and added Hepatitis-B vaccine to the expanding list of vaccines being routinely given to infants.

Edda West, co-founder of the **Vaccine Risk Awareness Network** (VRAN) argues that parents of newborns are not being told that the safety and efficacy of this vaccine is unproven; that the incidence of the disease is extremely low and declining in North America; and that the only possible justification for the use of the vaccine in newborns is if the mother is infected with the disease or is a carrier.

According to **Health Canada** statistics in 1996, there were only 61 reported cases of Hepatitis-B in Canada in children under 15. West found out that most if not all of these cases occurred in children who were born to infected mothers, or who lived in certain Asian immigrant communities where the infection was endemic. In the U.S. a similar situation exists, with 279 children getting Hepatitis-B in 1996.

The **Canadian Hepatitis Working Group** noted that the prevalence of Hepatitis-B infections in children in Canada is low, and confined to small well defined groups such as infants born to HBV women for whom prevention programs already exists. **Dr. Giles Delage**, from the **Canadian Pediatric Society** is concerned about adding three more needles to the infant vaccine schedule. (but vaccines combining hep-B with other infant vaccines are being developed).

Moreover, a point often overlooked is that the protection of HBV vaccine lasts for only ten years at the most. Thus the Hepatitis Group recommended vaccination of the 9 to 13 year group, since the incidence of infections starts to rise dramatically in the 15 to 19 year group and peaks in the 20 to 40 year group.

Meanwhile reports of serious side effects in adults given the vaccine continue to accumulate. In Ottawa, prominent chronic fatigue researcher, **Dr. Byron Hyde** and the **Nightingale Research Foundation** documented the cases of 57 people, mainly in Quebec, who had suffered disabling injuries of the central and peripheral nervous system following Hepatitis-B vaccination. The number of cases reported to Dr. Hyde is now over 100.

In 1990, Dr. Hyde notified **Health and Welfare Canada** of the 57 cases, but he became dismayed when he found out that none of the cases had been adequately investigated beyond a phone questionnaire administered to 17 of these patients. Health and Welfare, says Hyde, is not keeping sufficient or proper statistics on Hepatitis-B and is thus putting both adult and children's health in serious jeopardy.

In 1996, Immunology researcher **Dr. John Classen** reported a 60 percent increase in the incidence of diabetes following a massive Hepatitis-B vaccination programme for children under 16 in New Zealand.

In Houston Texas, **Dr. Bonnie Dunbar**, professor of cell biology at Baylor College of Medicine, reported the cases of two colleagues who developed "severe and apparently permanent adverse reactions as a result of being forced to take the Hepatitis-B vaccine." Her brother, **Dr. Bohn Dunbar** was one of these. He developed lupus like syndrome and multiple sclerosis like syndrome. The other colleague, a medical student went completely blind in one eye following two injections of the vaccine.

Dr. Dunbar obtained the **FDA** list of over 8,000 individuals who reported adverse reactions over the last four years for one vaccine brand. The other vaccine brand is reported to have a list of 15,000 adverse reactions. Adverse reactions include rashes, joint pain, chronic fatigue syndrome, neurological disorders, neuritis, rheumatoid arthritis, lupus like syndrome, and multiple sclerosis like syndrome.

In France 150 doctors worried about recent reports of MS and other neurological disorders in vaccinated patients appealed to the **French Academy of Sciences** to commission an independent study of the vaccine. In July 1998, 15,000 French citizens representing 17 associations filed a suit against the manufacturers of Hepatitis-B vaccine. In addition, France suspended its vaccination of school children (but not infants).

The current consensus of the medical profession is that the HBV vaccine is safe and that the benefits outweighs the risks. Unfortunately, safety data was based on short term studies and follow up of only 4 to 5 days post vaccine.

Since serious sequelae take weeks to months to develop, long term side effects have not been studied. Nonetheless, a new package insert states that the vaccine has been associated with MS, lupus, arthritis, and Guillain Barre Syndrome.

An editorial in the **Journal of Midwifery** poses some timely questions. "With the addition of the HBV vaccine to the list of recommended childhood vaccines, an infant will receive seven immunizations by the age of eight weeks (two HBV vaccines, one diphtheria, one pertussis, one polio, and one H-Influenza vaccine) Is there a point at which this infantile immune system is being asked to take on more that it can handle?... Is it possible that by attempting to contain one disease, other disease processes are evolving?... Are our infants being subjected to vaccination because of the failure of the system to identify and vaccinate the appropriate populations?"

The **Vaccine Risk Awareness Network** (Box 169, Winlaw BC, V0G 2J0, 250-355-2525), is a watchdog organization that gathers and distributes information and publishes a newsletter. Membership is $25. You can send for a free reading list with related net sites. Other sources for information are, **The Association For Vaccine Damaged Children** (204-895-9192), **The National Vaccine Information Center** (www.909shot.com) and the **Immunization Awareness Society** (www.netlink.co.nz/'ias/ias.htm).

CoEnzyme-Q10 Essential For Treatment Of Heart Disease

Cardiologist and researcher **Dr. Peter Langsjoen** ranks the discovery of the nutrient known as co-enzyme-Q-10 as one of the biggest advances of this century. "To ask cardiologists to practice without it would be like asking an internist to practice without antibiotics."

Co-enzyme-Q-10 or Co-Q-10 is an essential component of the mitochondria, the energy producing units of the cells of the body. It is involved in the production of ATP which is the fuel that runs all body processes. The role of Co-Q-10 is similar to that of the spark plug in a car engine.

Langsjoen is an expert in congestive heart failure and disease of the heart muscle. Speaking at an international conference on anti-aging held in Las Vegas in December 1996, he presented the results of his ongoing research since 1981. In one 1994 study, 424 patients with six different types of cardiac disease treated with Co-Q-10 were shown to have improved heart function, enhanced quality of life and decreased medication requirements.

Langsjoen believes his research refutes the common assertion that a stiffening of the heart muscle is irreversible.

But the father of co-enzyme-Q-10 research and the world's leading researcher on co-enzyme-Q-10 is without a shadow of a doubt, **Dr. Karl Folkers**, now in his nineties. In fact, Folkers was presented the highest award of the **Anti-Aging Academy of Medicine** at the conference.

In 1958, Folkers was the first to elucidate the structure of co-enzyme-Q-10 and worked tirelessly to prove its benefit in heart disease as well as many other conditions. Folkers biopsied heart tissue from patients with various heart diseases and showed Co-Q-10 deficiency in 50 to 75 percent of cases. He also proved the effectiveness of Co-Q-10 in treating seriously ill congestive heart failure patients unresponsive to any other treatment.

Dr. Steven Sinatra, author of **A Cardiologist's Prescription for Optimum Wellness**, (Lincoln Bradley, 1996) says that as a traditionally trained cardiologist he was not the least bit open to nutritional therapies, but after reviewing the research, he started to use it in his practice. He has now treated over one thousand patients with co-enzyme-Q-10, with excellent results.

Sinatra points to over 50 major research articles published in reputable journals on the use of Co-Q-10 in cardiac related diseases, especially congestive heart failure and cardiomyopathy (a disease affecting the heart muscle). Researchers estimate that if doctors gave co-enzyme-Q-10 to 1,000 patients with congestive heart failure for one year, it could reduce hospitalization for the condition by twenty percent.

Although some cardiologists are using it, Sinatra adds, the vast majority either know nothing about it or have a bias against it because it is not a drug. Dr. Langsjoen and Sinatra have formed a national coalition of cardiologists to disseminate information on Co-Q-10.

Co-Q-10 is bright yellow bordering on orange in colour and is available in capsules or tablets at health food stores. It is best absorbed in soft gelatin capsules that contain an oil base. Otherwise it is wise to take it with olive oil or flax seed oil. The dosage ranges from 30mg to 300mg with the usual dosage being 30mg three times a day. Although its safety during pregnancy and lactation has not been proven, it has an excellent safety profile, with no serious side effects with long term use.

Research has also shown Co-Q-10 is a useful adjunct in the treatment of gum disease, muscular dystrophy and diabetes. It also is an immune stimulator and antioxidant. It can reduce the heart toxicity of cancer drugs like adriamycin. It has caused a partial remission in a small number of breast cancer patients. It is also very useful in the treatment of chronic fatigue syndrome and fibromyalgia.

Co-Q-10 is one of the top six written prescriptions in Japan. If we pay attention to the Japanese experience, we will improve the health of many chronically ill patients and reduce health costs as well.

Slowing HIV Progress With Nutritional Supplements

Dr. Chester Myers is a Canadian scientist who devotes much of his time outside work to researching the nutritional aspects of AIDS and making this information available to the AIDS community. Dr. Myer's review of the scientific data to date has led him to the conclusion that it is tantamount to malpractice not to prescribe nutritional supplements to people with HIV/AIDS.

Myers, who backs his recommendations with extensive references from the medical literature, says, "It is easier to go over the cliff, then to get back on top." Two 1993 studies showed that supplementation was associated with significant slowing of HIV disease in terms of years, not just months. Says Myers, "Deficiencies in HIV/AIDS are common and may occur early. It is far better to prevent problems caused by such deficiencies than to treat them later."

Eating a well balanced diet is a good start, but not nearly enough. People with AIDS often have preexisting nutritional deficiencies or can develop them in the course of the disease. Reasons why people with HIV infection can develop nutrient deficiencies include loss of appetite, diarrhea, malabsorption, poor eating habits, past history of drug and alcohol use, smoking history, and increased nutrient requirements because of illness and/or medications used.

The most recently published data were from the John Hopkins School of Hygiene and Public Health. **Dr. Alice Tang** and her colleagues studied 310 gay and bisexual men. Those that had adequate blood levels of vitamin-B-12 remained free of the disease for about eight years compared with four years for those deficient in this essential nutrient. The same type of relationship was also proven for vitamin-B-6 and folic acid.

Vitamin-B-12 works with folic acid in many essential body processes including the making of DNA, red blood cells, and the myelin sheath that surrounds nerves.

Dr. Barbara Abrams and her colleagues at the **University of California** found that the daily use of a multivitamin supplement for six years was associated with a 40 percent reduction in the risk of a low T-cell count. In fact, those whose supplement consumption was within the highest third were about half as likely to develop AIDS compared to those in the middle or lowest thirds. Intake of vitamin-E and iron from supplements alone was also significantly associated with a reduced risk of AIDS. There was no association between AIDS risk and the intake of food alone.

An earlier 1993 study by Tang showed that progression rate to AIDS was also decreased in subjects with the highest intake for vitamins B-1, B-2, B-6 and C. "The apparent protective effects observed in the B-group vitamins were primarily due to the intake of vitamins from supplements rather than food," commented the researchers.

Another interesting nutrient for AIDS is N-acetyl cysteine (NAC). Cysteine is an amino acid required to make a compound called glutathione. Glutathione is a powerful antioxidant present in every cell and in high concentration in the liver and lungs.

"NAC supplementation has been shown to discourage muscle wasting, lower immune cell destruction, lower production of certain immune suppressive compounds, and enhance production of glutathione," says Myers. The usual recommended dosage is between 400mgs and 1.5gms a day.

A new whey protein concentrate, Immunocal (TM), may inhibit HIV replication while stimulating the production of glutathione. At **Montreal's McGill University**, **Dr. Sylvain Baruchel** and his colleagues have shown in preliminary trials that this whey protein is beneficial for muscle wasting in children and adults with AIDS. A double blind randomized controlled study of Immunocal (TM) in patients with AIDS and wasting syndrome is now in progress in Canada and France.

All the vitamins and minerals are required in balance. An individualized supplement programme should be geared to specific needs and problems. Among other important nutrients recommended by Myers are co-enzyme-Q-10, vitamin-E, zinc, selenium, magnesium, the amino acid carnitine and essential fatty acids.

Myers recommends the work of Washington DC researcher **Dr. Lark Lands**, "the original guru for promotion of good nutrition including aggressive supplementation among people living with AIDS." Both Myers's and Land's research articles are available through the **Community AIDS Treatment Information Exchange** at 1-800-263-1638 or www.catie.ca

Genetically Engineered Food
A Serious Health Threat

The **United Nations Codex Committee on Food Labelling** plans to pass regulations that would allow thousands of genetically engineered products to flood the food market all over the world. The huge biotech industry is lobbying Codex to pass internationally binding legislation allowing these experimental and potentially very dangerous foods in every country, without labelling or proper testing and mixed with other foods. The implications for the future of our health and that of our children are staggering.

As we found out in cloning experiments with animals, the results of manipulating genetic material are unpredictable. Some of the cloned sheep turned out to be monsters, too large to fit into their stalls or to be delivered by normal sheep mothers. If human organs are to be grown inside cloned sheep, there are still disturbing questions about whether the animal viruses contained in them can be transmitted to humans.

Now our very food supply is being threatened by genetic experiments never before performed in human history. Biologist **Dr. John Fagan** puts it this way: "If genetic engineering was precise and controlled it would give rise to reliable results. In fact, it isn't. There is always some uncertainty as to where the inserted gene will land... Other problems stem just from the immense complexity of living organisms... We cannot predict the range of interactions, nor can we control it. Therefore unexpected damaging side effects are inevitable."

These damaging side effects could include new toxins and allergens in foods; unnatural gene transfers between species, causing the spread of dangerous diseases across species barriers; increased use of stronger pesticide and pesticide combinations; and of course unknown long term effects.

Soy foods are now being promoted for disease prevention. However, soybeans and canola oil are being genetically engineered to be resistant to weed killing chemicals or herbicides. This allow farmers to spray higher levels of herbicides without damaging crops. The increased use of herbicides leads not only to increased contamination of food, soil and water, it is also toxic to animals, and the genetic alteration may spread to other weeds making them very difficult to eliminate.

Soybeans are used in approximately 60 percent of processed food. Canola oil is also used in a wide variety of food products.

Using the new genetic technology, genes that can be spliced into plants include bacteria, viruses, fish and even human genes.

The New Leaf potato from PEI contains a bacteria gene which creates a toxin in the potato to kill insects. Biotech supporters claim that this toxin becomes deactivated in humans, but tests have only been performed on animals. Long term effects are simply unknown.

In a recent article in **Health Naturally**, nutritionist **Carola Barczak** points out that genetically engineered tomatoes in imported canned products (purees, ketchups and pizza sauces) can carry anti-ripening genes, antibiotic markers, herbicide resistant genes and fish genes. Further she says that unlabelled U.S. approved squash targeted for the baby food market is spliced with a virus gene.

Dr. Fagan, who has done extensive research in the field of molecular genetics, has called for a worldwide fifty year moratorium on genetically altered food saying that "the entire population is in a dangerous global experiment in the interests of short term commercial gain by giant trans-national biotech companies that control large segments of the world's food supply."

In general, European countries have refused to let genetically engineered foods into their countries without labelling. A recent referendum in Austria showed strong consumer resistance to allowing genetically altered food into the food supply. Polls here show that 83 to 94 percent of consumers want clear labelling.

I believe we should take a cautious and moderate approach to the problem and enable consumers to make their own choice through proper labelling of such foods and a moratorium on the introduction of genetically manipulated foods until they have been properly tested. Consumers meanwhile can get information packages from **Greenpeace** or **The Natural Law Party**. Both have good internet sites.

In the native tradition, all are urged to consider the effects of their actions on seven generations to come. When these genetically altered foods enter the food chain, as many have already done, there will be no way to put the genie back into the bottle. For the sake of our children and ourselves, we must insist on our rights to clear labelling and freedom of choice.

Studies Finger New Heart Attack Villain, Homocysteine

In the future, it may be more important to know your homocysteine level than your cholesterol level. An elevated homocysteine level is proving to be a very accurate predictor of heart disease and stroke risk. The good news is that it is easy to lower your homocysteine levels through diet and vitamin-B supplements.

According to a recent cover story in **Newsweek** (August 11/97) most heart attack victims have normal cholesterol levels. Moreover, says reporter **Geoffrey Cowley**, there has been a steady decline in deaths from heart attacks despite the fact that cholesterol levels haven't changed much. "An avalanche of new studies show that an amino acid called homocysteine (pronounced HO-mo-SIS-teen) plays a critical role in destroying our arteries, perhaps as big a role as smoking and cholesterol."

Dr. Kilner McCully, a pathologist at the **Veteran Affair's Medical Center** in Providence, Rhode Island has conducted research on homocysteine for over 35 years. But due to the dominance of the "it's all cholesterol" school of thought, he's been like a voice crying in the wilderness. Now McCully's work has finally been vindicated in larger studies and McCully has just authored a book called, **The Homocysteine Revolution** (Keats, 1997).

Homocysteine is a sulphur containing byproduct of the essential amino acid methionine which is present in all protein. When methionine is broken down, it is converted to the free radical homocysteine. This free radical can cause damage to the arterial wall.

There are three ways you can get elevated homocysteine levels. The first is eating an excess of foods that contain methionine, which is plentiful in meat. The second is if you have a genetic defect that makes you unable to breakdown homocysteine. The third, and by far the most common, is if you have borderline vitamin deficiencies of three B-vitamins, folic acid, vitamin-B-12 and B-6.

A nutritional survey of older people conducted in Boston showed that most were deficient in not just one, but many nutrients. In the 60 to 69 year group, 65 percent were deficient in vitamin-D, 70 percent in folic acid, 70 percent in vitamin-B-12, 35 percent in calcium and 65 percent in zinc. B-6 deficiency was also widespread. Also as you age, the stomach makes less acid, and thus much less of the vitamins and minerals from our food are actually absorbed.

According to **Dr. Jeffrey Blumberg**, a senior scientist at **Tufts University** in Boston, homocysteine also functions like a brain toxin in the elderly. Elevated homocysteine levels, which are a sensitive indicator of deficiencies of vitamin-B-

6, and folic acid, can trigger such neurological changes as a drop in alertness and memory ability as well as numbness and tingling in the legs.

Meanwhile, numerous studies have documented the link between hardening of the arteries and elevated homocysteine levels.

Dr. Jacob Selhub is the author of one of the recent studies on homocysteine published in the **New England Journal of Medicine**. Selhub and his colleagues in Norway found that even after adjusting for age, cholesterol and the amount of blockage already found in the heart arteries, high homocysteine levels were associated with a higher death rate from heart disease.

"A blood test for homocysteine costs about $25 to $40." said Selhub, "and high homocysteine is easy to treat by ensuring that patients get enough folic acid and vitamins B-6 and vitamin-B-12."

In fact, right now there's plenty you can do to assure a lower level of homocysteine. First eat a low fat high fibre diet with lots of fruits and vegetables. Second watch how you prepare your food especially vegetables which should be steamed or baked. The three B-vitamins are destroyed during food processing, and also by high heat and freezing.

Thirdly don't hesitate to take supplements if you are not getting your 5 to 7 daily servings of vegetables and fruits. Take at least 75mgs of vitamin-B-6, 100 micrograms of vitamin-B-12 and 400 micrograms of folic acid daily as a preventative measure. For very little money, and with no harmful side effects, you will be lowering your risk for heart disease and stroke, according to the latest evidence.

As Selhub puts it, "Do not wait for the Messiah, we recommend that you eat more vegetables, but if you can't do that take a vitamin pill."

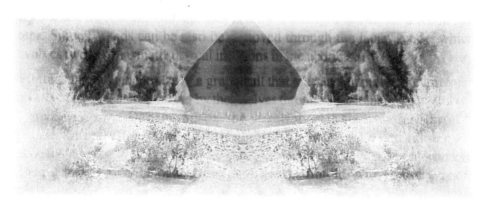

That Low Fat Diet May Cause Weight Gain

All carbohydrates are not alike. The current obsession with a low fat high carbohydrate diet may be misguided. For at least one third of the population or more, this diet, even when religiously followed, has been a disaster for weight loss. In addition, a significant minority of doctors believe this diet can be harmful for your heart.

The debate recently reached the pages of the **New England Journal of Medicine**. (August 21, 1997) **Drs. Katan, Grundy** and **Willett** point out that while concerns grew over high fat in the diet, "the perception grew that carbohydrates were innocuous."

First they point out that low fat high carbohydrate diets lower the good HDL cholesterol as well as the bad LDL cholesterol. "Replacement of fat by carbohydrates has not been shown to reduce the risk of coronary heart disease, and benefits are unlikely, because this change similarly lowers HDL and LDL cholesterol, and reduces the intake of vitamin-E and essential fatty acids."

The three doctors also point out that studies of people who are on a fat restricted diet show very little weight loss. In fact, the number of people that are overweight is increasing steadily while the total calories derived from fat is decreasing.

New York complementary medical doctor **Robert Atkins** was one of the first physicians to champion the cause of the low carbohydrate diet. Atkins believes that obesity is caused by a chronic state of high insulin secretion. High insulin levels cause sugar to be stored as fat and the body becomes less sensitive or resistant to the effects of insulin. This hyperinsulinemia is a major risk factor for both heart disease and diabetes.

Normally in the body there is a balance between two hormones insulin and glucagon. Glucagon causes sugar to be released into the blood stream from fat tissues while insulin removes it from the blood stream and stores it as fat.

New York doctors, **Richard** and **Rachel Heller**, authors of **The Carbohydrate Addict's Diet**, found that excessive carbohydrate consumption leads inevitably to addictive behaviour. A vicious cycle ensues in which high carbohydrate consumption leads to high insulin levels which in turn leads to a drop in blood sugar levels leading to increased cravings for carbohydrates which in turn leads to more carbohydrate consumption and eventually to obesity.

Rachel Heller was massively overweight. After twenty years of agony, ill health and being blamed by her doctor for her failure to lose weight, Heller finally found an effective diet that balances and redistributes carbohydrates throughout the day in order to create a stable constant level of insulin secretion. For two meals a day, you eat no carbohydrates. Then for the third meal, you eat a balanced meal with unrestricted carbohydrates at the same time every day.

Other diet books, such as, **The Zone**, by PHD researcher **Barry Sears** promote a diet with low carbohydrates and increased fat and protein. Sears maintains that this diet ensures a steady insulin level and good energy level as well as weight loss.

Sears also emphasizes certain carbohydrates with a low "glycemic index" versus those with a high "glycemic index". Glycemic index refers to the rate at which glucose enters the bloodstream after a carbohydrate is eaten. Examples of low glycemic index foods are rye breads, slow cooking oatmeal, lentils, many vegetables, and yogurt. Examples of high glycemic index foods are sugar, corn chips, rice cakes, puffed cereals of all kinds, cooked carrots, raisins, and white rice.

What does all this mean for the average person? First, if you have consistently failed at every weight loss diet, consider cutting down on carbohydrates. Especially important are sugars and refined and processed carbohydrates. This includes white bread, white pasta, sugar and refined flour products. This may be more important than reducing fat. Eating all carbohydrates at one meal may be another effective strategy.

Dr. Katan and her group advise overweight people to eat less sugar and highly refined starch. They recommend replacing unhealthy fats from meat, dairy and margarine with healthy fats such as olive oil. As for carbohydrates, they should be consumed "mainly in the form of fruits, vegetables, legumes and whole grains."

Why We Need Good Fats

In our obsession with low fat, we haven't always distinguished between "good" and "bad" fats. It's clear that bad fats, like margarine, shortening, animal fats, refined vegetable oils, rancid and overheated oils are harmful. But sometimes the good fats, like extra virgin olive oil, and the essential fatty acids like flaxseed and fish oils get overlooked.

Essential fatty acids are necessary for normal growth and development, but cannot be manufactured by the body. They must be obtained from the diet. There are two families of fatty acids known as omega-3's and omega-6's.

Omega-3 fatty acids are found in marine life such as fish, seal and whale, and plants such as flaxseed. Omega-6 fatty acids are found in evening primrose oil, borage, black currant, sunflower and safflower oils.

The typical North American diet results in widespread deficiency of essential fatty acids as well as an imbalance of omega-3's relative to omega-6's.

Health Canada recommends a ratio of omega-3 to omega-6 of between 1 to 4 or 1 to 7, versus the usual diet with its ratio of 1 to 20 to 1 to 60. The typical low fat diet may contribute to excess omega-6's fats. As a result, most health authorities suggest daily supplementation with one or more omega-3 sources.

People who consume a diet rich in omega-3 oils from either fish or plant sources have a reduced risk of heart disease. Studies of the Inuit and Greenlanders whose diet is high in meat and fat, mainly from seal, found they had a low rate of heart disease.

Inhabitants of Crete eat a typical Mediterranean diet with its large amounts of olive oil, vegetables, legumes, fruits, greens and wild plants. Cretan men have been found to be among the healthiest in the world. The Cretans also have a diet high in walnut oil, and a wild plant known as purslane- both high in omega-3's.

Hundreds of studies have demonstrated that either fish oil supplementation or consumption of fatty fish lowers cholesterol and triglycerides levels. Fish oils can also prevent heart attacks in those that already have heart disease, and lower the incidence of blood clots. Fish oil or flaxseed oil have both been shown to lower high blood pressure.

Dozens of studies have demonstrated that rheumatoid arthritis patients who take fish oil supplements daily have less morning stiffness and tender joints and can reduce medication.

Omega-3 oils have numerous other health benefits including improving insulin action in non-insulin dependent diabetics. They are also very helpful in a wide variety of conditions including Crohn's disease, ulcerative colitis, irritable bowel syndrome, chronic fatigue syndrome and multiple sclerosis.

Researcher **Udo Erasmus**, author of **Fats that Heal, Fats that Kill** prefers flaxseed oil for omega-3's. However, he believes that health conscious people can overdose on flaxseed oil and that maintaining a proper balance of omega-3's to omega-6's is important.

Steven Kripps, author of **Nutrition Alert**, advises that flaxseed oil is very sensitive to heat, light and oxygen. He recommends grinding your own organic flaxseeds, a two week supply at a time and storing them in your freezer. But no matter how you do it, it is wise to increase your intake of omega-3 fatty acids.

The Power Of Superfoods

Both **Sam Graci** and **Daniel Cristafi** are rare individuals who have studied the rules of natural healing and who have devoted their lives to letting people know how they can achieve their highest vision of health and well being. Both also share a deep concern for our planet and how our lifestyle choices affect our future and that of our children. Both believe that each of us can truly make a difference on this planet.

The choice of what we eat greatly impacts the planet. The average meat eater requires 20 times more land to support his habit than a vegetarian. In addition, much of our food has been grown on depleted soils with harsh pesticides, insecticides and chemical fertilizers. Some pesticide residues concentrated in the fat of meat and dairy can mimic the actions of estrogen, causing hormonal imbalance and even cancer. Even our organic soils are deficient in the trace minerals so necessary for optimal health.

Few of us are eating the five to seven servings of vegetables and fruits recommended in the food rules. Few of us are taking the time to make nutritious meals prepared in a loving and wholesome manner. The introduction of microwave cooking has caused further deterioration in the quality of our foods. This is why **The Power of Superfoods** is such an important book for healthy living.

This book covers the essentials of healthy eating including many different types of superfoods, the use of green drinks (which I recommend to all my patients), balancing acid and alkaline foods, drinking large quantities of pure water, making sense of current diet controversies and saying goodbye to dieting. Two separate chapters go into detail on super-nutrition for men and women.

At the same time, The Power of Superfoods avoids being self-righteous and does not suggest that a strict vegetarian diet is appropriate for everyone. It also gives lots of ideas for short cuts to healthy eating, so important in today's chronically time deprived world.

Some well known superfoods Graci discusses are organically grown grasses, sprouts, sea vegetables, sea algae, acidophilus, bee products, bilberries, grape seeds and soy lecithin.

Harvey Diamond, the world renowned author of **Fit For Life**, contributes an excellent chapter on a form of fasting and cleansing known as mono-dieting or eating only one kind of food at a time (which is easier to do than regular fasting).

The mind body connection is rightfully given a prominent place in this book. Sam Graci includes a helpful chapter on exercise emphasizing walking as an ideal exercise. Another important chapter is on breathing for relaxation and stress management. A key chapter includes a questionnaire to determine your spiritual fitness and how to improve it.

Jeanne Marie Martin whom I have known for many years, gives us the benefits of her vast experience preparing tasty and delightful meals at the end of this book.

In short, **The Power of Superfoods** by Sam Graci and **Les Superaliments** by Sam Graci and **Daniel Cristafi** (both Prentice Hall, 1997) provide the insight and guidance you need to fuel your body effectively for both physical nutrition and spiritual evolution.

Take Time & Consider Options After Breast Cancer Diagnosis

Getting breast cancer has a profound effect on your life but it's not usually a medical emergency. You can allow yourself the time to get centred, to organize good emotional support and to investigate your options.

Even experts disagree and thus you may be faced with difficult choices at an emotionally vulnerable time.

The first decision is what type of surgery to have to remove the cancerous lump (either lumpectomy, just having the lump removed or mastectomy, having the whole breast removed). Long term survival for lumpectomy is the same as for mastectomy.

With lumpectomy you have the advantage of preserving the breast and having sexual sensation still present. Some doctors may have a unscientific bias towards mastectomy. Nonetheless mastectomy may be the best option with a very large tumour or several tumours in the same breast, or if radiation is not feasible.

At the time of the lumpectomy, some or all of the lymph nodes are routinely removed for diagnosis in finding out whether the cancer has spread. The lymph glands are an important part of the defense system against cancer. Removing them does not appear to extend long term survival. Side effects may include pain, numbness, swelling, and a limited range of motion in the arm.

The Head of Surgical Oncology at the B.C. Cancer Agency, **Dr. Greg McGregor** notes that the value of lymph node removal is becoming an increasingly controversial topic. Dr. McGregor is chief investigator in a new trial to see whether lymph node conservation affects lymph node reoccurrence or overall survival.

Dr. Edward Fish, former assistant professor of surgery at the University of Toronto, also questions the routine removal of lymph nodes, especially for women who have a small breast lump and no palpable lymph nodes felt in the armpit.

American breast surgeon **Dr. Robert Kradijian**, author of **Save Yourself From Breast Cancer**, believes axillary dissection is unnecessary in many cases, including women who have decided firmly for or against chemotherapy before surgery. He suggests a full discussion of risks and benefits with your surgeon.

A new technique is being developed where a radioactive blue dye is injected close to the tumour before it is removed. The dye then travels through the axilla to a lymph gland called the sentinel gland. The sentinel gland is then removed and if it contains no cancer cells, the lymph nodes can be safely left intact.

Radiation is usually offered with lumpectomy but unnecessary with mastectomy. Radiation does not extend your life but does reduce local reoccurrence of the cancer in the same breast by about 15 percent.

The main radiation side effects are fatigue and skin changes (redness, itching, peeling and blistering). Some of the changes in the skin may cause ongoing problems.

Dr. Fish studied 100 women who had lumpectomy only. Women over 65 with a small tumour with no aggressive features, had a local reoccurrence rate of less than 5 percent and would thus not benefit from radiation.

Finally there is the question of "preventative" chemotherapy to prevent distant spread of the cancer. In his thoughtful book, **Breast Cancer** (Prima Press, 1994) naturopathic physician **Steve Austin** says most women have severely impaired quality of life from chemotherapy but relatively few benefits.

Toxic side effects include hair loss, nausea, vomiting, and a dangerous lowering of your white blood cells making you susceptible to infection.

If you have no lymph node spread, you have a 70 to 80 percent chance of surviving free of disease without chemo. If you are a postmenopausal woman with no nodal spread, chemotherapy has minimal benefit. If you are a pre-menopausal woman with lymph node spread, the benefits are modest, a ten percent increase in overall survival. With a large or rapidly growing tumour, chemotherapy may be strongly recommended. Each woman has to weigh the risks versus the benefits for herself.

Still confused? One of the most clearly written and illustrated guides to sorting out conventional breast cancer treatment was written by three B.C. cancer specialists. The book is, **Breast Cancer: All You Need to Know to Take an Active Part in Your Treatment**, by **Drs. Olivotto, Gelmon and Kuusk**.

Finally, women are increasingly demanding access to information about alternative treatments for breast cancer. At a recent meeting in Vancouver forty doctors from across North America agreed to study unconventional breast cancer treatments.

An excellent manual, **A Guide to Unconventional Cancer Therapies**, was funded by **Health Canada** as part of the **Breast Cancer Initiative Project** (905-727-3300).

Another valuable tool is the **Healing Choices Report**, by **Ralph Moss**, a thirty to fifty page summary of alternative therapies for your cancer type. (718-636-4433)

Cancer As A Turning Point

Dr. Lawrence LeShan researcher and clinical psychotherapist is the author of **Cancer as a Turning Point** (Plume, revised 1994) For over 35 years Dr. LeShan has worked with terminally ill cancer patients given up on by the medical profession, using a unique approach which has resulted in about half of them going into long term remissions and still alive when the book was published.

LeShan believes that the traditional psychological approach does not help cancer patients. When he used therapy based on the usual questions, (What is wrong with the person? How did she or he get that way? What can be done about it?) the person felt temporarily better but the outcome was always the same- they died.

LeShan developed a different approach focussed on the questions:

"What is right with this person? What is her special and unique ways of being, creating, and relating, that are her own and natural ways to live? What is her unique song to sing that when she is singing it, she is glad to get up in the morning, and glad to go to bed at night? What style of life would give her zest, enthusiasm and involvement? How can we work together to bring her dream into manifestation, and release blocks and other obstacles?" When the person was able to do this, LeShan discovered that they went into a long lasting remission.

LeShan's earlier research, reported in his book, **You Can Fight for Your Life** (Evans, 1980), found common clues suggesting a cancer prone individual. The strongest clue concerned the loss of the person's reason for being, or sense of purpose. The second was an inability on the part of the individual to express anger or resentment. The third factor was continuous emotional tension over the death of a parent.

The loss of hope that you can ever live your own life in a meaningful dynamic passionate and engaged way that makes a difference in the world, says LeShan, weakens your immune system and defeats any chance of recovery. LeShan evokes **W. H. Auden**'s definition of cancer as "a foiled creative fire."

"Over and over again, I found this pattern of loss of hope in between 70 and 80 percent of my cancer patients and in only 10 percent or so of the control group."

Psychiatrist **Jean Shinoda Bolen**, inspired by LeShan's work, began giving a series of workshops for breast cancer patients which eventually became the book, **Close to the Bone, Life Threatening Illness and the Search for Meaning** (Scribner, 1996).

"Illness is both a soul shaking and soul-evoking event for the patients and for all others for whom the patient matters. We lose all innocence, we know vulnerability, we are no longer who we were before this event and we will never be the same. We are in uncharted terrain, and there is no turning back. Illness is a profound soul event and yet this is virtually ignored and unaddressed. Instead, everything seems to be focussed on the part of the body that is sick, damaged, failing or out of control."

Bolen describes the experience of a life threatening illness as a descent into the underground, where we can undergo numerous ordeals, find strength and courage and have the potential to be reborn into a new sense of self and purpose.

Bolen uses myths and stories to describe the incredible and terrifying journey that anyone with a life threatening illness embarks on, willing or not. With understanding or not. With profound spiritual growth or not.

Nowhere is blame for your illness implied (one of those less than useful new age concepts). The complexity of illness can't be understood by facile assumptions about how the person's lifestyle, diet, stress levels or thought patterns somehow produced the cancer.

However, how we respond to illness, what we learn from it and how we engage the journey along the way can certainly impact the outcome. These two writers provide us with many lighted sign posts along the way.

How To Find Out About Alternative Cancer Care

More people than ever are dying of cancer, and one in three can expect to develop cancer. Alternative medicine offers some excellent options to prevent reoccurrence of the disease or as part of a treatment plan that includes surgery or finally as an adjunct to both chemotherapy and radiation.

However, when it comes to finding out about alternative cancer treatments and how to access them, patients often find themselves on their own, with a bewildering explosion of information, some reliable and some not.

Doctors themselves often lack reliable information about alternatives, and are fearful about drug interactions with herbs or vitamins. At the same time, they want to know what their patients are using.

With an estimated 10 to 60 percent of cancer patients using some form of complementary therapy, public demand for more information has been responsible for some recent initiatives to study cancer alternatives.

After the 1993 **National Forum on Breast Cancer**, the **Canadian Breast Cancer Research Initiative** formed a task force to advise it on how best to promote research into unconventional therapies. Chaired by **Dr. Elizabeth Kaegi**, former Director of the **National Cancer Institute**, the task force reviewed available literature for essiac, green tea, iscadora, hydrazine sulfate, vitamins A, C, and E and 714-X. Their information packages on these six topics are available free through the **Cancer Information Service** at 1-888-939-3333 or at their web site. Although the conclusions tend to be quite limited from an alternative perspective, they provide a good starting point.

In addition, the articles were published in the **Canadian Medical Association Journal**. Comprehensive summaries of all literature reviewed are available on request for doctors.

At an October 1996 conference held in Vancouver, forty doctors from across North America agreed to study unconventional treatments for breast cancer. One innovative study proposed comparing 100 women following conventional treatment to 100 women using conventional therapies plus alternatives.

The study would then measure differences in quality of life as well as rates of recurrence and survival for the two groups. Alternative medicine usually involves a multi-pronged approach. So it may be problematic to study a single therapy in isolation, as is usually proposed.

In Vancouver, a new multidisciplinary **Center for Integrative Therapy** offers complementary therapies for cancer. The Center will employ two full time physicians, **Dr. Roger Rogers** and **Dr. Hal Gunn**, and will include practitioners doing massage, body work, yoga, meditation, music therapy, art therapy, and therapeutic touch. Gunn sees the goal of the clinic as providing people with more options and helping bridge the gap between alternative and conventional medicine.

The Center will also be involved in researching non-traditional therapies. It will collaborate with the University of Texas and the **Tzu Chi Center for Complementary and Alternative Medicine** at Vancouver Hospital to study 714-X and essiac.

New York oncologist **Dr. Charles Simone**, author of **Cancer and Nutrition** (Avery, 1992) refers to over 200 peer reviewed articles which show that nutritional modification, including the use of antioxidants, decreases the side effects and complications of chemotherapy and radiation while increasing response rates to both therapies.

Several excellent reference books are available including, **The Alternative Medicine Definitive Guide to Cancer** by Diamond, Cowden and Goldberg, (Future Medicine 1997); **Cancer Therapy: The Independent Consumer's Guide** by Ralph Moss (Equinox, 1995), and **A Guide to Unconventional Cancer Therapies** by The Ontario Breast Cancer Exchange Program, funded by Health Canada (905-727-3300).

Ralph Moss, the author of ten books including **Questioning Chemotherapy**, and **Herbs Against Cancer**, provides a research service for cancer alternatives. For $275 U.S., **The Moss Reports** provides a detailed 30 to 50 page report specific to your type of cancer including the most promising alternative treatments, and how to obtain them. Call 718-636-4433.

Meanwhile, take the time to examine all your options. Too many people are making decisions based on fear and terror. Whatever type of therapy you choose, you still need to know and trust yourself.

Breast Cancer Linked To Toxic Environment

By the most conservative estimates, 80 percent of all cancers are related to environmental factors. This includes the food we eat, the water we drink, the air we breathe, and the heavy metals, industrial chemicals, pesticides, and radiation we are exposed to.

In fact, the **National Research Council** found no information at all on possible toxic effects of eighty percent of the 50,000 or so industrial chemicals used in the U.S. and Canada. There are also many unanswered questions about the remaining twenty percent.

Organochlorines like dioxin, PCP's, DDT and 10,000 other chemicals in the same family have been shown to disrupt the endocrine system and impair the reproductive abilities of animals. Organochlorines are highly persistent and toxic chemicals produced by industries that make PVC plastics, solvents, pesticides, refrigerants, and bleached white paper. They concentrate in the fatty tissues of animals and the humans who eat them. More than 177 organochlorines have been found in the tissues of the general population of Canada and the U.S.

Breast cancer has been linked with the use of pesticides, as well as exposure to radiation, and low level emissions from nuclear plants. Most studies have shown a connection between PCB and DDT exposure and breast cancer. One study that didn't show that link was a retrospective study on 240 nurses. However, the study is of limited value since it measured only a few chemicals in stored blood taken in 1989 or 1990. Larger well designed studies are now in progress.

Dr. Sandra Steingraber, author of **Living Downstream: An Ecologist Looks at Cancer** (Addison-Wesley, 1997) says there will never be absolute proof that chemicals cause cancer. Cancer has multiple causes, may take decades to manifest. Furthermore, large populations and control groups are needed to conduct reliable studies. Meanwhile, she believes that scientific evidence to date justifies action to eliminate major pollutants from our environment.

Co-author of **The Breast Cancer Prevention Program**, (MacMillan, 1997) and professor of occupational and environmental medicine at the University of Illinois, **Dr. Samuel Epstein** faults the **U.S. National Cancer Institute** for adopting a blame the victim mentality. He says the Institute concentrates too much on personal habits like dietary fat and too little on the avoidable carcinogens that accumulate in fat. Preventive research is being neglected, charges Epstein, in favour of a futile and lucrative quest for cures.

American **Greenpeace** researcher **Joe Thornton** says that "stopping organochlorine pollution of the environment and our bodies should be a priority of breast cancer prevention strategies." Women should urgently support Greenpeace and other groups to phase out the industrial use of organochlorines in the pulp and paper industry and in the manufacture, use, and incineration of PVC products.

Prudent avoidance of exposure seems the best policy. Women should refuse to use bleached paper products, including sanitary napkins and tampons (unbleached sanitary products are available in health food stores). Avoid the use of all chemicals and pesticides for home, lawn and garden. Get your family to take off their shoes at the door to reduce the tracking of lead and other contaminants into the house. Use alternatives to PVC building materials and PVC children's products which are listed on the Greenpeace website.

The main source of exposure to dioxin and other chemicals is in the fat of meat and dairy. Thus it's best to reduce or eliminate animal fat in your diet and concentrate on whole grains, beans, fresh vegetables and fruits.

Innovative Ways Of Dealing With Infertility

Both male and female infertility rates have risen dramatically over the last fifty years. More than three million visits each year to North American physicians are for infertility.

The increased infertility is mainly due to environmental pollution of our air, water and food. In addition, due to chemical agriculture, our food and soil is severely depleted in many essential nutrients especially trace minerals. We are also subjected to electromagnetic radiation through computers and high voltage power lines which affect basic biological rhythms like reproduction.

Over the last fifty years the male sperm count has dropped by fifty percent. **Dr. Niels Skakkebaek**, Professor at Copenhagen University Hospital, examined studies of more than 15,000 men in over sixty studies and found a steady downward trend in sperm quality. He also discovered that some men had 50 percent abnormally formed sperm.

Organochlorines and other industrial chemicals can unlock the estrogen receptor in the body, like a key fitting into a lock, and thus cause an estrogen like effect. In women, this may cause relative progesterone deficiency and contribute to a rising incidence of female reproductive problems including infertility. In men, this has been associated with a decreased sperm count, infertility, undescended testis and other developmental abnormalities in young boys, and finally, prostate and testicular cancer.

In 1978, **Lynn Barnes** founded the **Association for Promotion of Preconception Care** in England. Also known as the **Foresight Foundation**, its doctors have been able to prevent miscarriage and birth defects through a comprehensive preventative programme. Of the approximately 5,000 couples who followed their protocol, only one baby was born with a birth defect and one in 65 miscarried, compared to the usual ratio of one in four.

In May 1995, the **Journal of Environmental Medicine** published a Foresight study in which 367 couples participated. Among the 204 couples with infertility, 86 percent achieved a healthy pregnancy. There were no malformations and only one child was born with a low birth weight.

So exactly what did the Foresight doctors do? After taking a medical and environmental history of both partners, they performed standard blood and urine tests, cultures for infection, semen analysis, cervical smear and prostatic secretion analysis. They also conducted special tests to determine vitamin and mineral status and hair analysis to check for the toxic heavy metal level. Foresight doctors commonly found that the main cause of the infertility problem was an undiagnosed infection.

Doctors working for Foresight emphasized preventive education of prospective parents. They focussed on the dangerous effects of smoking, alcohol, medications, and recreational drugs on both fertility and the fetus. At the same time, they stress the need for treating allergies, digestive problems, malabsorption, candida, and parasites before conception. Future parents must also eliminate contact with environmental toxins by eating only organic foods, drinking clean water and taking high quality nutritional supplements.

Dr. Marja Trossel, a leading complementary medical doctor in Holland, tests the mercury load of the body. If the results are positive, she uses at least ten chelation treatments to eliminate heavy metals from the body and boost the immune system, after mercury fillings or work exposure to mercury have been dealt with.

According to Dr. Trossel, the most commonly occurring toxic metal is lead, which has a detrimental effect on reproduction, causes fetal abnormalities, malformed sperm, low sperm count, decreased motility of sperm and interferes with sperm production.

Her clinic also promotes a healthy bowel ecology to enhance detoxification, promote absorption of nutrients and decrease allergies. In addition, she recommends exercise, low temperature saunas and an environmentally clean home.

Dr. Patrick Kingsley, a prominent Foresight doctor in Britain, says that infertility and birth defects should be regarded as any other chronic disease. Adds Dr. Trossel, "It's a signal of the body just like allergy, rheumatism or bowel problems that something is wrong. And it can be treated! Detoxification is the answer."

Dr. John Lee author of **What Your Doctor Won't Tell You About Menopause** (Warner Books, 1996) believes that, "estrogen dominance and progesterone deficiency has caused a near epidemic of infertility among women in their mid-thirties." He advocates the use of natural progesterone skin cream to enhance fertility.

If you do nothing else, remember a recent randomized controlled study of more than 5,000 women. Those who received a multi-mineral and vitamin supplement for at least one month prior to conception had a higher rate of pregnancy.

Foresight American Foundation For Pre-conception Care can be reached at 215-529-9026.

Menopause "Wonder Drug" Must Stand The Test Of Time

TV reports on a new estrogen designer drug for menopause, the wonder drug that will have all the benefits of estrogen with none of the down side, came off sounding very close to the drug company's own press release. In fact, **Eli Lilly** just released preliminary data on its new drug, raloxifene. Mention of any possible long term negative effects was carefully avoided.

Raloxifene is the first among a new class of drugs called selective estrogen receptor modulators. Recent research has discovered that both natural estrogen and synthetic estrogen-like compounds interact with estrogen receptors in different ways.

The shape of the receptor changes to accommodate the shape of the estrogen like a water bed changes to conform to the body. The shape assumed by the receptor determines what type of action the estrogen will have on breast, uterus, heart and bone.

The new estrogen receptor modulators attempt to produce the positive effects of estrogen on heart and bone while preventing the cancer causing effects on breast and uterus.

Eleven thousand women taking raloxifene are being studied in more than 20 countries. Two years into a five year trial, raloxifene prevented bone loss in the spine and hips compared with calcium supplemented placebo. The effects on preventing fractures are still being studied.

For two years, the effects of raloxifene on cholesterol were evaluated throughout the trials and specifically in a six month trial of 390 women. So far, it has lowered total cholesterol and serum fibrinogens, a risk factor for heart disease. It did not appear to cause breast or uterine cancer to date.

Some prominent experts have raised concerns that raloxifene may block the protective action of estrogen in the brain, thus speeding up the onset of Alzheimer's in women at risk for contracting the disease. Right now this connection is still unproven but obviously very worrisome.

A few years ago, raloxifene's cousin, tamoxifen, a drug used to prevent breast cancer recurrence, was suggested as a safe alternative to hormone replacement therapy. Tamoxifen appeared to prevent breast cancer while helping preserve bone and having a positive effect on the heart.

However, when the proper long term studies were performed a different picture emerged. First of all, tamoxifen's protective effect against breast cancer lasted about five years. After five years, the breast tissue appeared to become resistant to tamoxifen and tamoxifen may have actually caused more cancer.

Meanwhile, it was found that tamoxifen increases bone loss in women taking it before menopause and stabilizes bone mass in women after menopause. As for tamoxifen's initial beneficial effect in preventing heart attacks, it was disproved in later studies. Tamoxifen also increases the risk of cancer of the uterus.

Tamoxifen does have a few annoying side effects. These include hot flashes, nausea, vomiting in 25 percent, and, less frequently, depression, skin rashes, irregular bleeding, blood clotting, visual problems and liver enzymes changes.

Why would a healthy menopausal woman want to take tamoxifen? This question arose in 1992 when healthy women were being urged to participate in a large tamoxifen trail for breast cancer prevention launched by the **US National Cancer Institute**.

In England, five deaths from liver disease were linked to tamoxifen. These deaths prompted Britain's **Medical Research Council** to refuse to back the tamoxifen prevention trial.

At that time, **Dr. Adriane Fugh-Berman**, Director of the **National Women's Health Network**, posed the question: "Is this disease prevention or disease substitution?" This question may have to be posed for raloxifene and its relatives.

It's too early to say whether raloxifene will turn out to be the new wonder drug. In about thirty years we will accurately know whether this new drug truly offers a good and reasonable option to the menopausal woman. The outcome of long term clinical trials on whether the benefits of HRT outweigh the risks for healthy postmenopausal women are still pending.

Sandra Covey, author of **The Menopause Industry** (Hunter House, 1994), says that the industry has constructed the illusion of choice, between death and deterioration and medications with serious side effects. Much of what passes for patient information, she argues, is actually a carefully constructed marketing exercise. Complex issues are minimized. Incomplete and confusing studies are presented as dogma.

Meanwhile, Canadian women are not flocking to take hormones, only about 15 percent of them versus about 50 percent of American women who take them. Baby boomers are looking long and hard at the alternatives and defining their own choices.

How To Cope With Persistent Bladder Infections

So many women suffer from recurrent bladder problems that until recently it was considered part of the fate of women. Natural remedies can play a useful role in both prevention and treatment. There are two distinct types of chronic bladder problems or cystitis. Infectious cystitis is due to reoccurring bacterial infections of the bladder. The other very different type is called interstitial cystitis, an inflammation of the interstitium, the space between the bladder lining and the bladder muscle.

According to Beverley Hills urologist **Dr. Larrian Gillespie**, author of, **You Don't Have to Live with Cystitis**, injury to your low back area can damage the nerves that go to your bladder causing your bladder not to empty completely. Thus some residual urine is always left, predisposing you to repeated infections. Gillespie recommends chiropractic adjustment to relieve the pressure and prevent infection.

Too much sex, too little sex, or oral sex, do not cause infectious cystitis. However, after sex it is important to urinate, but only after you have waited long enough to build up a good forceful stream to wash out the bacteria that have accumulated in the bladder.

Diaphragms that are too large can alter the angle of the bladder neck, making it difficult to empty the bladder completely. Make sure your diaphragm fits snugly, and be sure to urinate before you put it in and six hours later, after you remove it. Tampons can cause the same problem. So, if necessary, remove them before urination or use sanitary napkins. Use only unbleached tampons and pads.

The vagina itself is a balanced ecosystem. Friendly bacteria called lactobacillus acidophilus help keep the vagina acidic and resistant to infections.

Excess spermicide, foam, or lubricant, can also irritate the urethra and predispose you to infections. According to **Dr. Gregor Reid**, former Director of Urology Research, at Toronto General Hospital spermicides destroy a woman's friendly bacteria and increase the risk of bladder infections by as much as four times.

Dr. Reid and his colleague **Dr. Andrew Bruce**, Chief of Urology at Toronto General Hospital have been studying women with chronic bladder infections.

In the study, one group of 28 women with four proven bladder infections within the past 12 months, was treated with the acidophilus suppositories; the other group with inert suppositories. Another arm of the study treated 40 women with acute bladder infections with a three-day course of antibiotics followed by a three-month course of **Restoration Plus**, and compared it to results with 20 women treated with antibiotics followed by three months of placebo.

"When we looked at the two groups of women, those who did not have infections, had beautiful growths of lactobacilli," Dr. Bruce commented in the **Toronto Star** (Apr/13/92). "The lactobacilli seem to have a protective effect. A significant number of women who had repeated infections had a poor population of lactobacilli."

Restoration Plus is a unique vaginal suppository that contains two key strains of lactobacilli called lactobacillus casei and lactobacillus fermentum.

The results of this study have shown Restoration Plus to be a very effective preventative treatment for bladder infections. Acidophilus suppositories seem to stimulate the normal growth of lactobacilli in the vagina. The treatment is given once a week for six to 12 months. Dr. Reid estimates that the new treatment could save the North American health care system $150 million a year.

If you have repeated infections, you may want to try acidophilus suppositories placed in the vagina every night for a week, then once a week for six months to a year. You can use a high quality acidophilus powder available in any health food store, and put it in 00 gelatin capsules.

When symptoms first appear it may be helpful to drink one teaspoon of baking soda in a glass of water, one time only. More importantly, make sure you drink at least eight ounces of water a day. Avoid acid foods like citrus and tomatoes, sugar and sugar substitutes and use only buffered vitamin-C.

Research to date has shown that cranberry or blueberry juices make it harder for bacteria to stick to the bladder wall and also acidify the urine. One study showed that if you take 300cc of cranberry juice daily, you cut the rate of reinfection by half. Unsweetened juices are best.

Eliminating contributing factors and improving the body's natural defences provide more options for women with this troublesome problem.

Endo Under-Diagnosed And Difficult To Treat

"If a man had a disease which caused him to be unable to father a child and unbearable pain during sex and unbearable pain during bowel movements treated by feminizing hormones and surgery," says nurse **Nancy Petersen**, Director of the **Endometriosis Treatment Program** in Bend, Oregon, "endometriosis would be a national emergency in this country."

Fortunately there is an outstanding international group dedicated to supporting and educating women and their doctors about the diagnosis and treatment of endometriosis. The **Endometriosis Association** (1-800-426-2END) is sponsoring endometriosis awareness week March 23 to 28. The association is distributing yellow ribbons to spread the word to women who do not yet have access to information about the disease.

Endometriosis (endo) is normal tissue in an abnormal location. It occurs when tissue similar to that which normally lines the inside of the uterus, (the endometrium) grows in parts of the body where it doesn't normally grow. This happens most commonly in the bottom most part of the pelvis, the uterine ligaments, outside surface of the uterus, tubes, ovaries, lower end of the large bowel, and on the membranes covering the bladder.

Endometriosis may be the result of an auto-immune disease. This means that the body rejects the abnormal endometrial-like tissue that is located in the pelvis, with both local and generalized effects.

Recent evidence has shown that the immune system of endometriosis patients is depressed. This includes dysfunction of T-cells, B-cells, and natural killer cells.

The meticulous research of a gynecologist in a small city in Oregon has yielded a new and intriguing theory of what causes endo. **Dr. David Redwine** of Bend, Oregon, found no evidence that endo is a recurrent or progressively spreading disease.

In Dr. Redwine's theory, endo is a static disease that you are born with, as a result of cells left behind during fetal development. Later on, certain triggers activate the disease.

Some of those triggers could include environmental contaminants such as dioxin, other industrial chemicals and radiation; stress and emotional factors; a diet high in meat and dairy; iodine deficiency, deficiency of essential fatty acids; vitamin and mineral deficiencies; chronic yeast infections, sluggish liver function, and relative progesterone deficiency.

Women with endometriosis still have difficulty getting diagnosed. Petersen says that 75 percent of the women who came to Dr. Redwine's clinic with proven endo had been dismissed by their doctors as being neurotic.

Unlike what most doctors were taught, women with endo report a wide variety of types of pain and timing of pain. There is really no "typical" endometriosis pain and it can occur at any time throughout the cycle.

In Dr. Redwine's study, painful periods occurred in only 45 percent of women, painful sex in 37 percent and infertility in 27 percent. Other symptoms included pain with bowel movements, pain with aerobic exercise or jogging, and pain with posture changes. Twenty percent of women were asymptomatic.

The purpose of treatment is the relief of pain (it does not usually improve pregnancy rates). The choices offered are usually expensive drugs with serious side effects or surgery requiring much skill and expertise.

For some women, the painful symptoms of endometriosis can be alleviated through natural means. However, such approaches require time, patience and commitment. They are not as cut and dry as taking a pill or getting abnormal tissue cut out. There is no single panacea that works for all women with endo. It will probably be necessary to combine a number of different therapies and to allow sufficient time for them to work. It is also advisable to have a naturopathic physician to co-ordinate treatment.

It is also important to look at the emotional issues both caused by having a disabling disease and preceding the development of it. Working to change beliefs about illness, stress reduction and visualization techniques are helpful to anyone with chronic pain problems.

The new age attitude that we create our own reality, while it has merit, has resulted in people beating up on themselves or others who have chronic illness. The implication is that women with endo have done something wrong in their physical or emotional life that caused the illness. These attitudes can become an obstacle to healing.

Evidence On Endometriosis And The Environment

Thanks to the untiring efforts of **Mary Lou Ballweg**, founder of the Endometriosis Association, evidence on the link between radiation exposure, and organochlorine exposure, and the development of endometriosis has been brought to light.

The Endometriosis Association is renowned as a model of the successful self help group. Its mission is to provide support and information to women with endometriosis, to conduct research, and to educate doctors and the public.

Ballweg's quest led her to research published by **NASA**. In the mid 1960's, NASA had begun a long-term study to find out the effects of ionizing radiation on monkeys. Endometriosis developed in 53 percent of the monkeys after radiation exposure; and in only 26 percent of the monkeys not exposed to radiation.

Meanwhile, years ago, the Canadian government studied the effects of adding PCBs to monkey food. Researchers were surprised to find that the monkeys developed endometriosis. **Dr. James Campbell** told Ballweg that the addition of PCB to food seemed to increase the severity of the endometriosis rather than the numbers who got it.

Through Dr. Campbell, Ballweg tracked down another study. Since 1977, the **Environmental Protection Agency** had funded a long-term study on the effects of adding dioxin to the food of a monkey colony. Researchers noted immune dysfunction in exposed animals as well as difficulty in reproduction. In 1992, the funding for the project had become exhausted, and the animals were to be sold.

Under Mary-Lou Ballweg's leadership, the **Endometriosis Association** stepped in and bought the remaining animals. The Association then asked renowned endometriosis experts, **Dr. Dan Martin** and **Dr. Paul Dmowski**, to carry out laparoscopic and immunological studies on the animals. The results were published in the **Journal of Fundamental and Applied Toxicology** in Nov/93.

Seventy-nine percent of the animals exposed to dioxin in the study developed endometriosis compared to 33 percent in the control group. Most importantly the disease was dose dependant, that is, it increased in severity in direct proportion to the amount of dioxin exposure.

Currently, the **National Institute of Environmental Health Sciences** is carrying out a study to determine the blood levels of dioxin, furan and PCB's in women with endometriosis. PCB's have been linked to endometriosis and thyroiditis in a German study published in 1992. **The Environmental Protection Agency** is also carrying on a study to determine the effects of dioxin in rats who have had endometriosis surgically implanted in their bodies.

Definitive studies will take many years to complete. And as Ballweg says, with so many chemicals involved, and complex mechanisms of interaction within the human body, there will be no simple answer.

Meanwhile, it makes sense for women with endometriosis and their families to avoid exposure to all unnecessary radiation as well as exposure to dioxins and other industrial chemicals.

The main source of exposure to dioxin and other industrial chemicals is in the fat of meat and dairy products. Thus it is best to emphasize whole grains, and organic fresh vegetables and fruits and to cut down on fats from milk and meat products.

It also makes sense for women to stop buying bleached paper products (with possible dioxin residues) including toilet paper, diapers, sanitary napkins, tampons; and chlorine bleaches and cleaning agents. Ballweg suggests that before you throw out that last box of napkins or tampons, you call the toll free number of the company and tell them why you're switching. Alternatives include cloth pads, a rubber cup known as the keeper and unbleached tampons/napkins available at health food stores.

Ballweg speculates that, "The disease of endometriosis might have been a mild, mostly tolerable disease in the past (except presumably for a few unlucky souls) that has become severe and distinctly intolerable with the additional effects of modern pollutants in our bodies. These studies may help explain why there seems to be an **epidemic** of endometriosis world wide in this century."

Dealing With Hot Flashes Naturally

One of the most well known symptoms of menopause is hot flashes. Estrogen usually eliminates hot flashes. However, for women who choose not to take hormones either as a personal choice or because they have already had breast cancer, there are safe natural alternatives.

A hot flash is described as a sudden reddening of the skin over the head, neck and chest or even the entire body, accompanied by a feeling of intense body heat. The hot flash may last from several seconds to several minutes, rarely up to an hour. The frequency varies from rare to occurring every half hour. Some women sweat profusely; others just a little, or not at all. Hot flashes are usually preceded or followed by chills. Within two years after the last period, hot flashes will subside completely for the most part. However, for one third of women, they may continue well after that.

Hot flashes may be visible to others, but not usually. They can also be triggered by hot drinks, spicy food, alcohol, emotional stress, hot weather or overheated rooms. The key to handling hot flashes is to keep cool, dress in layers, carry a portable fan, avoid the triggering factors, and keep a sense of humour. The good news is that hot flashes are harmless.

Some women experience incapacitating hot flashes that seriously interfere with their sleep or work. They wake up drenched in sweat and have to change their nightgown and sheets three to four times a night. They may want to consider the risks and benefits of taking estrogen.

Alternative remedies, except for Ipriflavone, a patented soy derivative approved for the treatment of osteoporosis in Japan and Italy, have not been studied for their effect on bone loss. A recent New England Journal of Medicine article reported that soy protein reduces cholesterol. The antioxidant vitamins, especially vitamin-C and vitamin-E reduce the risk of heart disease.

Soy proteins contain 75 percent plant estrogens known as isoflavones which have been shown to relieve menopausal hot flashes. Two tablespoons of ground flax seed (which has a nutty taste) or two servings of soy foods daily should help get rid of hot flashes. A new cookbook entitled, **Estrogen the Natural Way, Over 250 Easy and Delicious Recipes for Menopause**, by **Nina Chandler** (Villard, 1997) provides new ways to add soy and flax seed to your diet.

In Chinese acupuncture, the twelve energy pathways of the body are balanced with acupuncture needles and herbs. Many women have had excellent relief of menopausal symptoms when they receive acupuncture and Chinese herbal treatments from an experienced practitioner.

Dong quai root (angelica sinensis) is famed in Chinese medicine for its affinity for the female constitution. It contains many plant estrogens that are about 1/400 as strong as prescription estrogens. Dong quai balances the amount of estrogen in the body and usually relieves hot flashes.

Panax ginseng, either Oriental or North American, will increase energy levels and metabolic rate, stimulate the immune system, and help normalize body functions. It works well for hot flashes, as well as stress, and mental and physical fatigue. It is not recommended for those who are anxious, or have insomnia or high blood pressure.

Vitamin-E enhances the effect of estrogen in the body and is helpful for hot flashes. One controlled study of 94 women showed that of women who received 200mg of vitamin-C combined with 200mg of bioflavonoids six times a day for hot flashes, 67 percent reported complete relief and 21 percent reported partial relief. Bioflavonoids have a very weak estrogenic effect about 1/50,000 that of estrogen.

Two food supplements, evening primrose oil and bee pollen are safe and effective for hot flashes.

Standardized black cohosh root has been well studied in Europe for over forty years. It improves all menopausal symptoms and has a good safety record. One randomized double blind study compared the results of 80 women selected to take Remifemin (black cohosh extract) premarin or a placebo. The first two groups both reduced their symptoms the same amount and both did better than the placebo group.

Natural remedies empower women with more choices during a challenging and often trying life transition.

Natural Remedies Can Ease Interstitial Cystitis

An estimated 450,000 people in the U.S. and 50,000 in Canada have interstitial cystitis (IC), a disabling disease that can be under-diagnosed and improperly treated. Ninety percent are women. The average age of onset is 40 years old, but 25 percent of these women are under age 30. A combination of conventional and natural remedies can provide help for this disabling problem.

A 1987 survey of IC sufferers by the **Urban Institute of Washington** showed that 40 percent were unable to work; 27 percent were unable to have sex due to pain; 27 percent had marriage breakdown; 55 percent contemplated suicide and 12 percent attempted suicide.

For **Dr. Vicki Ratner**, now an orthopedic surgeon, who developed an intensely painful bladder condition as a medical student, it took 11 months of desperate search and visits to ten urologists and two allergists before the diagnosis of IC was made. Dr. Ratner founded the **Interstitial Cystitis Association** (ICA) in 1984. It was born, as she says, out of patient desperation.

Now, thanks to the hard work of the ICA, both doctors and the public are much more aware of this incapacitating condition. ICA has also lobbied successfully for eleven million dollars in research funds for IC and related areas.

Typically, if you have this problem, you experience recurrent and disabling bladder pain and urinary frequency, but urine cultures keep coming back normal, that is, showing no signs of bacterial infection.

During these painful episodes, you feel a painful burning sensation when you pass urine. You can also experience urgency which means the urgent need to go to the toilet to urinate, but little result when you do. Most likely you also have urinary frequency, that is, you have to urinate more frequently than normal and often during the night as well. Some sufferers urinate as many as fifty times a day.

In interstitial cystitis, the interstitium, the protective layer that lines the inside of the bladder is damaged. Normally this layer protects the bladder from the acids and toxins in the urine and prevents bacteria from adhering to the bladder wall.

There may be other co-factors as well including neurological, inflammatory and auto-immune aspects, which may dictate different forms of treatment.

Treatment of IC requires the help of a urologist, preferably one who is experienced in treating IC. A natural substance known as dimethyl sulfoxide (DMSO) is the most common treatment used. DMSO is a liquid anti-inflammatory agent instilled in the bladder through a catheter. The patient holds the medication in her bladder for up to a half an hour. Approximately 50 to 90 percent of those with mild to moderate interstitial cystitis get improvement with DMSO.

Some women have been helped by very low doses of elavil (an antidepressant medication) in the range of 10 to 40mg a day, usually taken at bedtime. In these low doses, the drugs help by blocking pain, calming bladder spasms and reducing inflammation.

In clinical trials, the anti-histamine known as hydroxyzine has been shown to improve IC symptoms, especially those with a history of allergies, migraines and irritable bowel syndrome.

Elmiron or sodium pentosanpolysulfate is an expensive oral medication that is believed to coat the bladder and protect it from irritants. The major side effects are diarrhea and reversible hair loss. In **FDA** clinical trials, 38 percent of those treated with Elmiron for three months reported improvement of their symptoms.

Dr. Ramon Perez-Marrero believes heparin (a drug that decreases blood clotting) acts like elmiron in the bladder. Since heparin is far cheaper, Dr. Perez-Marrero feels it might make more sense to put heparin into the bladder.

In his experience with severe IC, instillation of heparin into the bladder helped 40 to 50 percent of people with severe IC. Patients can be taught to self-catheterize and do the daily treatments at home for three to four months.

For women who fail to respond to any other treatment a new and pricey product known as Cystistat (R) may be helpful. **Bioniche Inc** of London Ontario manufactures this product (1-888-567-2028 in Canada and 1-800-567-2028 in the United States).

Cystistat is instilled directly into the bladder. It acts as a temporary replacement for the defective bladder lining. Cystistat has been approved as a medical device. It is actually a solution of sterile sodium hyaluronate, a natural substance found in the body, which acts as a binding and protective agent.

A preliminary study of 21 patients, who previously failed to respond to all other treatments, showed that with Cystistat, 70 percent experienced significant relief and 30 percent had some improvement. Further studies are underway at ten medical centers across Canada. A FDA pilot study at the **New England Medical Center** in Boston is underway.

New research has shown that BCG (tuberculosis vaccine) can help IC. Several studies showed that six weekly instillations of BCG into the bladder produced a 60 percent response rate when compared to a 27 percent placebo response rate. Moreover, 89 percent of the positive responders maintained improvement two years after treatment.

In my experience, it is also important to determine food allergies through an elimination diet. Foods to which a person is sensitive definitely can trigger a bladder attack. So can artificial sweeteners like cyclamates or aspartame.

Other natural methods that can be used as an adjunct to treatment include TENS or "transcutaneous electrical nerve stimulation" which means using electrical stimulation of acupuncture points to reduce pain. A minimum four to six week trial should be tried. Biofeedback, hypnosis and bladder retraining may also be useful.

Studies have shown abnormalities of the fourth and fifth lumbar vertebrae in women with IC. Chiropractor adjustment of these vertebrae may result in improvement of pain and frequency of urination.

Some have obtained excellent relief using a combination of diet, herbs, vitamins and homeopathic remedies. Chinese medicine in the form of acupuncture and herbs works well for some. Good results for all these methods depends on the supervision of an experienced practitioner who can individualize your treatment program.

A recent study showed that taking an amino acid known as L-arginine in doses of 1.5 grams per day for six months resulted in a decrease of IC symptoms.

While there is still a lot we don't know about IC, much can be done to bring the problem under control and allow a person to lead a normal life.

For more information contact the **Canadian Interstitial Cystitis Society** at 250-758-3207 and the **Interstitial Cystitis Association** in New York at 212-979-6057. ICA's website has fact sheets on all the treatments at www.ichelp.org.

Natural Remedies For Yeast Infections

Vaginal yeast problems are a common and highly annoying problem for women. Natural remedies can be highly effective as well as cheap. In addition, chronic yeast infections can be part of a bigger picture which requires more intensive treatment.

In 80 to 90 percent of cases, vaginal yeast infections are caused by a yeast known as candida albicans. Lately, another candida species known as candida glabrata is showing up with increasing frequency, possibly due to widespread use of over-the-counter drugs for yeast infections. Candida glabrata doesn't respond as well to the commonly used drugs, but does respond well to something as simple as boric acid suppositories.

As many women know all too well, the main symptoms of yeast infections are vaginal discharge and itching of the genital area. The discharge is usually white, and varies from being a little to a lot, from being thin and mucousy to thick, curdy and cottage cheese-like (with anything in between being possible). The amount of itching varies, but can be severe enough to interfere with sleep and normal activities. Some women notice a characteristic odour suggestive of bread dough or the fermenting yeast smell of beer being brewed.

Other frequent symptoms are swelling, redness and irritation of the outer and inner lips (the labia), painful sex and painful urination due to local irritation of the urethra.

A woman with a full-blown yeast infection is acutely uncomfortable and requires immediate treatment if possible. If you suspect that you have a yeast infection see your doctor as soon as possible in order to get cultures of the vaginal secretions taken, before you take any over the counter medication. Other types of vaginal infections can co-exist or produce a similar picture of signs and symptoms.

Pregnant women with yeast infections should not use any douche or suppository or herb suggested below, but should seek treatment from their doctor.

Boric acid is an effective, inexpensive treatment for both candida albicans and candida glabrata infections. It costs under five dollars per bottle. Boric acid can be put in 00 gelatin capsules and inserted high into the vagina once or twice a day for seven days. As an alternative, a douche can be made using two tablespoons of boric acid to one quart of lukewarm water and used daily for a week.

Another natural over-the-counter drug is betadine douche or suppository, made from iodine and effective against both yeast and trichomonas. Trichomonas is caused by a pear shaped parasite and can cause symptoms which can mimic yeast infections.

Tea tree oil vaginal suppositories taken every night for seven to fourteen days is another remedy recommended for both yeast and trichomonas. The suppositories are available from health food stores.

A douche made of golden seal and myrrh once a day for three to five days is useful for resistant yeast infections. The douche is made by covering one teaspoon of golden seal powder and one teaspoon of myrrh powder with one quart of boiling water and letting it steep until cool.

Avoid using pre-made homeopathic suppositories for yeast, which can cause a terrible aggravation of symptoms.

Persistent reoccurring yeast infections may be part of a larger picture involving widespread overgrowth of yeast organisms in the whole body. This syndrome is not yet recognized by the medical profession, except in patients with severely compromised immune systems. Proponents say chronic yeast syndrome is common and causes symptoms affecting every system of the body. Symptoms include fatigue, brain fog, depression, irritability, diarrhea alternating with constipation, food and environmental allergies, menstrual problems including PMS, infertility, asthma and other respiratory illnesses.

Treatment involves taking the friendly bacteria known as acidophilus, and following a special diet avoiding sugar and highly refined foods, yeasted breads, fermented or mouldy foods and fruit juice. Natural or prescription anti-yeast medications (taken by mouth) for six weeks to six months are also usually recommended.

New Ways Of Dealing With Fibroids

Fibroids are benign tumours or growths of the uterus, which are dependant on the hormone estrogen for their growth. They are two to three times more common in Afro-American women. Fibroids are the number one reason for hysterectomies in both Canada and the U.S. accounting for one third of all hysterectomies.

Until recently, there were few options for women with problematic fibroids. However, the good news is that, if necessary, fibroids can be removed surgically by themselves, and the uterus saved. Natural therapies can be an effective option for fibroids, especially small and medium sized ones.

Fibroids are made of smooth muscle and fibrous tissue. They can vary from the size of a pea to a size of a melon. They are made of hard white grisly tissue that has a whorl-like pattern. Fibroids can be easily diagnosed through a pelvic ultrasound.

Fibroids can cause no symptoms at all, or cause irregular or heavy bleeding, and pressure symptoms. In fact, heavy or irregular bleeding is the most common presenting symptom of fibroids. Sometimes a large fibroid can cause symptoms by pressing on a pelvic organ. For example, urinary frequency may result from pressure on the bladder. Fibroids can also cause a sense of fullness in the rectum, lower back or abdomen. Usually these symptoms are annoying, but not harmful.

Small slowly growing fibroids which are causing no symptoms can be left alone. Symptomatic small fibroids can be removed through a new procedure known as hysteroscopy. Hysteroscopy refers to an operation in which a small lighted instrument (scope) is used to look inside the uterus (hystero).

Fibroids under 1 to 2cm (about an inch) in diameter, or that have a stalk, or that are protruding into the uterine cavity can be easily removed through the hysteroscope. Fibroids between 2.5 and 5 cm. (one and two inches) can be removed the same way, after they have been shrunk through medication. Fibroids larger than 5cm (two inches) must be shrunk medically, and then removed in two steps. Some fibroids can be also be removed through the laparoscope, which involves two to four small surgical incisions in the abdomen.

Fibroids larger than the size of a grapefruit that are causing pressure symptoms or severe bleeding can be cut out by themselves through abdominal surgery known as myomectomy. Depending on the location and size of the fibroids, myomectomies can be more complicated, take a longer time, and cause more blood loss than hysterectomies. It may take some research and input from women's groups to find a gynaecologist skilled at removing fibroids while preserving the uterus.

There is a new non-surgical technique being studied in Toronto called "embolization". This treatment involves injecting tiny granules of polyvinyl alcohol to plug up the tiny blood vessels that enable the fibroid to grow. The fibroids then shrink in size or sometimes disappear altogether.

During this procedure, a catheter is inserted through a vein in the groin area to the uterine arteries. The granules are then injected through the catheter and travel with the blood into the small blood vessels supplying the fibroids and block them up. The main uterine arteries may also be blocked, so this technique is not suggested for women who still intend to become pregnant. The fibroids then break down, and this can cause pain in the first few days following the embolization.

Dr. Andrew Common, head of vascular radiology at University of Toronto has successfully used this treatment to treat ten women at St. Michael's Hospital in Toronto, and more than 200 cases have been performed worldwide. A five year study involving four Toronto hospitals and enroling 400 to 500 women is in progress and will be completed in 2003.

Fibroids will grow larger if you are taking estrogen pills. Fibroids will also shrink after menopause. So if you are close to menopause, the best course may be to leave them alone until that time.

Some women have had success treating symptomatic fibroids naturally. The natural approach involves diet, nutritional supplements, natural progesterone and liver support. Improving pelvic circulation is also important through osteopathy, through "visceral manipulation" (a special type of chiropractic manipulation) hydrotherapy, and castor oil or clay packs to the lower abdomen. Usually the supervision of a skilled naturopathic physician or chiropractor is necessary to co-ordinate a multi-pronged approach.

PID Can Be Prevented

Pelvic inflammatory disease or PID will affect one is six women by the year 2000. In the United States, over one million women will get PID every year, and 300,000 women are hospitalized for the condition. In Canada, each year over 100,000 women will contract the disease. PID is the leading cause of preventable infertility and tubal pregnancy. Yet PID is perhaps the most ignored women's health problem.

Moreover, it can cause long-term health problems and complications. Scarring of the pelvic organs, chronic pain, tubal ovarian abscesses, and recurring infections are common after only one episode of PID.

The good news is that PID can be prevented. This is the urgent message of the **Canadian PID Society**, the only North American group which provides public education and prevention programs on PID.

"The most important measure that women can take to prevent PID is to use barrier methods of birth control." says **Jill Weiss**, co-ordinator of the PID Society. "Women can also protect themselves from PID by regular testing to ensure that they are free from cervical chlamydial infection or bacterial vaginosis which can cause PID."

Pelvic inflammatory disease is an infection or inflammation of a woman's reproductive organs (uterus, tubes, ovaries and surrounding tissues). It is caused by a number of different bacteria- the most common one being chlamydia. PID is usually acquired through sex. A common vaginal infection, bacterial vaginosis, is also associated with PID. Surgical procedures that open up the cervix like D-and-C's, abortions, and insertion of IUD's can predispose to PID.

Childbirth also opens the cervix and can result in PID. All pregnant women should be checked for cervical and vaginal infections and promptly treated. Women who have C-sections have a high risk of developing PID after surgery. Preventative antibiotics before a C-section or abortion drop the incidence of PID by 30 to 70 percent.

Symptoms of PID vary a great deal and do not give a good indication of the extent or even presence of infection. Most women with PID have normal temperatures, and most have only one or two mild symptoms. There is no specific lab test yet negative tests do not mean PID is not present. A high index of suspicion and willingness to investigate vague but suggestive symptoms is important.

At least fifteen studies have shown that clinical diagnosis is in error at least 40 percent of the time. In the United States, the **Center for Disease Control** estimates that at least 50 percent of women with PID are never diagnosed or treated. In addition, once diagnosed, women are often inadequately treated with a single antibiotic.

The Center for Disease Control recommends evaluation for PID if any of the following are present: fever, recent lower abdominal pain, increased pain or bleeding during periods, bleeding between periods, pain during sex, discharge that is not easily explained, tenderness of the tubes or pain when the cervix is moved during an internal exam or a positive test for chlamydia, or gonorrhea. Proper treatment requires multiple antibiotics taken for a full two weeks as well as treatment of partners.

An estimated 65 percent of Canadian teenagers use no protection during sex. Yet teenagers have the highest risk for PID. Each year, one in eight sexually active teenagers will develop the condition.

In spite of these appalling statistics, the prevention of PID is not only possible but highly effective. In Sweden, the rate of PID has decreased by 40 percent as the result of a widespread public education campaign which begins in elementary school. At the University of British Columbia in Vancouver, testing, education and increased condom use reduced chlamydial infection by 37 percent.

Women who regularly use condoms or diaphragms with spermicide have anywhere from 40 to 60 percent less risk of PID. The pill, on the other hand, causes changes in the cervix that make it more susceptible to infection.

To find out more about PID and its prevention, contact the **Canadian PID Society**'s free information line at 604-684-5704. An excellent book on PID is available through this group, the only one of its kind in North America.

Cat's Claw

Have you heard anything about a new herb called Cat's Claw? I've heard all sorts of claims for it.

Cat's claw, or uncaria tomentosa, has a long history of use by the native peoples of the Peruvian rain forest. For many centuries, the native tribes have used the inner bark and root to prepare a medicinal tea used for arthritis, cancer, gastritis, and female hormonal imbalances.

The group of plants known as cat's claw are woody vines that grow over 100 feet in length as they wind their way up through trees growing in the highlands of the Amazonian jungle. The name, cat's claw, is derived from the two carved thorns at the base of each leaf that resemble a cat's claw. In 1974, an Austrian by the name of **Klaus Keplinger** brought knowledge of the plant to the west. He had the active ingredients analyzed and patented them.

Dr. Julian Whitaker, in his newsletter **Health and Healing** (May 1995) states that "as late as 1993, cat's claw was not mentioned in any of the herbal or naturopathic reference books. Yet studies in Austria, Germany, England, Hungary and Italy were suggesting that the bark of this plant could be helpful in treating cancer, AIDS, and a host of other ailments, including arthritis and intestinal disorders."

Researchers have isolated many active constituents. One has been shown to enhance the immune system by improving the ability of white blood cells to attack foreign invaders. Another inhibits clot formation.

Studies so far indicate that cat's claw also has anti-viral effects. Thus, some doctors have used it successfully to treat genital herpes and herpes zoster and alone or in conjunction with AZT for AIDS. It also has been shown to reduce side effects of radiation therapy for cancer. Other beneficial effects include antioxidant and anti-tumour effects.

One of the most important effects of cat's claw is that it has a marked anti-inflammatory effect. It seems to improve the overall function of the gastrointestinal tract through a deep cleansing action, and has been successfully used for bowel disorders such as irritable bowel syndrome, Crohn's Disease and ulcerative colitis.

Only the inner bark is used so the plant can live on. The usual dose is one to three grams a day, available as a tablet or a tincture and taken preferably on an empty stomach. The quality of herb available on the market is highly variable. Make sure that the herb you are taking is from a reputable source and most importantly, that its active ingredients are standardized. It is a slow acting herb, requiring at least 30 to 60 days before there will be noticeable improvement. The most common side effect is diarrhea. In this case, the dose should be lowered until there is no diarrhea.

While some claims about this herb still need to be proven, cat's claw is an exciting addition to our herbal pharmacopoeia. More high quality research needs to be done on this herb. Remember that this herb should not be used during pregnancy and nursing, or for transplant patients or those with auto-immune diseases. Treating yourself for a serious illness with this herb should be done only under the supervision of your family doctor or other qualified practitioner.

Chronic Fatigue Syndrome

What is Chronic Fatigue Syndrome? Is it really illness or is it just a psychological problem?

Chronic Fatigue Syndrome (CFS) or Chronic Fatigue and Immune System Dysfunction Syndrome (CFIDS), is a very real and very disabling physical illness that causes profound fatigue and muscle weakness following a viral illness. This syndrome is also known as Myalgic Encephalitis (ME), post-infectious neuromyasthenia, post-viral syndrome, yuppie flu, or formerly chronic Epstein Barr virus. CFIDS can cause injury to the brain, the immune system and the muscles of the people who suffer from it.

CFIDS was formerly thought to be caused by the Epstein Barr virus, but this has not been proven. Other viruses may also be associated with this syndrome, including herpes-6 virus, enteroviruses (coxsackie-B virus, poliovirus, echovirus, etc) hepatitis virus, influenza virus, adenovirus, and cytomegalovirus. For the viral infection to take hold, the immune system is usually already weakened by a number of causes, including the overuse of antibiotics and cortisone, major stress, poor diet and chronic yeast infections.

Dr. Byron Hyde, a leading Canadian CFIDS researcher, notes that like poliomyelitis, the incidence of CFIDS goes up after immunization, and also in late summer and early autumn. He strongly recommends that "individuals do not go to work in third world countries or start work in hospitals or schools during the first four weeks after immunization."

The official diagnosis of CFIDS can be made only after a thorough medical history, physical exam, mental status exam and laboratory tests are done to exclude other underlying or contributing conditions that require treatment. Then the patient must fulfil both of the following criteria:

The first criteria is six months or greater duration of clinically evaluated, unexplained persistent or relapsing chronic fatigue that is of new or definite onset (ie not lifelong), is not the result of ongoing exertion, is not substantially alleviated by rest, and results in substantial reduction in previous levels of occupational, educational, social or personal activities.

The second criteria is the concurrent occurrence of four or more of the following symptoms: substantial impairment in short term memory or concentration; sore throat; tender lymph nodes; muscle pain; multi-joint pain without joint swelling or redness; headaches of a new type, pattern or severity; unrefreshing sleep; and post-exertional malaise lasting more than 24 hours. These symptoms must have persisted or recurred during 6 or more consecutive months of illness and must not have pre-dated the fatigue. **Annals of Internal Medicine** (Dec 15/94-121;953-959).

People with CFIDS can be so tired they do not have enough energy to get out of bed. Brushing their teeth can become a major effort.

Dr. Hyde emphasizes the muscular component of the chronic fatigue syndrome. He defines the condition as, "a chronic illness of at least six months in duration, that develops after an acute infectious disease, in a well and physically active person. In this disease, the patient develops an unusual form of muscle failure experiencing fatigue, pain, or exhaustion in the exercised muscle."

Other important features of this illness, according to Dr. Hyde, are sleep disturbances, variability and fluctuations of symptoms, serious difficulty processing information (memory loss, lack of concentration, slurred speech, disorientation, loss of coordination) and generalized malaise.

Fibromyalgia, the "sore all over" syndrome may be part of CFIDS, with pain being a more prominent symptom than fatigue. In this condition, which affects mainly women in their late 30's and forties, there is generalized pain and aching throughout the body, morning stiffness, fatigue, disturbed sleep, and multiple tender spots on the body.

Specialized types of brain scans have shown decreased blood flow to the brian of CFIDS patients. After exercise, brain scans show even more drastic decreases in blood flow and brain function. In addition, some researchers have noted white abnormalities in certain areas of the brain.

Most blood tests are normal in CFIDS, but there may be abnormalities of immunoglobulins and T-cell function. In particular, there may be a decrease in natural killer cells, or an increase in helper cells or an increase in the ratio of helper cells to suppressor cells.

Dr. Byron Hyde has published a comprehensive 750 word textbook on CFIDS for doctors entitled, **The Clinical and Scientific Basis of ME/CFS** which is available through **The Nightingale Research Foundation** at 613-729-9643.

Tryptophan and Sleep

I've heard that tryptophan is helpful for sleep problems. Where can I get some and how should I use it?

L-tryptophan is one of the eight essential amino acids, one of the building blocks of protein. I have found it an extremely helpful sleep aid in my practice for all sorts of sleep problems, including the sleep disorders of fibromyalgia and chronic fatigue syndrome, for grief reactions, and for PMS and for menopause. It can also be used as part of a treatment programme for migraines and eating disorders.

It also has a useful role in treating depression, either by itself or in combination with antidepressant drugs like prozac where it counters the insomnia side effect and prevents the need for increasing the dosage.

In November 1989, the **FDA** recalled all tryptophan from the health food stores due to a serious illness induced by one contaminated batch of L-tryptophan. The illness and subsequent fatalities were solely caused by the contaminant. Uncontaminated L-tryptophan was never allowed back in the market in the U.S. Some American doctors believe that the banning of tryptophan helped pave the way for the domination of the market by the new antidepressants like prozac, zoloft and paxil.

The same thing may be happening right now in Canada as another very useful sleep aid, melatonin is removed from the market. Melatonin is a cheap and effective sleep aid in doses of .1mg to 6mg per night.

Currently in Canada, all prescription tryptophan is manufactured by one company, **ICN Canada**, whose product has never been associated with any problem. The cost is about $1.00 per 1,000mg tablet. Pure tryptophan without any fillers is also available from specialized pharmacies for people with allergies.

The usual dosage ranges from 500mg to 4,000mg at night one before bedtime with a carbohydrate snack. My usual recommended dosage is 2,000mg at bedtime. It is best not to take tryptophan with protein as it competes with tryptophan for absorption, but it can be taken with a carbohydrate snack. Combined with vitamin-B-6 and magnesium, there is an enhanced effect. It should be combined with niacinamide for chronic pain or depression.

Tryptophan should not be taken by people who have hepatitis or other liver disease or by pregnant women.

In the U.S. tryptophan is available by prescription from compounding pharmacists. An alternative to tryptophan known as 5-hydroxy-tryptophan or 5-HTP (50mg of 5-hydroxy-tryptophan equals 500mg tryptophan) is available without a prescription. In the body, tryptophan is converted to 5-HTP and ultimately to serotonin. Well known naturopathic doctor and educator Dr. Michael Murray has written a book on the many uses of 5-HTP called **The Natural Way to Overcome Depression, Obesity and Insomnia** (Bantam, 1998).

Headaches And Fibromyalgia

I am trying to find a solution to severe headaches prior to and up to 2 to 4 days after the beginning of the menstrual cycle. I am writing on behalf of someone who has been diagnosed with fibromyalgia but I'm not convinced.

Fibromyalgia or the "sore all over syndrome" may be part of chronic fatigue syndrome, with pain being a more prominent symptom than fatigue. Symptoms of fibromyalgia include generalized pain and aching throughout the body, morning stiffness, fatigue, disturbed sleep, and multiple tender points on the body. Headache is a possible symptom, but the other symptoms mentioned above are more important for diagnosis.

Fibromyalgia affects mainly women in their late 30's and early 40's (ten women for every man). About 25 percent of those affected are depressed before the illness, and one third suffer from anxiety or depression during the illness. There is no evidence that depression causes fibromyalgia.

Treating chronic fatigue syndrome, if present is the first step. This often involves treating chronic yeast infections first. Changes in diet and vitamin and herbal supplements are necessary to boost the immune system. Helpful supplements include oil of evening primrose, cod liver oil, co-enzyme-Q-10, B-12, zinc, magnesium, echinacea or astragalus combinations, vitamin-B, vitamin-C, vitamin-E, and pantothenic acid. Adrenal and thyroid support may also be necessary. Superfoods containing green foods and algae, are rich in nutrients and trace minerals, and are an important part of recovery.

Severe headaches in the first few days of the period may have multiple causes. Women are fortunate to have a natural period of cleansing during the period. You can assist it greatly by eating only fruits, vegetables and whole grains the first few days of the period. In addition, food allergies are a common contributing factor for headaches. An elimination diet will reveal foods which you should avoid or rotate.

Remedies for Bloating and Gas

I feel bad every time I eat something. Each morning my stomach is flat and quiet but after breakfast it is bloaty, gurgling and fizzing and I burp constantly. At day's end, my clothes are digging into me and my fingers and feet are swollen. This is after three normal size meals (no snacks). I exercise, eat a healthy diet and take supplements. I hope you have an answer for me because nothing I try seems to work.

Bloating and gas after meals can be due to a variety of causes including multiple food allergies, poor digestion, low stomach acid, candida and parasite infections, and improper food combining.

The bloating itself is caused by gas produced by bacteria in the large bowel. The gas is caused by undigested protein, candida fermentation, or an imbalance of bacteria in the gut.

Many people have unrecognized food allergies. Delayed sensitivities to dairy, wheat, corn, soy, caffeine and sugar are common. The cheapest and most effective way to find out about your food allergies is through an elimination diet.

Dr. Ralph Golan, author of **Optimal Wellness** (Ballantine, 1995), suggests you make a list of foods and beverages that you eat repeatedly, that you suspect make you feel bad, and that you crave i.e. that you think you cannot do without. Then you eliminate all these foods if feasible (or two to three at a time) for 10 to 14 days.

Another simple elimination diet is to eat only fish or chicken or brown rice plus steamed vegetables for one week. Then add your other foods back, one item every two or three days.

There are also several electo-acupuncture diagnostic machines that can screen for large numbers of foods and do a computer print out listing the suspected foods. However, RAST blood tests for food allergies are the most accurate, but are only available from nutritionally orientated doctors.

A digestive stool analysis will give you much information about your digestion, absorption, bacterial balance, and intestinal function as well as the presence of abnormal bacteria, yeast or fungi. It is available through naturopathic doctors or through having your doctor call **Great Smokies Diagnostic Lab** at 1-800-522-4762.

Poor food combinations, especially eating fruit with other foods can lead to fermentation and gas. Fruits should always be eaten alone one-half hour before meals or two hours after meals. Check at your local health food store for a detailed food combining chart.

In addition, yeast and parasite infections are much more common than most people believe, and can cause major digestive disturbances. These infections have to be properly treated before bowel function can return to normal.

Digestion enzymes are always helpful for digestive problems. In some cases, supplemental hydrochloric acid and pancreatic enzymes may have to be prescribed. Lactobacillus acidophilus and other friendly bacteria are also necessary to reestablish a healthy balance in the bowel.

Some people do very well on a specific carbohydrate diet which eliminates all complex carbohydrates and gives the digestive system a rest. **Elaine Gotschall** has written about it in her excellent book entitled, **Breaking The Vicious Cycle** (revised, 1998).

Finally, **Dr. Zoltan Rona** author of **Return To The Joy Of Health** (Alive, 1995) suggests that a bowel detoxification programme including juice fasting, psyllium, flax seed oil and bentonite may be needed to re-establish intestinal balance. Strengthening the abdominal muscles through exercises also helps the digestive process.

Dealing With Stubborn Acne

My son, now aged 16, has had an acne problem that has been bothering him for about three years now and still hasn't completely disappeared. He has been seeing a dermatologist for the last two years, who has prescribed Minocin, Benzagel cream and soap, vitamin-A lotion and Staticin. The Benzagel soap and Minocin cause a burning sensation. The dermatologist suggests that the reason for all this is because of hereditary oily skin. The doctor doesn't prescribe anything now, and my son is doing much better. He drinks water every hour, and gets lots of sleep. It seems he's improving, yet, during the day, his face looks oily, although he washes his face every three hours. We would appreciate some natural healing suggestions.

First of all your son's condition is complicated by the fact that he has been taking long term antibiotics in the form of minocin, which is a form of tetracycline, and staticin, which is a lotion form of erthyromycin. Long term use of antibiotics can lead to an overgrowth of a fungus called yeast.

Symptoms of yeast can manifest as skin problems, fatigue, digestive problems, and a decline in concentration and learning ability at school among many other symptoms.

Treatment involves an anti-yeast diet with avoidance of sugar, fruit, dairy, yeasted bread products and fermented foods for at least six weeks, as well as taking the friendly bacteria called acidophilus by mouth. Acidophilus should be taken any time you are on antibiotics. Natural anti-yeast medicines include garlic capsules, caprylic acid capsules, or grapefruit seed extract.

It's not a good idea for him to wash his face every three hours. Once a day with pure water and no soap may be sufficient. In fact, frequent washing strips the natural oils, causing the body to produce more oil, resulting in increased oiliness.

Specifically for the acne, benzagel and vitamin-A lotion are both natural products and relatively safe to use. A burning sensation is to be expected while taking this combination which can also cause redness and peeling. Afterwards, the acne usually improves. Dermatologists also use up to 50,000IU's of vitamin-A daily, by mouth, to treat acne. This high dose should only be used under supervision.

It is important for your son to find out if he has any food allergies through an elimination diet. At his age, he probably will not want to give up pop including diet pop, sugar and junk food, but he probably needs to. A diet which eliminates refined foods, fatty foods, milk, cheese and iodine rich foods, may be beneficial for acne.

In addition, your son can safely take zinc pincolate, Vitamin-E and Vitamin-C, trace minerals (especially chromium and selenium), flax seed oil and oil of evening primrose, all of which are taken by mouth. For further advice consult a naturopathic physician.

Vitiligo
And Auto-Immune Disease

I have a friend who has long struggled with vitiligo. Are there any natural remedies or dietary supplements that can ease this condition? Should she consult a natural health care practitioner?

Vitiligo is a skin disorder in which patches of skin lose their pigmentation. Depigmented white patches are particularly obvious in dark skinned people, appearing on the face, hands, armpits, and groin. Affected skin is very sensitive to light. Vitiligo usually occurs in early adulthood and affects one in 200 people. Spontaneous remission can occur in 30 percent of people.

A common fungal infection of the skin (tinea versicolor) can result in white patches in the skin over the trunk that do not tan, and should be distinguished from vitiligo. Treatment consists of applying selenium sulphide lotion from the neck to the waist daily and leaving it on for 20 minutes for 7 days, then weekly for month. The alteration in pigmentation may take months to fill in.

Vitiligo is thought to be an auto-immune disease. It can also be associated with adrenal or thyroid dysfunction. In addition, vitiligo is strongly associated with a lack or insufficiency of hydrochloric acid (HCL), which can then lead to multiple nutrient deficiencies especially vitamin-B-12.

Treatment may involve the use of hydrochloric acid and pepsin under the direction of a practitioner. Swedish bitters are often useful to improve digestion.

Dr. Elson Haas, author of **Staying Healthy With Nutrition** (Celestial Arts, 1992) suggests as an alternative to HCL tablets, that you drink the juice of half a lemon squeezed in water, or a teaspoon of apple cider vinegar in a glass of warm water, twenty minutes before meals.

Many nutritional doctors believe that there is a strong relationship between auto-immune disorders and food allergies, candida infections and parasite disorders.

Treatment of auto-immune disorders involves a multifactorial approach including high doses of vitamin-C, vitamin-E and bioflavonoids, testing and treatment of food allergies, treatment of candida and parasites as well as adrenal support. Supervision by a practitioner skilled in natural medicine is essential.

Nutritional support of the adrenal glands includes licorice root tea; vitamin-C and pantothenic acid 500mg of each four times a day; adrenal glandular tablets two twice a day at 8 a.m. and between 3 and 4 pm.

Gerovital H-3 face cream from Rumania has been reported to give excellent results.An ancient Mediterranean plant known as khella (amni visnaga) has also been studied. Oral and topical use with subsequent exposure to sunlight has stimulated melanin synthesis and repigmentation in about one third of patients.

I've just had silicone breast implants removed? What can I do to get better? Are the new saline filled implants any better?

First of all, it is believed that when silicone implants rupture or leak, the white blood cells of the body break down bits of silicone and carry them into the blood stream and then into the tissues of the joints, muscles and brain. In the case of saline implants, the implant is coated with silicone, which can still be broken down by the white blood cells and cause the same type of problems. Although it is true that the silicone filled implants cause greater problems, there is no good scientific data that proves the safety of any type of implant.

However, those women who have already had breast implants for whatever reasons should not blame themselves for their decision. Seeing a therapist or councillor is often helpful to deal with feelings of guilt, anger and sadness.

Indications that leakage is occurring include symptoms of chronic fatigue syndrome and the triggering of auto-immune diseases such as lupus and rheumatoid arthritis or neurological illnesses like multiple sclerosis. Although not proven, the implants may either cause or accelerate these disease processes in predisposed individuals.

Other symptoms include memory loss, poor concentration, sleep disorders, severe weight loss, hair loss, liver dysfunction, lymph node swelling, weakness, breast and nipple inflammation, circulation problems, joint pains, chronic muscle pain and stiffness.

Before healing can begin, the transplant has to be surgically removed. Secondly, a detoxification programme must be started including supervised fasting, colon therapy, baths with ozonated water, and lymphatic massage. Other aspects of treatment include antioxidant supplements, cellulase enzymes, nutrients to support the liver and kidneys, and intravenous vitamin and mineral therapy. At least this is one highly successful programme developed by **Dr. W. Lee Cowden** of **Integrahealth** in Dallas, Texas.

In a recent article in the **Alternative Medicine Digest** (#10), Dr. Cowden says that "Women going through this detoxification process see white powdery flakes coming out of their urine and stools, usually in a matter of days to weeks, after which their symptoms start to lift and dramatically improve."

Talk TV host **Jenny Jones** was one of the first to break the silence about breast implants. In a recent article in Alternative Medicine #23, Jones says that after five surgeries over ten years, her breasts were rock-hard, disfigured by scarring, leaking silicone, and chronically painful yet completely numb. In 1992 Jones finally had her implants removed.

The well known actress **Mariel Hemingway** also had chronic ill health after breast implants at age 19 and she eventually had to have them removed. Afterwards, she recovered her health using alternative medicine.

Ultimately, Jones says she believes the solution lies in changing the messages that women receive about their bodies. "Show your daughters how beautiful they are the way they are. Show them that the body is only a small part of it. It's your character and your heart and soul that are important. That's what being a woman is all about."

Silicone Implants, How To Get Well Again After The Implants Come Out (Issue #10), and **Got Silicone? Jenny Jones Doesn't, Anymore** (Issue #23), are from **Alternative Medical Digest** magazine available from 1-800-333-HEAL or 206-922-955. Jenny Jones has founded **The Image Foundation** Box 3630, Chicago, Illinois, 60654.

Eyestrain And Computers

My eyes are sore, burning, and watery and my job requires me to work six hours a day at the computer. What can I do?

You are suffering from eyestrain, and this condition has many different causes. Eyestrain means sore, burning, dry, itchy, tender, watery, or irritated eyes. It can also mean the sensation of heavy or twitching eyelids or pulling or drawing of the eye muscles. Other common eye problems of computer users include difficulty focusing, double vision, blurred vision and seeing coloured fringes or a pink after image.

To find the cause of the eyestrain, you have to consider computer screen design, office lighting, and work regimens. You should also get your eyes checked by your optometrist or eye doctor.

It is crucial to have a screen that is clear and easy to read, with proper lighting and absence of glare. Windows should be at right angles to the screen, lighting should be recessed and not direct, and all surfaces around the computer should be free of glare.

Dr. Helen Feeley, an Ottawa optometrist, says glare and uncorrected vision problems are the two main causes of computer related eyestrain. Dr. Feeley has written an excellent trouble shooting manual entitled, **The VDT Operator's Problem Solver**. (available from **The Planetary Association for Clean Energy**, 100 Bronson Avenue #10001, Ottawa, Ontario, K1R 6G8. 613-236-6265).

Intensive computer work should be limited to 50 percent of the work day. Computer work should be interspersed with other types of work.

To protect your eyesight, some suggest that yellowish green letters on a darker green background are easier on the eye. Others find white on black helpful for long periods of work.

In addition, you should schedule breaks for ten minutes for every hour of visually demanding work (columns, figures, rapid entry of data) and 15 minutes minimum for every two hours of less demanding work.

During breaks, is important to focus into the distance. Look at your hand and then at a distant object, back and forth 15 times. You can also rest your eyes by rubbing your palms together vigorously and cupping them over your eyes, while visualizing a peaceful scene in nature or just pitch blackness. This should be done for two or three minutes several times throughout the day, and is very restful for the eyes. Remember to blink often during breaks. And finally, practice moving your eyes through their whole range of movement five to ten times a day.

Glaucoma Treatment And Prevention

Are There Any Natural Treatments For Glaucoma?

Glaucoma is a condition in which the optic nerve is damaged by toxins, lack of circulation or abnormally high fluid pressure. Usually chronic and painless, glaucoma causes no symptoms except for loss of peripheral vision resulting in tunnel vision. It often begins at age 40 to 45 in about one percent of the population and if left untreated will lead to blindness by age 60 to 65. By age 80, it may affect up to 80 percent of the population.

Glaucoma is usually detected by routine eye exams that include the measurement of eye pressure. In most cases, blindness can be prevented by early diagnosis and treatment. According to a noted glaucoma researcher, seventy percent of the vision loss occurs prior to the first doctor visit.

Information on natural treatments for serious eye diseases is difficult to find. Fortunately, I recently came across the work of medical journalist, **Bill Sardi**. In a three part series for **The Townsend Newsletter for Doctors and Patients** (Fall 1995 to January 1996: for back issues call 360-385-6021.) Sardi says that the current approach to eradicating glaucoma is so fraught with side effects that it is difficult to separate the treatment from the disease.

Sardi states that, "a holistic non-pharmacological approach to this blinding ocular disorder that includes dietary measures, exercise, lifestyle changes and nutritional supplements may come closer to resolving this mysterious eye disease than standard medical therapy..."

Like many areas of medicine, the disease category known as "glaucoma" has been thought of as separate from the health of the rest of the body. Yet, as Sardi says, the causes are multifactorial and not limited to the eye.

Causes include free radical damage from ultraviolet radiation, allergy, auto-immune disease, decreased blood supply to the eye (caused by low blood pressure, vasoconstriction, or hardening of the arteries) elevated eye pressure, and toxic influences on the optic nerve (caused by various drugs, alcohol, artificial sweeteners, MSG, tobacco and vitamin-B-12 deficiency).

Chronic use of steroid eye drops can also cause glaucoma. Even the use of steroid skin creams can contribute to glaucoma. In fact, as Sardi notes, steroids are the primary cause of glaucoma caused by doctor-prescribed medications.

Benzalkonium chloride is a preservative used in tiny amounts in anti-glaucoma drops and artificial tears. Researchers found that half of the surgical failures from glaucoma surgery due to scarring and inflammation of tissues were the result of using benzalkonium chloride containing eye drops. Sardi also says that this substance may even accumulate within soft contact lens "to a concentration beyond safe levels."

Alternative treatments address the many factors involved in causing glaucoma. This includes a healthy diet, finding and eliminating allergies, improving digestion, ultraviolet protective eyewear, daily brisk walking, the B-vitamins, antioxidant vitamins, co-enzyme-Q-10, magnesium (nature's own calcium channel blocker) at least 1,500 micrograms of vitamin-B-12 a day, flax seed and omega-3 fish oils, and quercitin for allergy.

One of the finest herbal remedies for glaucoma is marijuana. In fact, it is more effective than any drug for lowering abnormal pressure within the eye, which is the main aim of treatment. Marijuana has been legalized in California and Arizona for this and other medical indications.

Finally, Sardi has found that there may be a place for surgery in the treatment of glaucoma since there may be less side effects and better long term results than with medical or laser treatment.

Eye specialist **Dr. Gary Price Todd**, author of **Nutrition, Health and Disease** (Whitford Press, 1985) says that most patients with open angle glaucoma, the most common type, have deficiencies of vitamin-A and the enzyme nicotinamide adenine dinucleotide or NAD. NAD or co-enzyme-1 is related to energy production in the cell. NAD levels can be boosted by taking reduced co-enzyme-1 or through increasing levels of co-enzyme-Q-10, magnesium, and N,N-dimethylglycine. Dr. Todd also tests for thyroid deficiencies using the basal temperature test and for mineral deficiencies using hair analysis. Dr. Todd can be reached at 1-800-426-7581 or 704-648-9400.

In 1937, an American physician by the name of **Emmanuel Josephson** pioneered the treatment of glaucoma using cortin or adrenal glandular extract, and found it was helpful in 72 percent of the cases for the preservation of useful vision. Nutritional physician **Dr. Jonathan Wright** has found the therapy useful, although not in all cases. Josephson's book, **Glaucoma, And Its Medical Treatment with Cortin**, is available only through fax from Dr. Wright office at 206-850-5639.

Bill Sardi has written an excellent three volume book set on all aspects of eye diseases and their natural prevention and treatment called, **Nutrition And The Eyes** (Health Spectrum Publishers). Volume I deals with cataracts; volume II with macular degeneration and volume III with glaucoma and diabetic eye disease. They are all out of print right now, but Sardi has a new book incorporating the same information called **How to Keep Your Eyes Healthy Naturally** (Avery, 1999).

Treating Cataracts Naturally

Can I do anything to prevent cataracts?

A cataract means that the crystalline lens of the eye is becoming cloudy, which is a gradual process occurring with age. The most common symptom is blurry vision. Over four million Americans and 300,000 Canadian suffer from cataracts, which can cause blindness. Fifty percent of those between 54 and 65 have cataracts, with cataract surgery being the most common surgery performed on those over 65.

Incredibly, there is good scientific data to show that taking antioxidant vitamins can prevent and slow the formation of cataracts. The risk of cataracts increases substantially with low blood levels of vitamin-E, vitamin-C, and betacarotene.

According to **Jane Heimlich** in her chapter on cataracts in **What Your Doctor Won't Tell You** (Harper and Collins, 1990), **Dr. Otto Hockwin**, a leading cataract researcher in Europe, believes that age is only one of many risk factors for cataracts. Other risk factors include ultraviolet radiation, nutritional deficiencies, medications and chronic diseases like diabetes.

Dr. Gary Price Todd is a rare breed of eye specialists whom Heimlich found treated cataracts with nutrition. Dr. Todd, author of the book, **Nutrition, Health And Disease** (1-800-426-7581 or 704-648-9400) does a hair analysis to check for heavy metal poisoning (one study showed that cadmium concentrations are two to three time higher in cataracts lens) and trace mineral deficiencies which he has found in over 35 percent of his patients. He then uses vitamin-C 1,200mg, Vitamin-E 400 IU, zinc 20mg, betacarotene 15,000 IU, in addition to glutathione 200mg and selenium 600 micrograms by mouth for six to twelve months.

Another Californian eye specialist that Heimlich interviewed, **Dr. Stuart Kemeny** has successfully treated over 7,000 cataract patients, and co-authored a book with **Dr. Alex Duarte** called **Cataract Breakthrough** Dr. Kemeny uses a comprehensive nutritional programme similar to Dr. Todd, as well as eye drops containing phenoxazine carboxylic acid and glutathione.

Bilberry or vaccinium mrytillus is a shrubby perennial plant that grows in Europe and produces a blue black berry. The plant contains special flavonoids known as anthocyanosides. They are extremely powerful antioxidants with a special affinity for the eyes. British air force pilots reported improved night vision on bombing raids after consuming bilberries. Research showed that healthy subjects who took bilberry extracts had improved night vision. One study of 50 patients showed that bilberry extracts plus vitamin-E stopped progression of cataract formation in 97 percent of patients with age related cataracts. The usual dose is 40 to 80mgs of bilberry extracts containing 25 percent anthocyanosides three times a day.

Dr. Jonathan Wright also recommends iodine supplementation which can specifically improve clogged arteries in the eye due to hardening of the arteries.

Researcher **Bill Sardi** has a new book out dealing with glaucoma, cataracts and macular degeneration called **How to Keep Your Eyes Healthy Naturally** (Avery, 1999) This book is loaded with practical nutritional and preventative advice.

Don't expect your eye specialist to know anything about nutritional prevention of cataracts. Most have never studied nutrition nor reviewed the latest research. As one specialist told Jane Heimlich, "Cataract surgery is big business." Fortunately, prevention is cheap.

Saint John's Wort Herb for Anxiety and Depression

I regularly use vitamin/minerals, herbs, homeopathic remedies etc. At the present time, I have been experiencing anxiety and depression after a stressful year. I tried the herb, St. John's Wort (hypericum perforatum) for several weeks, but it did not help. Because I use homeopathic remedies often, I ordered some homeopathic hypericum and have been using the tablets for a few weeks. It is working well, but I don't know how long I should take it. Why isn't the homeopathic remedy being recommended for anxiety and depression?

St. John's Wort in its herbal form is an excellent remedy for mild to moderate depression. A comprehensive overview of 23 randomized trials on St. John's Wort was published in the August 1996 issue of the **British Medical Journal**. The authors concluded that hypericum extracts were more effective than placebo for the treatment of mild to moderately severe depressive disorders. The researchers also reviewed six studies that compared hypericum to a low dose of tricyclic antidepressants and found it to be equally effective. **Dr. Michael Murray** reports in his comprehensive book, **Natural Alternatives To Prozac**, (William Morrow, 1996) that a total of 1593 patients have been studied in twenty five double-blind studies with consistently favourable results. St. John's Wort has a low incidence of side effects and can be safely used for six to eight months or more. The dose can be reduced after two or three months where possible.

So why didn't it work for you? First of all, it doesn't work for everyone, only an estimated 70 percent of people. Secondly, there is a delayed onset of action, sometimes up to four weeks. So it may have worked if you had persisted for longer. Thirdly, the quality of the St. John's Wort currently available varies greatly and some preparations may contain no St. John's Wort at all. At a recent conference, Dr. Murray pointed out that there was more St. John's Wort being sold than there is raw material available.

Check for high quality whole herb preparations that contain .3 percent of one of the active ingredients known as hypericin. Another form of the whole herb that is highly effective is wild harvested in Greece and extracted during more than 1,000 hours of sunlight in extra virgin olive oil. I have had consistent good results with this St. John's wort oil which is manufactured by **Flora**.

Also St. John's Wort is not as effective for anxiety as it is for depression. Kava is a very useful herb for the treatment of nervous anxiety, restlessness and insomnia. Kava is a member of the pepper family native to the South Pacific.

Homeopathic preparations of St. John's Wort contain the herb in highly diluted form, and there are no side effects on a short term basis. Homeopathic remedies work in a completely differently manner than herbal remedies and are used for different reasons. Homeopathic hypericum is used for injury to nerves and trauma of the spine, head and tail bone. It can be also recommended for neuralgia, sciatica and headache after injury. It is used for depression but usually for depression that occurs after trauma, injury or surgery. Homeopathic hypericum should not be taken longer than 2 months without consulting with a homeopathic practitioner for further help and advice.

Finally, depression usually has a multitude of factors feeding into it. Other important aspects of a holistic approach to depression include improving the overall diet and eliminating coffee, alcohol, sugar and sugar substitutes. Food allergies can contribute to depression and can be determined through an elimination diet. There are often nutritional factors in depression. Deficiencies of folic acid, vitamin-B-12 vitamin-B-6 and essential fatty acids are very common. Regular exercise, and learning some stress management technique like meditation are also recommended.

Natural Remedies For Eczema

Just after my daughter was born, I developed eczema on my hands. Doctors have prescribed various creams, ointments and cortisone, but my eczema is spreading. They say diet has no effect on eczema. I am now turning to alternative medicine hoping for an answer. What do you suggest?

Eczema affects an estimated 2.4 to 7 percent of the population. Eczema is an itchy inflammatory condition of the skin. It is commonly found on the face, wrist and insides of the elbows and knees. It can occur at any age, but is most common in infants. Fifty percent of infant cases will clear up by 18 months of age.

The skin is the largest organ of elimination, and its vital role in eliminating toxins is usually completely overlooked. Skin elimination can be promoted by daily skin brushing and hydrotherapy. Hydrotherapy consists of alternating hot and cold showers. (one minute of each, for 15 minutes) In general, skin problems require time and patience to treat because the solution involves long term changes including internal cleansing and lifestyle changes.

Homeopathic remedies will address the specific symptoms and the constitutional makeup, as well as the inherited tendencies. Healing takes place in a certain order of priority. So, in the case of skin disease, the internal problems have to be addressed first and older unresolved symptoms may arise in the process.

The chronic use of cortisone creams leads to an imbalance in the whole body, including chronic yeast infections and adrenal gland dysfunction. These last two problems can then lead to allergies and chemical sensitivities.

There is a strong allergic component in eczema. Studies have shown that most patients have food allergies. Symptoms improve on a diet which eliminates common foods that cause allergies such as milk, sugar, corn, citrus, and peanuts. There are many ways to determine your food allergies including an elimination diet, specialized RAST blood tests, and electro-acupuncture testing.

Low stomach acid is common in people with eczema. This can be remedied by taking digestive enzymes or Swedish Bitters on your own or by using hydrochloric acid under the supervision of a practitioner.

Most people with eczema have an essential fatty acid deficiency. Treatment with oil of evening primrose is essential. It can be taken internally and also applied directly to the affected areas of skin. It is also important to increase your intake of fish and fish oils.

Other important supplements that can be used daily for skin health include vitamin-A 25,000IU's Vitamin-C 500mg and zinc pincolate 25 to 50mg. Bioflavonoids have an anti-inflammatory effect and up to 1,000mg a day is recommended.

Pizzorno and Murray, in their **Encyclopedia of Natural Healing**, (Prima, 1998) recommend oral burdock root with its long history of use in the treatment of eczema. The authors say that inulin, the primary active component, tends to correct the underlying defects in the inflammatory mechanisms and immune system as well as helping control the staph infections so common in eczema.

Topical herbal preparations of camomile or licorice root have been proven effective for eczema. Traditional Chinese herbal formulas containing licorice root have been tested in two double blind studies and shown to be effective.

A new supplement known as methylsulfonylmethane or MSM may be very helpful for chronic stubborn eczema. MSM makes the bonds between cell walls more flexible, and improves allergies, liver function and digestion. MSM lotion can be applied two or three times a day and taken orally as well.

Finally, it is also important to address stress and emotional conflicts which can precipitate or aggravate eczema. Meditation, visualization and breathing exercises are beneficial.

Dealing With Childhood Asthma

*I read an article in which **Dr. Jonathan Wright** referred to an experiment where 90 percent of children with asthma were helped or cured by supplementing with hydrochloric acid (HCL). We are anxious to try this as soon as possible with a seven year old girl, but could find nothing on the shelves at the local health food store to give guidance in administering HCL to children. Also we are having difficulty finding an alternative medical doctor in our area. Can you give us some direction?*

Many studies have shown that food allergies play an important role in asthma. Obvious food allergies produce an immediate reaction such as hives, swelling, sneezing, wheezing, headache or stomach upset. The usual culprits are nuts and shellfish.

However, delayed food allergies, which are harder to detect, are much more important. These allergies can be best detected through an elimination diet. Common delayed food allergies include dairy, sugar, wheat, citrus and food colouring. Diet is the key to controlling asthma. Pediatrician **Dr. William Crook**'s book, **Detecting Your Hidden Allergies** (Professional Books, 1988) describes how to plan an elimination diet for your child.

Dr. Jonathan Wright's program for asthma stresses a multifactorial approach starting with diet. As you mentioned, one important facet of Dr. Wright's programme is the use of hydrochloric acid to ensure proper digestion of food and thus prevent any additional burden on the immune system.

According to Dr. Wright, in his **Nutrition And Healing Newsletter** (1-800-528-0559), a 1931 study showed that 80 percent of asthmatic children had lower than normal production of acid and pepsin in their stomachs. Wright says that this impairs digestion, lowers the absorption of vitamins and minerals from food, and gradually increases allergies to food. Meanwhile, food allergies, especially to cow's milk can cause low stomach acid, and thus a vicious cycle is set up.

To break the cycle, hydrochloric acid is prescribed. Hydrochloric acid is ideally taken under the supervision of a naturopathic doctor. The usual recommendation is to start by taking one-half to one hydrochloric capsule (10 grains) at the two largest meals of the day. The dose may be increased very slowly to two or three capsules per meal or until your child feels a sensation of warmth in her tummy. If your child feels a sensation of warmth, this means she has taken too much hydrochloric acid for that size of meal. The aim is to find the largest dose she can tolerate at the two largest meals of the day without feeling any warmth in her stomach. This becomes her maintenance dose.

Other supplements that may be taken instead of or along with the hydrochloric acid include Swedish stomach bitters to improve digestion, and digestive enzymes.

Dr. Wright also emphasizes the importance of daily vitamin-B-12 injections, since the stomach malfunction also impairs vitamin-B-12 metabolism. Dr. Wright recommends vitamin-B-12 injections 1,000 to 3,000mcg per day for a thirty day trial. Results can be dramatic. He also advises additional magnesium, vitamin-B-6, cod liver oil capsules, Vitamin-E, selenium and high doses of buffered vitamin-C, all taken by mouth.

Vitamin-C acts like a natural anti-histamine and also seems to reduce the tendency of the bronchial passages to go into spasm. Usually the amount of Vitamin-C necessary is determined by starting with 500mg every day. Then you increase each daily dose by 500mg until your daughter gets diarrhea or her stools start to soften. Then you cut back to the highest daily dose that she can take and still have normal bowel movements. Usually asthmatic children need a lot higher dose of vitamin-C than healthy children.

To find the closest holistic medical doctor to you, call **The American Academy For The Advancement Of Medicine** at 1-800-532-3688 or 949-583-7666 fax 949-455-9679. To find the naturopathic doctor closest to you, call the **American Association Of Naturopathic Physicians** at 206-323-7610.

In Canada, you can contact **The Canadian Complementary Medical Association**, at 403-433-0481 (fax 403-433-0481), or **The Canadian Naturopathic Association**, at 416-233-1043.

Childhood Headaches

My six year old son has started to experience migraines. He also has a history of middle ear infections. Some possible reasons for the migraines are genetics, weather changes and sinuses. He did have a CT scan to rule out all possibilities. I'm beginning to wonder if it's allergies. I would greatly appreciate your help.

For children with headaches, the number one thing I would look for is food allergies. Your child's recurrent sinus congestion and ear infections also point to food allergies. The most common offenders are sugar, milk, wheat, corn and soy. These allergies can be detected through specialized testing including blood tests and electro-diagnosis. These can be obtained from a physician practising natural medicine. Conventional allergy tests from an allergist are not useful.

You can also determine allergies through a food elimination diet described well in **Dr. William Crook**'s Book, **Detecting Your Hidden Allergies** (Professional Books, 1988). **Dr. Zoltan Rona**'s book, **Childhood Illness And The Allergy Connection** (Prima, 1997), is also recommended. Environmental allergies such as to dust and mould may also have to be checked.

Recurrent sinus and ear infections are very significant. Repeated courses of antibiotics cause the child's whole system to go out of balance. In particular, antibiotics wipe out the friendly bacteria in the gut and cause an overgrowth of yeast which can then cause digestive problems, fatigue and headaches.

Your son should be treated by replacing the friendly bacteria by taking acidophilus capsules specific for his age, dietary changes (especially eliminating sugar and dairy), and taking natural anti-yeast remedies like garlic or caprylic acid. **The Complete Candida Guidebook** by **Jeanne Marie Martin** and **Zoltan Rona** (Prima, 1996) gives specific diets designed for children and reviews many different types of natural treatments.

It may be important to consult with a chiropractic doctor to check your son's spinal alignment, especially if he has had any injury or fall. Cranial-sacral therapy to gently adjust the cranial bones and spine is also worthwhile, especially if your son experienced birth trauma.

Acupuncture can also play an important role in migraine treatment and prevention. A small acupuncture machine can be rented or purchased for pain relief at home. One well designed machine with phone support can be purchased through **Acumed** at 1-800-567-PAIN or 416-252-6060.

The herb feverfew has been shown in many studies to reduce the frequency and severity of migraine headaches. It will not help a headache once it is started.

Once the headache has started, you can try hot castor oil packs, ice packs, extra Vitamin-C and bioflavonoids, extra calcium and magnesium, ginger capsules and white willow bark. Aspirin is derived from white willow bark, but the natural product is milder and has fewer side effects.

In addition your child should be taking daily a high quality multi-mineral vitamin, cod liver oil, and extra zinc, vitamin-C and bioflavonoids.

Treatment of migraines in children does require a multi-pronged approach, time and effort but the effects are so worthwhile. Children usually respond faster to natural treatments and also will have the benefit of good health habits begun early.

Trigeminal Neurlagia

I have a friend who has been suffering from trigeminal neurlagia. The only relief she gets is to stay on doctor prescribed medications. Lately even the medication isn't helping all the time. Is there anything else she can do?

This condition is a disorder of the fifth cranial nerve or trigeminal nerve and causes severe stabbing pain of the lips, gums, cheek, or chin on one side of the face. The pain seldom lasts more than a few seconds or up to two minutes. The pain may be so intense that the patient winces, hence the other term for this condition, painful twitch or tic douloureux.

The cause is unknown. The condition is most common in middle and later life and affects women more than men. Most sufferers are over age 50. In younger people it may be associated with multiple sclerosis.

Attacks typically occur in bouts throughout the day and night for several weeks at a time. Pain free intervals tend to become shorter with time. The pain always starts from one point on the face and can be precipitated by touching the face, washing, shaving, eating, drinking, drafts, or even talking.

The usual treatment is anti-convulsive drugs. Surgery is reserved for severe cases.

The good news is that trigeminal neuralgia responds very well to a series of at least six acupuncture treatments. It is best to choose an experienced acupuncturist. **The World Health Organization** recognizes trigeminal neuralgia as one of the conditions that can be successfully treated by acupuncture. Treatments should be continued on a regular basis.

A small hand held acupuncture machine can be rented or purchased and appropriate acupuncture points can be stimulated at home on a daily basis. You can order a properly designed device from **Acumed** at 1-800-567-PAIN or 416-253-6060 as well as other reputable companies.

Other treatment modalities that may be helpful include myofacial release therapy, chiropractic, osteopathy and laser acupuncture.

Daily vitamin-B-12 injections have proven helpful for some. Extra B-vitamins, folic acid, lecithin, choline and inositol are also recommended.

If your friend decides to go off her drugs, she should slowly wean off them while adding in natural treatments at the same time.

ElectroMagnetic Protection

How can we protect ourselves from electro-magnetic fields, especially extremely low frequency waves?

Extremely low frequency (ELF) electro-magnetic waves are produced by high voltage power lines, neighbourhood transformers, and from the front, sides, and back of the computer screen.

Electrical appliances also give off ELF waves which drop off rapidly within a short distance of the appliance. Most appliances are only used for a short period of time. However, hairdressers who use blow dryers for hours at a time may be at increased risk. It may be helpful to point the back of the dryer away from the user's body.

In contrast, electric blankets and electrically heated water beds expose people to continuous potentially harmful ELF electro-magnetic fields. Both can be safely used but should be turned off at night. One study showed that sleeping on a water bed caused an increased rate of miscarriage.

Most recently, concern has focused around the long-term health effects of ELF electro-magnetic waves on body structure and function since these waves can penetrate to the cellular level. Studies done to date show that chronic exposure to ELF waves may cause lowered immunity and adverse effects on the nervous system, blood cell growth, and fetal growth.

To minimize exposure to ELF waves from the computer, make sure you and your children are at least 71 centimeters (28 inches) from your computer screen and at least an arm's length (91-101 centimeters or 36 to 40 inches) from any other computer terminal. Monitor the total amount of time your children spend in front of a video screen (computer, TV and video games) and make sure they take frequent breaks.

Computer work practices are extremely important. There should be regularly scheduled breaks for ten minutes for every hour of visually demanding work (columns, figures, rapid entry of data) and 15 minutes minimum for every two hours of less demanding work. During these breaks, it is important to leave the computer, stretch, gaze into the distance and drink lots of water. Breaks should never be skipped. Intensive computer work should be limited to 50 percent of the work day.

Rosalie Bertell suggests that you outline the electro-magnetic fields for yourself using a hearing aid which emits a high pitched sound when in the field. In this way, you could figure out the best distance to sit from your computer and from any other co-worker's computer near you.

The **Tesslar Watch** helps protect you from such radiation. This device and others like it are available through **Essentia Communications Inc** at 613-238-4437 or fax 613-235-5876. Essentia Communications has an extensive catalogue which includes various types of computer screens and measurement devices, as well as the books mentioned below.

The **Q-Link** which can be worn around the neck and a special clock device that covers a ten foot radius neutralizes electro-magnetic radiation. They are available from **Clarus Systems** at 1-800-223-1998 or 714-489-9904.

For more information, consult **Paul Brodeur**'s book, **Currents Of Death: Power Lines, Computer Terminals and the Attempt to Cover Up Their Threat to Your Health** (Simon and Shuster, 1989) and **Dr. Samuel Becker**'s book, **Crosscurrents** (St. Martin's Press, 1990).

My book, **Take Charge Of Your Body**, (Well Women Press, 1997) has a chapter on the health hazards of computers. **Microwave News**, edited by **Louis Slesin**, is the definitive source of the latest information on the health effects of electro-magnetic fields (www.microwavenews.com or 212-517-2800).

Natural Remedies for Lupus

A friend of mine has just been diagnosed with lupus. Does natural medicine have anything to offer her?

Lupus erythematosus is an auto-immune disease, in which the body's immune system attacks the connective tissue of the body as if it were foreign, causing inflammation. The connective tissue is the matrix, the glue that surrounds body structures and holds them together.

The most common type, discoid lupus erythematosus or DLE affects exposed areas of skin. The more serious form is known as systemic lupus erythematosus (SLE) and affects the whole body including the skin, eyes, blood, nervous system, heart, joints and kidneys.

Lupus affects nine times as many women as men, usually those of childbearing age. The incidence is higher in certain ethnic groups such as blacks and Chinese, where it reaches one in 250 women. Over one million Americans and 50,000 Canadians have SLE.

Certain drugs, including anti-convulsants, penicillin, sulfa drugs and the birth control pill can trigger SLE. Other triggers include stress, exposure to sun, immunization, infections and pregnancy.

Chronic infections with yeast or parasites, delayed food and chemical allergies, mercury fillings, heavy metal hypersensitivity and the leaky gut syndrome are important triggers often overlooked in conventional medicine.

Natural medicine has much to offer, but supervision by an experienced practitioner is recommended.

Eliminating food allergies is one of the first steps. The best way to determine allergies is through an elimination diet or specialized allergy testing. Blood tests for food allergies will not be accurate if you are taking prednisone or aspirin.

Systemic lupus and other auto-immune diseases are often associated with hydrochloric acid deficiency in the stomach. Remedies include taking hydrochloric acid, the enzymes betaine and pepsin, or Swedish stomach bitters. Another alternative is to take half a lemon or a teaspoon of apple cider vinegar in a glass of warm water 20 minutes before meals.

Your natural health practitioner can order a comprehensive digestive stool analysis. This test can identify candida, parasites or bacterial infections as well as digestive weakness, which can then be corrected with natural remedies.

Dr. Zoltan Rona in his book, **Return To The Joy Of Health**, (Alive, 1995) recommends the antioxidant vitamins to protect against tissue damage. He suggests mixed carotenes, grape seed extract, bioflavonoids, vitamin-C, vitamin-E, N-acetyl cysteine, glutathione, methionine and co-enzyme-Q-10. He also notes that high doses of Vitamin-E have an immune suppressive effect (above 2,000IU's daily).

At the University of Stellenbosch in South Africa, **Dr. Patrick Bouic** has done extensive research on plant sterols and sterolins, which were first isolated in the lab in 1922. Plant sterols and sterolins are the plant fats which are usually bound to plant fibres, making them difficult to digest. Bouic found that these compounds decrease the inflammatory response in auto-immune diseases, while at the same time decreasing the antibody response to the body's own tissues. This makes the recently released product Sterinol (TM) valuable for treating both lupus and rheumatoid arthritis.

According to nutritional physician, **Dr Jonathan Wright**, vitamin-B-12 injections 1,000 to 2,000 micrograms twice weekly are very helpful. In addition, he recommends very high doses of vitamin-B-6, between 200 to 500mg three times a day which must be taken under the supervision of a doctor who can monitor for signs of nerve toxicity.

Wright says that over 80 percent of SLE patients have severe deficiencies of hydrochloric acid and 100 percent have food allergies. Additionally, in his experience, over 50 percent of women have low levels of DHEA and testosterone and improve when they take these hormones in appropriate doses.

Other important supplements include a high quality multi-mineral vitamin, a supergreen drink, B-complex, vitamins E and C, flaxseed oil, fish oil, zinc, selenium, calcium, magnesium, and bioflavonoids.

Diet Key To Managing Irritable Bowel Syndrome

I'm 29 years old, and have been suffering from severe cramps and diarrhea for about three years. This usually occurs within minutes after eating any meal, spicy or not. I went to a family doctor and she just shrugged it off as irritable bowel syndrome. I eat well and take supplements. Could birth control pills be causing my problem?

First of all, since you have had these symptoms for three years, I suggest you request a referral to a gastroenterologist, (a specialist in diseases of the GI tract including stomach, small intestine and colon). This specialist will do a complete set of investigations including barium enema and colonoscopy. You should also get at least three stool cultures for bacteria and three cultures for parasites to determine the cause of your diarrhea (each culture taken two days apart). Occasionally birth control pills can cause gastrointestinal symptoms, but this is uncommon.

Irritable bowel syndrome or IBS is a condition in which diarrhea alternates with constipation accompanied by hyper-secretion of mucous, abdominal pain, bloating and gas. Other diseases with similar symptoms include ulcerative colitis and Crohn's disease.

Once the specialist has confirmed the diagnosis of IBS, then it would be wise to seek out a naturopathic doctor to supervise your care.

Diet is key in management, in spite of what your doctor might tell you. It is important to determine your food allergies through an elimination diet or specialized testing from an alternative practitioner. Recent research has confirmed the connection between IBS and sensitivity to certain foods.

First described in 1951 by **Drs. Sidney and Merrill Haas**, the specific carbohydrate diet has been successful in treating and curing thousands of cases of ulcerative colitis, Crohn's, celiac disease and IBS. This diet is described and explained along with delicious recipes in **Breaking the Vicious Cycle**, by **Elaine Gotschall** (Kirkton Press, 1998). The basic principle of this well balanced diet is that no food should be ingested that contains carbohydrates other than those found in fruits, honey, properly prepared yogurt and certain vegetables and nuts.

Enteric coated peppermint has been shown to relax gastrointestinal muscles. Powdered ginger in capsules has a soothing effect on the gut. Powdered activated charcoal in tablet or capsule form helps gas and absorbs toxins from the gut.

Robert's formula is an old naturopathic herbal formula with a long history of use for inflammatory disease and other causes of diarrhea. The herbs include marshmallow root, slippery elm, wild indigo, echinacea, geranium, goldenseal, poke root and comfrey. Capsules of the formula are available at selected health food stores.

Other useful supplements include vitamin-A, vitamin-E, vitamin-C, zinc, folic acid and flax seed oil. Vitamin-A is a regenerator of the bowel mucosa. Plant enzymes help in the break down of food. The amino acid L-glutamine helps regenerate the cells of the digestive tract.

Often the gut flora are disturbed and acidophilus and other friendly bacteria should be taken on a regular basis. Chronic candida of the gut can be an important co-factor and also must be treated if present. Finally, acupuncture and Chinese herbs can be very effective medicine for IBS.

ALS
Lou Gehrig's Disease

A friend of mine has just been diagnosed with Lou Gehrig's disease and I wonder if there is anything he can do? His doctor didn't give him any hope of recovery.

Lou Gehrig's disease or amyotrophic lateral sclerosis (ALS) causes progressive degeneration of the nerves within the central nervous system that control muscular activity. The disease generally occurs after age 50 and is more common in males. About 5 to 10 percent of cases run in families.

The first symptoms usually involve weakness and then wasting of the muscles of the hands and arms. Muscular fasciculations (spontaneous irregular contractions of small areas of muscle) and muscle spasms are also common. The throat muscles can be involved making speech difficult and eventually eating as well. The prognosis is usually bleak, with progressive decline and death within 3 to 5 years. However about 20 percent survive more than 5 years and 5 percent more than 10 years.

While ALS is very challenging to treat, a comprehensive programme of natural treatments may prove very helpful and may slow or even stop the progression of the disease. A qualified health practitioner experienced in treating neurological problems is essential.

One of the most important aspects of treatment is to check for heavy metal toxicity. Heavy metals, especially mercury, are very toxic to the nervous system. Mercury fillings usually have to be replaced with white fillings. Since mercury is released when the old fillings are removed, intravenous vitamin support, high doses of vitamin-C and homeopathic mercury are recommended after every dental session.

Following the removal of mercury fillings, it is imperative to have 10 to 20 sessions of intravenous chelation therapy to pull out all the heavy metals from the system. Some studies have shown that people with ALS have high levels of manganese, mercury and aluminum in their systems, and low levels of calcium and magnesium. Chelation therapy as well as appropriate mineral supplements will correct this.

A complete nutritional program is vital with particular emphasis on lecithin, oil of evening primrose, fish oils, a high quality multi-mineral and vitamin supplement and a supergreen drink containing spirulina or other sea algae. Daily injections of vitamin-B-12 and folic acid are often very helpful. Vitamin-B-12 and folic acid are known to improve nerve cell function. Taken orally, these two vitamins are less effective.

Dr. Andrew Eisen of the Neuromuscular Unit at Vancouver General Hospital is conducting a trial in which he is giving men with ALS large doses of DHEA. His previous research indicated that a low level of DHEA or more probably a rapid rate of decline of DHEA may result in a male preponderance of ALS.

Dr. Hans Nieper of Hanover, West Germany has documented excellent results in the long term treatment of ALS with intravenous and oral calcium EAP (calcium 2-aminoethanol). Calcium EAP is the component of the cell membrane needed for the binding and flow of electrical charges. It also inhibits the auto-immune response.

Nieper has treated thousands of MS patients successfully with this compound and it is an officially recognized treatment for MS in Germany. In his book, **Dr. Atkin's Health Revolution**, (Bantam Books, 1990) New York physician, **Dr. Robert Atkins** discusses his successful treatment of ALS and MS with the use of calcium EAP, which he believes should be approved by the FDA on compassionate grounds.

In addition to all of the above, all dietary and lifestyle stresses must be eliminated. Food allergies, candida and parasites must also be treated appropriately. Special attention must also be paid to improving digestion and liver function.

In his patient report in the **Townsend Newsletter** (June, 1997), **Peter Ganzel** says he believes that ALS is caused by a severe acid base imbalance and outlines a detailed treatment programme. One of the recommendations is the use of **Edgar Cayce**'s wet cell (which sends low voltage electrical impulses into the system) to help restore acid base balance. Peter can be reached at Pganzel@aol.com or 516-352-5522.

Excessive Facial Hair

I have a friend who suffers from hirsutism. She must shave her beard twice a day. The medication she took didn't work. I have since met three others who suffer from this rather embarrassing condition. Is there a natural product that could help them?

Hirsutism means excessive hair growth, and it usually occurs in women. It is a coarse type of hair, and can grow on the face, trunk, arms and legs. With any significant increase in hairiness, it is worthwhile to check in with your physician to have a complete history and physical. You may also have to have your hormone levels checked, especially testosterone.

Hirsutism can occur in certain medical conditions such as polycystic ovaries, adrenal tumours and other serious adrenal conditions.

However, most of the time there is no cause is found. Hirustism seems to run in families, and also tends to occur more in dark haired women. especially of East Indian or Hispanic descent.

Around the time of menopause, facial hair may increase. This is usually due to hormone imbalances, in particular progesterone deficiency or testosterone excess. Blood or saliva tests can determine your levels of estrogen, progesterone, free testosterone and DHEA. Individualized natural hormone therapy may decrease the regrowth of the hair. Some women have also found it helpful to apply natural progesterone to the face daily.

Meanwhile, there are several different ways to remove unwanted hair. Waxing works well, but needs to be repeated every three to four weeks. It can also be painful. Another good method is "sugaring" where a special sugar paste is applied to the skin and the unwanted hair pulled off using paper strips. (like waxing only with sugar) The ingredients of this paste are all natural, so there are no side effects. Like waxing, it has to be repeated every three to four weeks.

Electrolysis is the only permanent method, in which electric current is used to destory the growing part of the hair. You should make sure it is done by a certified technician. The downside is that it is expensive and time consuming.

Be cautious of hair removal creams, as they contain usually contain harsh chemicals which can be absorbed through the skin, causing toxicity or local irritation.

Panic Attacks

Are there any natural treatments for panic attacks?

Panic attacks are defined as a brief period of intense anxiety. These anxiety attacks can be accompanied by an overwhelming fear of dying or losing one's mind. Panic attacks usually occur suddenly and unpredictably without warning, but if they continue, they tend to become associated with certain places or situations. The attacks are usually associated with physical symptoms such as difficulty breathing, chest pains, rapid heart rate, light-headedness and dizziness, sweating and trembling.

Agoraphobia is one type of panic attack that causes incapacitating anxiety on travelling away from the safety of home or being in crowded places.

Emotional trauma, surgery, infections, medications and chemicals such as MSG can trigger panic attacks. Caffeine, sugar, and sugar substitutes may cause symptoms similar to panic attacks. In addition, it is useful to determine the food sensitivities through an elimination diet.

Several natural remedies may be helpful. Rescue remedy is a combination of five Bach flower remedies. These remedies were discovered by British medical doctor Dr.Edward Bach. Rescue remedy can stop panic attacks quickly. The recommended dosage is 5 to 10 drops every few minutes until the panic attack stops. Rescue remedy can be used in all cases of shock, terror, panic, sudden bad news, grief, and major and minor accidents.

Kava Kava is a shrub in the pepper family that grows in the South Seas. It has an anti-anxiety effect roughly equivalent to the effect of valium. However, Kava Kava does not cause drowsiness, or reduction in mental acuity, performance or memory.

The main active ingredients have been identified as kavalactones. The usual dosage is 100mg two or three times a day of Kava Kava standardized to contain at least 55 percent kavalactones.

A trial of mega-B vitamins 50mg and or with each meal may be helpful. Niacinamide 500mg three times a day may also be tried.

British physician **Dr. Claire Weekes** has written a very helpful book entitled, **Hope And Help For Your Nerves** (Signet, 1991) It is a simple and successful step by step programme that helps people understand their illness, markedly decrease their symptoms and resume a normal life without the use of medications.

Fibromyalgia
And Magnetic Therapy

Do you think magnetic therapy is safe? What about its safety?

Magnetic therapy has many promising applications, particularly in chronic painful conditions. Small magnets can be useful for painful areas on the body. They work by signalling the brain to produce more electricity and blood flow for healing. Magnetic devices are popular in Germany and some are designated medical devices and covered by medical insurance.

All magnets have two poles: positive or south and negative or north. The north pole has a calming effects and helps normalize metabolism. Thus it is useful for to decrease inflammation or swelling.(the north pole side should be placed directly on the painful or injured area) The south pole has the opposite effect, and thus it is useful for increasing circulation and metabolism in hypoactive states.

Two preliminary studies have been done on fibromyalgia and the use of unidirectional magnetic mattress pads. One was a small pilot study of six patients who had been diagnosed with chronic fatigue syndrome. Many of these patients had symptoms of fibromyalgia. All of the patients showed improvement in their symptoms over the four months. The second study was a placebo controlled study involving 29 patients diagnosed with fibromyalgia. The patients with the real magnetic mattress pad showed 2.4 times the improvement as the placebo group.

Dr. Dean Bonlie is an experienced researcher in the field of biomagnetism who designed the sleep pad used in this study. There are several kinds of sleep pads available on the market. Dr. Bonlie's is the only one that provide unidirectional magnetic fields. In my opinion, this type of sleep pad is the only safe one to use on a continuous long term basis.

Other sleep pads are designed to provide a bipolar magnetic field to the body. According to Dr. Bonlie, this unnatural magnetic field provokes and emergency response which decreases blood and electrical flow to the body. On a short term basis, this is very helpful, but on a long term basis, it uses up the body's reserves. These type of pads should never be used on a continuous basis, but with frequent breaks.

There is evidence to show that there has been a steady decline in the earth's magnetic field. With a decline in the earth's magnetic field, there is a decrease in the body's ability to heal and regenerate. The sleep pad designed by Dr. Bonlie is designed to replicate the earth natural magnetic fields, It enhances molecular action by speeding up the electrons and protons of the atoms.

This mattress has been found to help many conditions including PMS, arthritis, insomnia and recovery from injuries. Dr. Bonlie is now conducting research into the effects of large electromagnets on spinal injuries, stroke, cerebral palsy, multiple sclerosis, muscular dystrophy, and amyotrophic lateral sclerosis.

In the future using powerful electromagnetic fields may prove regenerative, especially for chronic neurological and muscular diseases previously considered incurable. To contact Dr. Bonlie call 1-800-265-1119.

The Dreaded Cellulite

What can I do about the dreaded cellulite? Nothing I do seems to help.

Cellulite occurs mainly in women and consists of dimpled fat that clings to the hips and thighs. If affects both the thin and the overweight. No amount of exercise or massage will get ever get rid of it. Even dieting combined with exercise will not budge it.

As **Leslie Kenton**, author of **Cellulite Revolution**, (Ebury Press, 1994) says at the beginning of her book, "Cellulite is no simple cosmetic problem of concern only to vain women who have been sold a bill of goods by the beauty industry. It is a sign that internal pollution is present in parts of your body which can not only reduce your energy levels but mar your physical beauty as well... You can be sure that you body is telling you that something within needs attention."

Nutritionist **Carola Barczak**, owner of **Nutritional Body Care** in Toronto, says that "cellulite fat is an estrogen controlled **emergency ration** for breast feeding during famine and ...that cellulite is burned for energy only when starvation sets in. This makes it unresponsive to diet and exercise."

Nonetheless, Barczak advises that excess starch and sugar form a flabby, soggy, waterlogged layer of cellulite while too many animal fats cause a more pitted texture.

Barczak stresses that essential fatty acids in flax oil, primrose oil, borage oil, and fish oils are "necessary to liberate stored fat so it can be burned off." These oils are part of what Barczak calls common sense nutrition for women.

Essential fatty acids and iodine from seaweeds are common ingredients in anti-cellulite pills. Barczak believes it's cheaper to supplement them yourself if necessary.

At her Toronto clinic, Barczak has had excellent results using electro-muscle stimulation (EMS) which exercises the muscles by alternating contraction and relaxation; but only if heat is applied during the treatment and a reducing diet is followed at the same time. Carola has documented that a series of 10 EMS treatments and a reducing diet can reduced the thighs by one to two clothing sizes.

Barczak also uses vacusage, which is a lymph drainage treatment developed in France that uses heat with vacuum suction. "This breaks up the deep micro-scars that cause the uneven texture of cellulite". At least 25 treatments are recommended.

Barczak suggests you look for a reputable clinic in the yellow pages under weight loss clinics that advertise cellulite treatments. "Call and ask if heat is applied during EMS or if they offer vacusage. Although expensive, these treatments do yield results. Anything else just isn't worth your money."

In her book, Kenton outlines a comprehensive programme that includes a cleansing and detoxification programme, daily skin brushing, and epsom salt baths. She also promotes increased lymph drainage through specialized massage and through using the mini-trampoline at least ten minutes a day. She advocates the daily use of aloe vera juice, spirulina, silica, and seaweeds.

Kenton has devised a cheap but effective anti-cellulite lotion. It is made by using 350cc. of aloe vera liquid combined with 25cc. each of cola vera liquid extract (14 percent caffeine, burns fat) and fucus vesiculosus (bladderwrack). Kenton advises applying the lotion twice a day to the cellulite areas, followed using a special anti-cellulite glove or roller over these same areas.

Drs. **Michael Murray** and **Joseph Pizzorno** in their book, **Encyclopedia of Natural Medicine** (Prima, 1998) recommend oral centella asiatica (gotu kola) 30mg twice daily and aesculus hippocastanum (horse chestnut) 500mg of the bark of the root three times a day and escin (compound isolated from the seeds of horse chestnut) 10 to 20mg three times a day. They also advise an ointment made with .5 to 1.5 percent cola vera extracts; .25 to .75 percent bladderwrack, and .5 to 1.5 percent escin.

One study of 65 patients who had cellulite showed 58 percent had very good results and 20 percent had satisfactory results using oral gotu kola alone.

In March 1999, a new anti-cellulite pill known as Cellasene was introduced to the market. It was invented by an Italian scientist named **Dr. Gianfranco Merizzzi**. It consists of bladderwrack, grape seed extract, sweet clover, ginkgo biloba extract, bioflavonoids, borage oil, fish oils, and lecithin. Three unpublished studies have been conducted in Italy involving just 90 patients. One small Australian study showed that 69 percent of women benefited from taking cellasene. It remains to be seen how effective this pill will turn out to be on the long term.

There are some good solutions to getting rid of cellulite, but it seems that time, money and commitment is required.

Listen to Your Body by **Carola Barczak** is series of ninety minute videos that discuss 55 different nutritional factors in depth (705-746-7839). Carola's **Nutritional Body Care Clinic** is in Toronto at 416-960-6200.

Pregnancy Supplements and Nausea

I am 29 years old and seven weeks pregnant for the first time. I am concerned about taking an appropriate multivitamin mineral supplement. A recommended maternal brand from the health food store taken 3 times a daily with meals seems to aggravate my frequently occurring nausea and causes me to vomit. A commonly used drugstore maternal brand (though containing fewer nutrients and inferior in quality) is only taken one time daily and I seem to tolerate it better. (They are taken with meals). My vomiting has occurred on days when no vitamin was taken. I am keeping most food down but I find fresh vegetables nauseating. Fresh fruit is fine. Can I be confident that I am getting the required nutrition for a healthy baby?

First of all, even with continuous nausea and vomiting, and even if you can't take vitamins until the nausea subsides, (usually around the fourth or fifth month) let me reassure you that your baby is getting the nutrition that it needs.

Personally, I recommend high quality natural prenatal supplements which contain not only all the necessary vitamins and minerals but soothing and safe herbs for pregnancy such as red raspberry leaf. Red raspberry leaf tones the uterus and contributes to an easier delivery. Some brands of drugstore prenatal vitamins contain forms of iron which can upset the stomach. It is best to take your supplements with meals.

However, it's OK if you don't start the prenatal vitamins until after the third or fourth month of pregnancy, with the exception of the B-vitamins including folic acid, which must be taken prior to and during the whole pregnancy.

For morning sickness, you can try powdered ginger root, available in capsules in most health food stores, three or four a day followed by a glass of water, first thing in the morning. This can be repeated several times throughout the day, as necessary.

Slippery Elm is a soothing and strengthening herb for the stomach. It possesses as much nutrition as oatmeal and is so gentle it can be retained by the most sensitive stomach. It can be taken in powdered form in capsules or made into a gruel with water or milk.

Vitamin-B-6, 50 to 100mg a day is a very effective anti-nauseant. It should be taken as part of a mega-B-50 capsule with breakfast and with lunch.

Why Take Supplements?

I have a good diet and I exercise regularly. Why should I take supplements?

If you are living in a stress free environment in the country, eating only organic foods grown on mineral enriched soil, drinking pure water, and experiencing an abundance of energy and vitality, then you don't need to take any supplements.

Unfortunately, most of us live in highly polluted cities, exposed to high levels of electro-magnetic radiation and noise. We eat less than five to seven servings of fruits and vegetables a day. In addition, most of us are stressed by our rushed frenetic pace, lack of time off and leisure, emotional conflicts and financial stresses. Meanwhile, the onslaught of chemicals in the environment, most of whose effects are unknown, continues to affect us daily through our food, water and air.

You may be experiencing non-specific but distressing health complaints such as fatigue, headaches, joint pains, sinus congestion, indigestion, and heartburn.

On the other hand, if you have developed specific illnesses like arthritis, migraines or hypertension, you absolutely require nutritional supplements as an essential part of treatment.

Your nutritional programme has to be tailored to your individual needs and requirements. In general, for a base line maintenance programme, I suggest the following: a high quality multivitamin and mineral combined, antioxidant vitamins and a supergreen drink. For specific illnesses, more supplements and herbs should be added appropriate to that particular illness.

The multi vitamin and mineral should be as high quality as you can afford, preferably in the form of two capsules with each meal. A minimal antioxidant regimen would include the main antioxidant vitamins daily: Vitamin-C 500mg Vitamin-E 400IU and betacarotene 30,000IU. Green drinks containing sprouts and blue green sea algae like spirulina supply essential trace minerals, antioxidants, and easily digestible protein. If you have a weak digestion, taking high quality plant enzymes with meals is also highly recommended.

Women over 35 should also take calcium magnesium supplements, preferably at bedtime. The usual recommended dose is 800 to 1,200mg of calcium and 400 to 600mg of magnesium.

Daily consumption of miso can protect you from the harmful effects of radiation. Green drinks also offer protection from the harmful effects of radiation, chemicals and other toxins.

Of course, a healthy diet is still the most important part of maintaining good health. I recommend a diet of organic fresh fruits and vegetables, whole grains and beans, supplemented, if necessary, with low fat yogurt, organic chicken and cold water fish.

Early Breast Cancer
Soy Foods and Tamoxifen

I am 37 years old and was recently diagnosed with early stage breast cancer. I had a partial mastectomy and 12 nodes removed with clean margins and no node involvement. I will undergo radiation soon. My tumour is both progesterone and estrogen positive. I would like to know which estrogen rich foods to avoid. Tamoxifen may be recommended but I worry it will increase my chances of uterine cancer?

I am not sure what a partial mastectomy means, but readers should know that lumpectomy, (removing only the lump), plus radiation yields the same survival rates as mastectomy (removing the whole breast). What readers may not know is that lymph nodes are removed for diagnosis primarily, and not for treatment. If the breast tumour is small, as yours was, and there are no hard lumps in the armpit, some women choose not to have any lymph nodes removed. Radiation does not prolong your life, but does decrease the chance of local reoccurrences.

In a new book on how to prevent breast cancer, **Fit for Life III** (Prentice Hall, 1998) **Harvey Diamond** emphasizes the critical role of the lymph glands, to trap and destroy cancer cells and limit further spread. Diamond also outlines how women can keep the lymph drainage system in top shape through reducing its load of toxins by proper diet, cleansing, and exercise, including jumping on the mini-trampoline for at least five or six minutes a day.

Pesticides contain chemicals which mimic the action of estrogen in the body. These pesticides tend to be concentrated in the fat of meat and dairy. Several studies have found a higher level of pesticides in the fatty tissues of women with breast cancer. Avoidance of animal fat, especially that of beef and dairy is important. All food should be organic when possible.

Vegetables and fruits are protective for breast cancer. Antioxidant vitamins like vitamin-E, vitamin-C, betacarotene, and selenium have a proven anti-cancer effect.

Soy beans contain genestein, a plant estrogen that interferes with the formation of new blood vessels that supply the cancer, and thus has an anti-cancer effect. As far as we know, soy products are safe and beneficial for breast cancer patients to take. Flaxseeds have the same positive effect. Some scientists believe that genestein and other plant estrogens act like tamoxifen, but without the side effects. Certain types of iodine also act like tamoxifen and can be taken for breast cancer prevention.

Tamoxifen has both anti-estrogenic effects and pro-estrogenic effects. Side effects include menopausal symptoms, menstrual irregularity, blood clotting disorders, eye problems, twice the risk of uterine cancer, depression and a possible small risk of liver cancer. For premenopausal woman with estrogen positive nodes, potential benefits from taking tamoxifen are small.

Much of the information for this answer comes **Breast Cancer, What You Should Know About Prevention, Diagnosis and Treatment** (Prima, 1994) written by a naturopathic physician, **Dr. Steve Austin** and his wife, **Cathy Hitchcock**, who had breast cancer. Two other general books on cancer that I highly recommend are **God I Thought You Died**, (McClelland and Stewart, 1986) by **Claude Dosdall** and **Cancer As A Turning Point**, (Dutton, 1989) by **Lawrence LeShan**. I also suggest you see a naturopathic physician to supervise a natural prevention programme. Dealing with breast cancer is emotionally demanding, and a good support network is important.

Breast Cancer And Natural Alternatives

I was the victim of breast cancer, for which I had surgery and chemotherapy. At the time, I did not know about alternative treatments. I lost my hair and had the usual terrible side effects. My question is that: If a friend were diagnosed with breast cancer, what could I tell her about natural alternatives?

One in three people will get cancer over the course of their lifetime. Thus, it's inevitable that all of us will have a friend or loved one develop cancer. The time to get familiar with alternative treatments is well before this crisis develops. Otherwise, you will be swept up in the fear and panic of the moment, and not be able to reasonably consider all the possibilities both conventional and alternative.

To prepare ahead of time, I highly recommend **Burton Goldberg**'s book, **An Alternative Medicine Definitive Guide To Cancer** (Future Medicine, 1997) and **Ralph Moss**'s book, **Cancer Therapy: The Independent Consumer's Guide** (Equinox, 1995). Make sure these books are part of your family library.

Even with respect to the usual treatments offered for breast cancer there are important choices to be made. Breast cancer usually develops slowly and by the time a lump has appeared it may already be too late to use alternatives alone without resorting to surgery. Certainly, it makes sense to have a small cancerous lump removed and then use alternatives to prevent reoccurrences. In your case, even having received standard treatment, you still need to make major lifestyle and emotional changes as well as to start using natural therapies to prevent reoccurrences.

It's important to remember that lumpectomy for breast cancer (removing only the lump), plus radiation yields the same survival rates as mastectomy (removing the whole breast). Lymph nodes are removed for diagnosis primarily, and not for treatment. If the breast tumour is small, and there are no hard lumps in the armpit, some women may opt not to have any lymph nodes removed. Radiation does not prolong your life, but does decrease the chance of local reoccurrences.

An excellent book that covers all surgical and medical options for breast cancer as well as alternative treatments and prevention from the point of view of a naturopathic physician, is **Breast Cancer, What You Should Know (But May Not Be Told) About Prevention, Diagnosis and Treatment**, by **Dr. Steve Austin** and his wife, **Cathy Hitchcock**, who had breast cancer (Prima, 1994).

The **Ontario Breast Cancer Information Exchange Project** has published an excellent well referenced book on alternative therapies for breast cancer, entitled **A Guide To Unconventional Cancer Therapies** (order through 905-727-3300). **Susun Weed**'s new book, **Breast Cancer, Breast Health, The Wise Woman Way** is an excellent comprehensive alternative guide to breast cancer prevention and treatment.

Ralph Moss also provides a research service for cancer alternatives. For $275 US, the **Moss Reports** provides a detailed 30 to 50 page report specific to your type of cancer including the most promising alternative treatments, and how to obtain them (718-636-4433).

If you decide not to get surgery at all, limit the amount of time you will try the alternative therapies without considering surgery. It doesn't make sense to let an easily treated small breast lump develop into an inoperable mass. It is relatively easy to treat the first appearance of a cancer. Preventing a reoccurrence is the most important issue in the long run.

You needn't choose between alternative or conventional therapies, both can be successfully combined. The key is becoming informed on the range of choices available and what you feel comfortable and safe doing. The decision on what type of therapy to employ is a personal one, and as a friend, your role is to support whatever choice is made even if you don't agree with it. (See the book chapter and column for more information).

Tight Bras
And Breast Cancer

I heard that wearing a tight bra might cause breast cancer. This seems unbelievable. Is there any truth in it?

While it makes sense that restrictive bras worn for long periods of time can contribute to breast cancer, there is no definitive proof.

Sydney Ross Singer and **Soma Grismajer**, authors of a recent book, **Dressed to Kill** (Avery, 1995), are researchers in the field of medical anthropology. Together they interviewed 4,500 women, about half of whom had breast cancer. They found that women who had breast cancer were more likely to have worn their bras for twelve hours or more a day, were less happy with the size and shape of their breasts without a bra, and more often their bras caused red marks or irritation. Twenty percent of women with breast cancer also wore their bras to bed.

The authors speculate that a tight bra worn for long periods of time cuts off lymphatic drainage and keeps the breast in contact with toxins for longer periods of time.

Their questionnaire results do suggest further well designed studies may be worthwhile. For large breasted women, wearing bras may be essential, but their use could be modified. The authors also pointed to the constant exposure to toxins in the diet and in the environment.

However, they downplay the importance of external estrogen in adding to breast cancer risk, like hormone replacement therapy for menopause and the many industrial chemicals that mimic the action of estrogen. In fact, a recent study published in the **New England Journal of Medicine** (June, 1995) by a well known researcher showed a 40 percent increase in breast cancer risk for women who had taken estrogen for six or more years.

There are four excellent books on breast cancer prevention. One is, **Fit for Life III** (Prentice Hall, 1998) by **Harvey Diamond**, who emphasizes the importance of a low fat vegetarian diet, fasting, and improving lymphatic drainage through using the mini-trampoline. **Susun Weed**'s new book, **Breast Care, The Wise Woman Way**, (AshTree, 1996) offers a comprehensive approach to breast cancer treatment and prevention using herbs and natural treatments including breast massage. **Dr. Ross Pelton** and radiologist **Dr. Vinton Vint** and **Taffy Pelton**'s book, **How To Prevent Breast Cancer** (Fireside, 1995) offers a more conventional but very useful approach to breast cancer prevention including antioxidants, melatonin, diet and non-sexual breast massage.

Finally a new book called **The Breast Cancer Prevention Programme** by **Dr. Samuel Epstein and David Steinman** (MacMillan, 1997) details how to avoid all environmental, occupational and prescription cancer causing agents.

The message in all this is to pay attention to your body's signals, avoid prolonged use of tight bras and practice breast self massage to promote lymph drainage (or get a loving partner to help).

Women And Alcohol

Do Women Handle Alcohol Differently From Men?

Yes, a woman's body handles alcohol very differently from a man's. The female body breaks down alcohol more slowly. A woman's body also contains less water. Therefore there is less dilution of the alcohol. That means, on the average, a woman gets drunk faster and on fewer drinks than a man.

During the premenstrual period and near the time of ovulation, the absorption of alcohol is accelerated even more. At such times a woman may get drunk on fewer drinks than usual.

For women, alcohol has a much quicker and more devastating effect on their health. Women develop cirrhosis of the liver and mental deterioration at about half the alcohol consumption of men.

More women die as a result of their alcoholism than men. Alcoholic women have a death rate three to seven times that of women who don't drink. On the other hand, alcoholic men have a death rate only twice than of non-drinking males.

Recent studies have linked alcohol to the development of breast cancer. The studies show that there is a 50 to 100 percent increased risk of breast cancer from as little as one or two drinks daily.

Heavy drinking also affects the whole hormonal and reproductive system of women. Menstrual periods and ovulation can become more erratic. The production of various types of female hormones is also altered.

Pregnant women who drink can cause serious damage to their babies. The risk to the baby is directly proportional to the amount of alcohol consumed.

No one knows for sure how many drinks per week is safe for the baby so it is probably wisest for a woman not to drink at all once she has confirmed her pregnancy.

Anemias, especially those due to deficiencies of iron and folic acid, are much more common in women drinkers than male drinkers by a ratio of three to one. Women alcoholics are also at a much higher risk for osteoporosis.

Women drinkers are more prone to nerve inflammation caused by lack of vitamin-B-1. Women are also more likely to develop the shakes or DT's during alcohol withdrawal. Mental deterioration from alcohol is three times as prevalent in women as in men.

In contrast, women drinkers are less prone than men to problems such as stomach ulcers and inflammation of the pancreas.

When a woman finally goes to her doctor for help, the chances are that he won't recognize that she is an alcoholic. He is also likely to prescribe tranquilizers, thus causing a dual addiction.

Is There Help For Premature Menopause?

Six years ago I was diagnosed with premature menopause and given both premarin and provera for life. I was told that if I stopped these drugs I'd be prone to stroke or heart attack. Recently, I went to a naturopath in Manitoba, who replaced my old drugs with angelica and vitamin-E. I haven't started to take them yet but, when I do, I must continue with the drugs for one month before stopping them. Am I now putting myself at risk and what changes should I expect in my body, if any?

In my experience, premature menopause is a much harsher experience than naturally occurring menopause. Most women go into menopause somewhere between 40 and 59, with the average age being between 45 and 55. Premature menopause occurs between 35 and 40 in one in a hundred women. Surgically induced menopause caused by removing the ovaries occurs in about 7 to 8 percent of women before age 40.

Early menopause seems to bring more problems including severe hot flashes, difficulty concentrating, disorientation, mood swings and insomnia. What's worse is that your friends of the same age won't know what you're talking about and your doctor may not suspect the diagnosis at first.

The risk of heart disease and bone loss increase after both natural and premature menopause. However, in the case of premature menopause, you are without your hormones for longer and the risks of heart disease and bone loss are greater. Increased risk of stroke has not yet been associated with menopause.

Taking premarin and provera will lower your risk of heart disease and bone loss, but may increase your risk of breast and ovarian cancer and other complications.

The most important prevention for heart disease and stroke is a high fibre low animal fat diet, the antioxidant vitamins-E, C and betacarotene, regular exercise, and dealing with feelings of alienation and loneliness.

Dr. John Lee, author of **What Your Doctor Won't Tell You About The Premenopause,** (Warner, 1996) California, found that bone loss could be prevented or reversed through regular use of a natural progesterone skin cream. The cream can be ordered through **Transitions For Health** at 1-800-648-8211. A soy derivative known as ipriflavone has been extensively researched and shown to prevent and reverse bone loss. It is available at health food stores.

It is important to go off premarin slowly over about a month. Alternate a full dose with a half dose for a week, then a half dose daily for two weeks, then a half dose every second day for a week. Meanwhile, you can start the angelica or dong quai and vitamin-E which should relieve the hot flushes. You can also add bee pollen, evening of primrose oil, and Vitamin-C with bioflavonoids.

The herb black cohosh can also be used instead of dong quai. A black cohosh extract known as Remifemin has been studied extensively in Europe and shown to alleviate all the symptoms of menopause. Its effect on hot flashes and vaginal dryness are equivalent to premarin.

Another alternative for premarin and provera is natural estrogens combined with natural progesterone. These natural hormones are derived from soybean and wild yam and you can get them by prescription only from any compounding pharmacist through the **International Academy of Compounding Pharmacists** at 713-933-8400 or 1-800-927-4227; the **Women's International Pharmacy** at 1-800-279-5708 or **Madison Pharmacy Associates** at 1-800-558-7046;

You may be pleased to be rid of the side effects of provera (mood swings, depression and bloating). Natural progesterone has few side effects by comparison. I usually advise taking natural progesterone even when taking herbs like dong quai and black cohosh to balance the net estrogenic effect of these herbs.

For further information refer to my book chapter on menopause.

I've been taking two 1,000mg capsules of flax oil each day for over a year. It has helped greatly with my eczema, arthritis and weight problem. I'm now going through menopause and refuse to take synthetic hormones. I tried oil of evening primrose to alleviate menopausal symptoms, but it gave me heart palpitations so I've discontinued it (vitamin-E capsules have the same effect). I read that if you overuse flax oil, it can upset your essential fatty acid levels, and you therefore have to take oil of evening primrose to restore balance. I'm concerned about overdoing flax oil, but it's helped me so much I don't want to give it up. What do you suggest?

Essential fatty acids are necessary for normal growth and development, but cannot be manufactured by the body. Thus they must be obtained from the diet. There are two families of fatty acids known as omega-3's and omega-6's. Flax seed contains about 60 percent omega-3 fatty acids and 16 percent of omega-6 fatty acids. However, the body can make more omega-6 fatty acids from flax seed through a series of enzyme reactions. So if your enzymes are working well, you may not need more oil of evening primrose, which contains mostly omega-6 fatty acids.

The typical North American Diet results in widespread deficiency of essential fatty acids as well as an imbalance of omega-3's relative to omega-6's. **Health Canada** recommends a ratio of omega-3 to omega-6 of between 1 to 4 or 1 to 7, versus the usual diet with its ratio of 1 to 20 to 1 to 60.

Omega-3 fatty acids are also found in marine life such as fish, seal and whale as well as flaxseed. Omega-6 fatty acids are found in evening primrose, borage, black currant, sunflower and safflower oils. Most health experts suggest daily supplementation with one or more omega-3 sources.

Researcher **Udo Erasmus**, author of **Fats That Heal, Fats That Kill**, prefers flaxseed oil for omega-3's. However, he believes that people can overdose on flaxseed oil and that maintaining a proper balance of omega-3 to omega-6 is important. So if you think you are taking too much flaxseed oil, you could balance it with another source of omega-6 oils. You may want to experiment with other brands of oil of evening primrose including those derived from borage or black currant.

Meanwhile, there are several herbs that you can use that will successfully relieve menopausal symptoms. Black cohosh extract has been studied for over forty years in Europe and has been shown to eliminate all the symptoms of menopause including hot flashes. Dong Quai is well known in China as the foremost female tonic. It has the effect of balancing the estrogen in the body. Take two capsules two or three times a day with meals or ten drops of the tincture in one-quarter cup of water three times a day. Panax Ginseng, another Chinese herb, will increase energy levels and metabolic rate, stimulate the immune system, and help normalize body functions. It goes well with vitamin-E. It works well for hot flashes, as well as stress, and mental and physical fatigue. However, it should not be used if you feel high strung or jittery, have insomnia or high blood pressure. The dose for ginseng is the same as for dong quai.

Herbalist **Susun Weed** in her book **Menopausal Years** (Ashtree, 1992) suggests taking dong quai for four weeks, followed by ginseng for two weeks and repeating this cycle for two years or as long as necessary.

VITAMIN-E enhances the effect of estrogen in the body. It usually doesn't cause palpitations. Experiment with different brands and perhaps make sure you take it after meals, when it is better absorbed. Start with 400IUs (international units) daily. You can increase up to 1,600IUs a day, if necessary. Don't use vitamin-E in high doses if you have high blood pressure, or if you are on drugs that decrease blood clotting.

Bee Pollen is another useful and safe food supplement. Start with two capsules or chewable tablets a day. Work up to as many as 12 or more until the hot flashes stop. Take it throughout the day, whenever it suits you. Test first to make sure you aren't allergic to bee pollen.

Irregular Periods

I'm 20 years old and was very active in competitive swimming for four years. The summer before I started competition, at age 14, I had my first period. Since then, I haven't had a monthly period for longer than a four month span. Although I haven't swum competitively for almost a year, I haven't had a period for about nine months except for one stimulated by Provera. My doctor prescribed it to see if it would normalize my cycle but it didn't. All results for various tests proved normal. Can you give me some insight?

In natural medicine, a healthy, normal, and regular period is considered an important sign that the female hormones are balanced and functioning well. Thus, it is worrisome that your periods have stopped altogether. One cause can be intense athletic training and competition.

If you are missing your period or having irregular periods, it is essential to know if you are ovulating. **Dr. Jerilynn Prior**, a professor of endocrinology at the University of British Columbia, and other researchers, have found that irregular cycles, or cycles with no periods, may lead to bone loss from a deficiency of the female hormone progesterone.

One of her patients, a competitive runner developed stress fractures of the small bones of her feet after one year of no periods. Women can inexpensively find out if they are ovulating by measuring their basal temperature daily.

The good news is that you can regulate and balance your hormonal cycle and prevent bone loss, through the use of natural progesterone skin cream or oral capsules. Unlike the synthetic progesterone your doctor put you on (which is the correct conventional treatment) the natural progesterone has very few side effects. You will have to take the natural progesterone for six months to a year.

In addition there are many wonderful herbs that help you. Among them is dong quai which is a well known treatment in China for periods that have stopped altogether. (amenorrhea) Dong Quai root is famed in Chinese medicine for its affinity for the female constitution. It contains many natural plant estrogens and balances the amount of estrogen in the body. Take two capsules two or three times a day with meals. As a herbal tincture, use ten drops in one-quarter cup of water three times a day.

Another very useful herb is Vitex Agnus Castus, also known as chaste tree, which is a slow acting tonic for the female system. The usual dosage is twenty drops of the tincture twice a day for three to six months at a time.

Other important aspects of treatment include treatment of chronic yeast infection, herbs that support liver function, and nutritional supplements. You may also need the guidance of a skilled health care practitioner.

Fibroid Removal

I am a forty seven year old women and my periods have recently become heavier and longer. A pelvic ultrasound showed a 3.5 cm. fibroid located in the wall of the uterus (a submucous fibroid). My doctor wants to do a hysterectomy if it grows any bigger. Can you tell me about the new surgical techniques to remove fibroids and preserve the uterus?

Fibroids are benign growths in or on the uterus. Smaller fibroids like yours can be removed through a new procedure known as hysteroscopy. Hysteroscopy refers to an operation in which a small lighted instrument (scope) is used to look inside your uterus (hystero).

Fibroids under one or two centimetres, that have a stalk, or are protruding into the uterine cavity, can be easily removed through the hysteroscope. Fibroids between 2.5 and 5 centimetres can be removed the same way after they have been shrunk through medication. Fibroids larger than 5 centimetres must be shrunk medically, and then removed in two steps.

A recent article by Dalhousie professors **Drs. Robert and Farrell**, reviewed over 1,000 cases of submucous fibroids and polyps. They found that both could be removed safely through the hysteroscope, with over 80 percent of women experiencing good results.

Slowly growing fibroids which are causing no symptoms can be left alone. Fibroids larger than the size of a grapefruit that are causing pressure symptoms or severe bleeding can be handled through myomectomy which means removal of the fibroid tumour with preservation, and if necessary, reconstruction of the uterus. These operations can be more complicated, require a longer time, and cause more blood loss than hysterectomies. Usually it will take some research and input from women's groups to find a gynecologist who is skilled at removing fibroids, even in a large city.

Natural treatments for fibroids aim to decrease levels of estrogen in the body. Excess estrogen can come from many sources including high animal fat diets, pesticides and other chemicals which mimic the action of estrogen, sub-optimal liver function, nutritional deficiencies and bowel problems. Treatments include low fat high fibre diet, hot castor oil packs to the abdomen three to four times a week, iodine supplements, herbs to support and detoxify the liver, and natural progesterone cream. Homeopathy and Chinese medicine can also be helpful. Usually, especially for large fibroids, the supervision of a skilled professional is necessary.

Fibroid growth will be stimulated by taking estrogen. Fibroids will also shrink after menopause. So as you are probably approaching menopause, the best course may be to leave them alone until that time.

Natural And Synthetic Progesterone

I've heard a lot about natural progesterone lately. What's the difference between natural and synthetic progesterone?

Natural progesterone is one of the two main female hormones made by the female ovaries. The other main hormone is estrogen which occurs in the female body in three main forms: estrone, estradiol and estriol. Natural progesterone, on the other hand, has only one form but many beneficial roles in the female body. It is essential during pregnancy, and predominates during the second half of the menstrual cycle. It can be turned into other hormones inside the body, including adrenal hormones, estrogen and testosterone.

According to **Dr. John Lee**, in his book, **What Your Doctor May Not Tell You About Menopause (Warner, 1996)**, other functions of natural progesterone include a natural diuretic, a natural antidepressant, promoting the action of thyroid hormones, normalization of blood sugar levels as well as copper and zinc levels, stimulation of bone building, restoration of proper cell oxygen levels and finally protection against both breast and uterine cancer. Dr. Lee believes that environmental pollution with chemicals and pesticides that mimic the action of estrogen has caused many women to be in a progesterone deficient state by the time they are in their mid thirties.

By contrast synthetic progesterone (actually called progestins and not progesterone, but everyone uses the words inter-changeably, causing much confusion) does not resemble the body's own progesterone and may cause many undesirable side effects. These include mood swings, irritability, depression and bloating. After menopause, progestins can also cause bleeding or spotting.

Natural progesterone is destroyed by stomach acid and thus can only be absorbed in the form of a skin cream, vaginal suppository or specially made oral capsule.

In the 1950's it was discovered that wild yams contain plant estrogens but no natural progesterone. What wild yam does contain is a substance called diosgenin, which can be made into natural progesterone through a three step chemical process.

A confusing number of wild yam creams all claim to contain natural progesterone, but with no concrete information at all to support that claim. Make sure if you are using a natural progesterone cream, you know how many milligrams of actual natural progesterone is contained in each jar.

Natural progesterone can be used as part of a treatment programme for endometriosis, fibroids, PMS, cystic breasts, irregular bleeding and menopause. Be sure to have your care supervised by a qualified practitioner.

Candida Infections

I was recently diagnosed by a naturopath as having candida albicans. It has infiltrated from the colon into the liver. Apparently candida has caused the nauseous attacks, body aches, violent headaches and depression I have suffered for years. After my digestion has been sufficiently stabilized by a complete dietary change, I will be taking a natural yeast killer to destroy the overgrowth. My concern is that if the source of the candida growth is not removed, won't the problem just start up again?

Candida albicans is the name of a family of one cell fungus which belongs to the plant kingdom and is normally present in the skin, mouth, gut and vagina. Some researchers believe that in its one cell form it may be involved in a beneficial role in hormone regulation.

However, under certain conditions (such as a sugary diet high in refined foods, birth control pills or prolonged or repeated courses of antibiotics or cortisone) the one cell form can put out a long tube with branches which can penetrate into the cell wall and secrete up to 79 different toxins.

Infection with this form of candida can cause local infections such as thrush (a mouth infection) in infants or vaginal infections in women, which may clear up right away with treatment. However with some people the infection becomes chronic or recurrent. This can cause fatigue, depression, mood swings, brain fog, digestive difficulties, menstrual problems, muscle aches, headaches, bladder pain and frequency, allergies, chemical sensitivities, repeated ear aches, hyperactivity and learning disabilities in children.

Candida can be accurately diagnosed through a blood test or specialized stool culture. Otherwise diagnosis can be suggested through a good medical history or by using one of the various electro-acupuncture machines. It's likely that your naturopath has screened you for candida, and the results showed a possible generalized yeast infection. However, there is no way to prove that this yeast infection has infiltrated your liver or colon.

Treatment is aimed at restoring the good bacteria in your gut and also at restoring an environment inside your body that prevents reinfection. The treatment plan suggested by your naturopath is a sound one. Through proper diet and taking friendly bacteria like acidophilus which help rid you of yeast, you can improve your digestion and allow a natural anti-yeast preparation like garlic capsules, caprylic acid or grapefruit seed extract to work most effectively.

Pregnancy Over 35

I am 38 years old and would like to become pregnant for the first time. Do you think it's safe at this age?

If you are 35 or over and considering pregnancy for the first time, you are joining an ever-growing group of contented older mothers who are rising to the different challenges that motherhood at that age presents. With advances in prenatal care, as well as the improved nutritional and fitness status of older mothers, pregnancy after 35 is no longer any riskier than pregnancy at an earlier age.

A recent large scale study showed no increased risk for older mothers, just different kinds of risks than for younger mothers. Women over 35 were no more likely to have a premature baby, or to have babies that were small for their age, or to have babies with low APGAR scores at birth (this score measures the vigour of the baby at birth). Women over 35 were also no more likely than younger women to have babies die in the womb, or shortly before birth.

However, the incidence of all chromosomal abnormalities slowly increases with age. The most common abnormality screened for is a cause of mental handicap known as Down's Syndrome. Ninety five percent of Down's Syndrome cases are age-related. At age 30, the incidence of Down's syndrome is about 1 in 1,000; at age 35, it is about 1 in 350 births; and at age 40 the chance of having a Down's child is about 1 in 100.

Dr. Patricia Baird, professor of medical genetics at the University of British Columbia, studied 26,859 children with birth defects. She excluded children with chromosomal abnormalities. She found there was no association between any other type of birth defect and the age of the mother. This also holds true for structural defects, including neural tube defect in which the bone forms incompletely over the spinal chord or brain. Most structural defects can be ruled out by ultrasound. Chromosomal abnormalities can be ruled out through amniocentesis.

Neural tube defects affect 300,000 to 400,000 infants per year worldwide, with 2,500 to 3,000 per year in the United States, and 800 in Canada. Numerous studies have shown that taking folic acid supplements can reduce this incidence by at least 50 percent.

All women of child bearing age should take .4mg folic acid daily or the dietary equivalent starting immediately after they stop using birth control, until at least ten to 12 weeks after a missed period. During pregnancy, women should take at least .8 to 1.0mg of folic acid daily.

Folic acid is present in dark green leafy vegetables, brewer's yeast, whole grains, legumes and organ meats, but it is very sensitive to heat and light and any type of cooking. Since low dose folic acid supplements are very safe, it is wisest to take these supplements on a continuous basis throughout the childbearing years to ensure adequate levels of folic acid.

Infertility And Chasteberry Herb

One in six couples in America have an infertility problem, and we are one of the unfortunate couples. My husband and I have been trying for another child through medical intervention for four years. I cannot tell you the amount of heartache and physical pain we have been through. Doctors finally found that I have a very strong uterus and reproductive organs but poor quality egg production. My ovaries are small and therefore stimulate poorly with extra hormones. Could you suggest any herbs to help egg production?

Infertility is indeed a heart wrenching problem for the women and men who experience it. Treating your problem through natural means requires time, patience, a complete change of lifestyle, and the supervision of a trained naturopathic practitioner as well as your family doctor. Even then there are no guarantees.

If you came into my office, I would look at the physical factors first. I would urge you to follow a diet low in pesticides and additives, namely a low animal fat diet emphasizing fresh fruit and vegetables, whole grains and beans, supplemented with small amounts of organic chicken and fish. Sugar, coffee, tea, white flour and all refined food would be cut down or eliminated. In addition, hot castor oil packs applied to the lower abdominal area five times a week would help improve the functioning of the ovaries.

Secondly, I would suggest nutritional supplements include a super green drink and high quality combination multi-mineral and vitamin supplement. In addition, I would suggest 400 to 800IU's of vitamin-E, extra trace minerals, zinc and folic acid. Ovarian and adrenal glandulars are also useful and should be taken for three to six months.

Dr. Serafina Corsello, a New York women's specialist, and author of **The Ageless Woman** (Corsello Communications, 1999) has had good success treating infertility using injections of magnesium, potassium, B-vitamins, zinc, manganese, and chromium combined with oral adrenal support and natural progesterone skin cream.

In addition, the herb chasteberry (vitex agnus castus) has helped some women with fertility problems. At a recent conference on women's health, naturopathic physician, **Dr. Donald Brown** presented research showing that chasteberry was especially useful in infertility due to progesterone deficiency. It is used as a tincture (i.e. the herb preserved in alcohol, or powdered form in capsules) four drops on an empty stomach with some water in the morning or one capsule of 175mg a day. This herb is slow acting, so should be taken for three to six months, or more.

Also important to take are herbs that improve the function of the liver, where estrogen is broken down.

If you are not already aware of the changes in temperature and mucous throughout your cycle, it would be useful to contact a fertility awareness teacher or take a course on the net in order to be able to recognize and treat subtle irregularities in your cycle. You can also consult books such as **Fertility Awareness Handbook: The Natural Guide To Avoiding Or Achieving Pregnancy** (Hunter House, 1997) by **Barbara Kass-Annesse** and **Hal Danzer** or **Taking Charge Of Your Fertility: The Definitive Guide To Natural Birth Control And Pregnancy Achievement** (Harper Collins, 1995), by **Toni Weschler**.

Finally, I would look at the emotional factors such as negative body image, low self esteem, mixed messages about motherhood and being a woman etc. I would also suggest that you work on visualization daily. I highly recommend the book, **Getting Around The Boulder In The Road: Using Imagery To Cope With Fertility Problems**, by **Aline Zoldbrod**, 1990.

A good resource is **Resolve Inc**, 1310 Broadway. Somerville, MA 02144-1731 (Helpline 617-623-0744 Web Site www.resolve.org). This is a national infertility organization with over 50 chapters in the United States and offers referrals, newsletters, and fact sheets. This group published a book entitled, **Environmental Toxins and Fertility**, (Resolve, 1995). In Canada, you can contact **The Infertility Network**, 160 Pickering St. Toronto, Ontario, M4E 3J7 (416-691-3611 or 416-690-8015).

Endometriosis And Depo-Provera

I was diagnosed with fairly severe endometriosis just over a year ago. I had minimal physical symptoms of the disease until an ovarian cyst ruptured and eventually led to the diagnosis. My gynecologist has put me on Depo-Provera, more to protect my fertility than for pain management. I'm advised to stay on the hormone until I plan to have children. Along with gaining six to seven pounds from Depo-Provera, my abdomen is excessively swollen all the time and especially uncomfortable after eating. Food intolerances have been identified and dealt with, and I don't have a candida problem. Can anything relieve this "swelling" to make the hormone treatment livable, or are there other options to staying on the drug for possibly a number of years?

The main symptom of endometriosis is usually but not always severe disabling pain during periods, or any time in the cycle.

In the past, it was thought that endometriosis caused infertility and that pregnancy would improve endometriosis. Neither of these concepts have been proven to be true.

Furthermore, minimal to mild endometriosis is not associated with infertility and does not benefit from treatment. With moderate to severe disease, anatomical distortion of the ovaries and the tubes may interfere with conception.

If you are not having any pain or other symptoms there is no reason to continue the depo-provera. "Protecting your fertility" is not a valid reason to take a potent drug with lots of side effects like depo-provera.

Depo-provera is a long acting form of synthetic progesterone, usually given as an injection every three months for birth control purposes. This means it can take months to clear out of your system. Side effects of depo-provera include weight gain, bloating and abdominal distension, nausea, acne, hair loss, irritability, mood swings, depression and irregular bleeding. Furthermore, it is possible that depo-provera might contribute to long term infertility for some women.

Fortunately, there are other drug options as well as natural remedies. There is a natural progesterone skin cream which has none of the side effects of depo-provera. There are also natural progesterone oral capsules which can achieve the same results as depo-provera.

Many women have also found a series of acupuncture treatments helpful. Other natural treatments, including herbs, homeopathy, cleansing and diet, under the supervision of a naturopathic physician, can improve and even arrest the disease.

You need to become an expert on the disease as well as educating your doctor. You should contact 1-800-426-2END to get information from **The Endometriosis Association**. The mission of this Association, one of the world's most successful self help groups, is to provide support and information to women with endometriosis, to conduct research, and to educate doctors and the public. It will also provide you with the name of the support group in your area, which can provide referrals to doctors experienced in treating endometriosis.

Discovering Alternative Medicine

More and more people are turning to alternative medicine for problems for which conventional medicine has no satisfying answers, and also as an alternative to unnecessary drugs and surgery.

Philosophy Of Alternatives

~The body has the innate ability to heal itself.

~Remedies stimulate this ability and boost the immune system.

~Remedies seek to address the root causes of illness.

~Natural remedies safer, fewer side effects.

~Spiritual, mental, emotional and physical aspects of illness taken into account.

~Mind body connection important.

~Individual responsible for getting informed and changing lifestyle and diet.

Naturopathy: This is a broad term, referring to a whole range of natural therapies. A naturopathic doctor has four years post graduate training in all branches of natural medicine including nutrition, herbal medicine, acupuncture, homeopathy, hydrotherapy, manipulation, counselling and lifestyle modification. Some specialize in one area, most use a combination.

Homeopathy: This is system of natural medicine discovered at the end of eighteenth century by Dr. Samuel Hahnemann. It uses very dilute preparations from the plant, mineral, and animal world to stimulate a sick person's natural defences, to correct the cause of underlying symptoms, and bring the body back into balance.

Chiropractic: This is the largest drugless healing profession in the world, and it focuses on the musculoskeletal system. Chiropractors receive four year post graduate training, including 4,500 hours in basic and clinical sciences. Chiropractic is based on the belief that misaligned spinal vertebrae impinge on nerves exiting from the spine to various body parts, causing discomfort and disease. This problem is corrected through spinal manipulation, a series of quick, painless thrusts that mobilize fixed or immobile joints.

Herbology: This is the art and science of using whole plant remedies to relieve symptoms, to stimulate the body's innate healing powers, and to cleanse and tone organs. Plant medicines are also powerful allies to prevent illness, to balance body functions, and to restore health. Used since ancient times, plants are the source for many modern medicines. Plants have low toxicity if used correctly.

Acupuncture: This is a 5,000 year old Chinese medical system in which health is determined by the flow of chi or vital life energy in 12 major pathways called meridians. The meridians are linked to specific organs and organ systems. Small sterile needles are inserted into the 365 main acupuncture points to help correct and rebalance the flow of energy, thus relieving pain and/or restoring health.

There are many excellent high quality studies which show the value of acupuncture for pain relief and addiction. But it is also used to treat and prevent a whole range of illnesses. It is usually combined with individually determined Chinese herbal medicines.

Body Work: Pioneers like **Dr. Milton Trager, Dr. Moshe Feldenkrais**, and **F.M. Alexander** found that through a system of exercises and posture changes, the connection between the brain and the muscles could be retrained. **Ida Rolf** invented a system of deep massage to release emotional patterns held deep in the muscles. All of these therapies are performed by practitioners after extensive training and apprenticeship.

Ayurvedic Medicine: This is a five thousand year old medical science from India, which examines the patient in terms of the five elements of fire, earth, air, water and ether. There are three possible body mind types. Imbalances and illness are treated with diet, herbs, minerals, animal products, exercise, yoga and meditation.

Shamanic Healing: Native healers look for the spiritual cause of illness and use ritual, prayer, dreams and herbs to bring the person back into balance.

Environmental Medicine: Sometimes known as clinical ecology, environmental medicine seeks to identify and treat the underlying dietary and environmental causes of physical and mental symptoms. Various testing procedures are used, and treatment includes avoidance, desensitization shots, oral and intravenous nutritional supplements, and other therapies to boost the immune system.

Aromatherapy: The branch of herbal medicine that uses the medicinal properties of plant essential oils. Essential oils are the subtle volatile liquids of plants extracted by steam distillation or cold pressing i.e the essence of the plant. The oils have a whole range of therapeutic properties depending on their chemical make-up including anti-bacterial, anti-viral, anti-fungal, anti-inflammatory, immuno-stimulant, antidepressant, sedative and stimulating.

Herbology

Herbology is the art and science of using whole plant remedies to relieve symptoms, to stimulate the body's innate healing powers, and to cleanse and tone organs. Plant medicines are also powerful allies to prevent illness, to balance body functions, and to restore health.

Used since ancient times, plants are the source for many modern medicines. Plants have low toxicity if used correctly. Improved standardization of plant extracts has allowed accurate identification and research. However, it is always preferable to use the whole plant as medicine rather than isolated active ingredients.

Preparations

Tea Of Leaves And Flowers: Boiling water poured over them, allowed to sit in a non-aluminum container for 5 to 15 minutes.

Roots: Boiling water added to roots, and cooked for 20 minutes.

Tinctures: Fresh or dried herbs preserved in alcohol, lasts for long periods of time.

Poultices: Crushed fresh herbs wrapped in gauze and applied to skin.

Other: Tablets, capsules, baths, syrups, inhalations, suppositories, ointments, salves, lotions, and oils.

Herb Usages

Echinacea: Purple coneflower or echinacea functions like herbal antibiotic and immune stimulant, useful for colds, flus and recurrent infections.

Dong Quai: Chinese herb, female tonic, for irregular, painful or heavy periods, and menopausal symptoms.

Stinging Nettle: Eaten freshly picked and steamed, rich in vitamins and minerals, great spring tonic.

Dandelion Leaves: are higher in Vitamin-A than carrots, while the roots are an excellent tonic and food for the liver.

Red Raspberry Leaves: Rich in iron, one cup daily during pregnancy helps relax the uterus, making for an easier delivery.

Slippery Elm: Soothing strengthening herb for the stomach, sore throats, possesses as much nutrition as oatmeal.

Plantain: Chewed leaves applied to skin relieves sting of insect bites.

Feverfew: Reduces frequency and severity of migraines.

Precautions

~Test small quantity for allergic reaction.

~Avoid prolonged use without supervision.

~Some herbs unsafe in pregnancy.

~Choose highest quality available.

~See your doctor for proper diagnosis.

Naturopathic Medicine

Naturopathic doctors (ND) were the first to recognize the connection between diet, lifestyle, environment and disease. Naturopathic medicine began at the turn of the century, based on Hippocrates's principle of the healing power of nature. In the 1920's and 1930's, ND's warned that poor eating habits especially low fibre, high red meat and refined diets would contribute to an increased rate of heart disease and cancer. In recent years, science has proven them right.

Basic Beliefs

~Body has innate ability to heal itself.

~Individually chosen natural therapies stimulate this ability without harmful side effects.

~Symptoms represent body's effort to restore balance, and if possible, should not be suppressed.

~Physical, mental, emotional, socio-cultural, environmental, and spiritual aspects of illness considered.

~Prevention is possible before disease appears.

~Patients are encouraged to be informed and take responsibility for changing their lifestyles.

Natural Living Laws

~Natural unrefined foods.

~Balance of rest and activity.

~Moderate paced lifestyle.

~Constructive mental attitudes.

~Avoiding polluted environments.

~Attention to proper elimination.

~Use of whole plant extracts.

Training

Four year post graduate training in naturopathic medicine including clinical nutrition, botanical (plant) medicine, acupuncture, homeopathy, hydrotherapy and manipulation.

Diagnosis

Naturopathic doctors do a detailed history, physical examination and laboratory testing. In addition, they may use additional assessment techniques which can include: urine and blood tests, food sensitivity testing using a type of electro-acupuncture; hair analysis to detect mineral deficiency and heavy metal poisoning; and stool analysis to detect yeast, parasite and bacterial overgrowth and poor digestion.

Pointers

Sometimes the most optimal choice may be to combine a drug or surgery treatment with a natural treatment.

Natural treatments work gradually. For chronic illness, allow at least one to four months for every year you have been sick.

A good practitioner will know his or her limits and get a second opinion or refer to a medical doctor if necessary.

Naturopathic physicians have a governing board which set standards and discipline practitioners. To find the ND closest to you call: **The Canadian Naturopathic Association** at 416-233-1043 or, **The American Association of Naturopathic Physicians** at 206-323-7610.

Chiropractic Medicine

Chiropractic medicine is the largest drugless healing profession in the world and it pioneered the holistic approach to health care.

The word chiropractic comes from Greek, meaning treatment by hand. Canadian Dr. Daniel Palmer brought the practice to North America. He believed that misaligned spinal vertebrae impinged on nerves exiting from the spine to various body parts, causing discomfort and disease.

Scientific Basis

Two double blind studies have showed that chiropractic manipulations produced better relief of low back pain than treatment in a hospital orthopedic department or by a family doctor.

A recent report commissioned by the Ontario government found that chiropractic management of low back pain was much more cost effective than medical management. Chiropractic treatment resulted in fewer complications and quicker return to work.

Training

Modern day chiropractors receive four year post graduate training, including 4,500 hours of full time training in basic and clinical sciences. Chiropractors refer to other health care providers, if the condition is outside their scope of practice.

Who Uses Chiropractic?

One in three persons in both Canada and the United States has had chiropractic treatment. There are sixteen accredited chiropractic colleges in the United States and one in Canada.

In a recent survey, three quarters of Canadians using chiropractors believed they are as competent in their field as doctors. Seventeen percent believed chiropractors are more competent.

Reasons For Visits

~50 percent of people consult for low back pain.

~25 percent consult for neck and arm pain.

~10 percent for other problems.

~15 percent for other painful conditions of the joints, or muscles.

Diagnosis

~Specialized history.

~General examination including nervous system, bone, muscle and joint testing.

~Examination of the motion of the spine, arms and legs.

~X-rays used if needed.

Treatment

~Spinal manipulation is a series of quick, painless thrusts that mobilize fixed or immobile joints.

~Other treatments include massage, heat, light, ultra-sound, electrotherapy, and special exercises.

~A holistic approach to address exercise, posture, nutrition, footwear and lifestyle factors.

Resources

To find a chiropractor in Canada, call the Canadian Chiropractor Association at 416-781-5656. In the United States, call the International Chiropractors Association at 703-528-5000 or the American Chiropractic Association at 703-276-8800.

Therapeutic Touch

Therapeutic Touch (TT) is a non-invasive holistic approach to healing based on an energy reaction between people. Developed by New York nurse **Dolores Krieger** and her mentor **Dora Kunz** in the 1970's, it is practiced by thousands of nurses, health professionals and lay people worldwide.

TT induces relaxation, reduces pain and anxiety and speeds up healing. It can be helpful for any illness or injury, or for normal processes like childbirth. It also helps the dying and those with chronic disease.

Research to date shows faster wound healing, reduction of headache pain and reduced need for post operative pain medication.

Theory

~In health "life energy" flows freely in, through, and out of the body in a balanced manner.

~In illness or injury, this flow is obstructed, depleted or disordered.

~TT attempts to restore the flow to the healthy pattern.

~The practitioner balances the energy field surrounding a person to assist their natural healing process.

How It's Done

~Practitioner moves hands around patient's body from head to foot (patient stays fully clothed).

~Hands move in a gentle flowing motion a few inches from the body.

~Full session lasts up to 20 minutes and is healing and energizing for both giver and receiver.

Who Does It

~Thousands of nurses and health professionals in hospitals and private practice.

~Can be learned by anyone.

~Check for TT practitioners at your hospital.

~To find a practitioner or recommended teacher contact the **Therapeutic Touch Network** at **416-65-TOUCH** or Fax **416-656-3948** (www.therapeutictouchnetwk.com).

Healing With Aromatherapy

Aromatherapy is that branch of herbal medicine that uses the medicinal properties of plant essential oils. Essential oils are the subtle volatile liquids of plants extracted by steam distillation or cold pressing (the essence of the plant).

Essential oils have been used for healing since the time of ancient Egypt. The oils are inhaled, applied through the skin or taken internally.

How Essential Oils Work

~They regenerate, oxygenate and protect the plant.

~They have a unique fat soluble structure, enabling them to pass through cell membranes of the skin and diffuse into the bloodstream.

~Through the sense of smell, they act on the limbic system in the brain.

~The limbic system controls heart rate, blood pressure, breathing, memory, stress levels, and hormone balance.

Chemical Properties

~200 types of oils with several thousand chemical constituents have been identified.

~Eugenol found in cinnamon, clove, and basil is antiseptic, stimulating and acts as a local anesthetic.

~Esters found in lavender, rose, and geranium are calming and sedating.

~Phenols found in oregano and thyme are anti-bacterial, anti-fungal, and antiseptic.

~Sesquiterpenes found in sandalwood and frankincense are soothing to inflamed tissue, immune stimulating, and cross the blood brain barrier to improve brain function.

Other Actions

~Improve adrenal function.

~Balance thyroid function.

~Aid digestive problems.

~Clear sinus and chest congestion.

Clinical Studies

~Lavender oil effective for burns, also calming effect.

~Diluted tea tree oil effective for trichomonas vaginal infections.

~Study showed that oil blend (clove, cinnamon, melissa and lavender) as effective in treating bronchitis as antibiotics.

~Russian study showed eucalyptus oil effective against influenza.

~German studies found clove, cinnamon and thyme had anti-inflammatory effects useful in treating arthritis.

Cautions

~Buy oils of highest quality.

~Otherwise oils may be diluted with harmful contaminants.

~Do not ingest oils without supervision.

~Conifers, citrus, spice oils must be diluted in a neutral oil before applying to skin.

References

~**Aromatherapy, The Essential Beginning**, by **Gary Young**.

~**The Practice Of Aromatherapy**, by **Jean Valnet**.

~**People's Desk Reference for Essential Oils** by **Gary Young**.

~**Natural Home Health Care Using Essential Oils** by **Daniel and Rosemare Penoel**.

~**Advanced Aromatherapy: The Science of Essential Oil Therapy** by **Kurt Schnaubelt**.

What Is Homeopathy?

Homeopathy is the art and science of using natural substances from the animal, plant, or mineral world in very diluted forms to stimulate a sick person's natural defences. Homeopathy is very useful for first aid, flu, allergies, arthritis, headache, digestive problems, etc. Chronic or complex illnesses require the advice of a homeopathic doctor.

Principles

~Body has innate healing abilities.

~Symptoms represent positive response to stressors.

Like Cures Like: A remedy that causes certain symptoms in a healthy person will cure those very same symptoms when given to a sick person. Works like a natural vaccine and immune booster to induce the body to heal itself.

~Remedies unique for each person after detailed mental, emotional and physical history.

~Treats root causes of illness and inherited weaknesses.

~Trauma and grief important triggering events.

Practitioners

~Over 4,000 medical doctors, naturopaths, chiropractors, and licensed homeopaths in North America.

~In England, 42 to 48 percent of medical doctors refer to homeopaths.

~In France, 25 percent of prescriptions are for homeopathic medicines.

Is It Science?

~107 controlled studies on homeopathy, 81 showed that remedies were effective; 24 showed they were ineffective and 2 were inconclusive.

~Placebo effect, due to the patient's and doctor's positive expectations, account for 40 percent of the effect of any medicine.

~New double blind studies show its effectiveness for childhood diarrhea, recurrent colds, fibromyalgia, and diabetic retinitis.

First Aid Homeopathy

Arnica Montana: For trauma, shock, injuries, after surgery or childbirth.

Apis Mellifica: For swelling and insect bites.

Metallum Album: Gastroenteritis, food poisoning.

Carbo Vegetabilis: Gas and bloating after eating, "homeopathic corpse reviver".

Calendula Officinalis Tincture: Antiseptic for scrapes, scratches and burns.

Rhus Toxicodendron: For sprains, joint stiffness, poison ivy rash.

Hypericum Perforatum: Nerve injury, injuries of tail bone and spine.

Magnesium Phosphate ("Homeopathic Aspirin") For aches and pains, toothache, cramping period pains.

Oscillococcinum: Most popular flu remedy in France, shortens duration of flu.

Mercurius Solubilis: Almost a specific for ear infection, tonsillitis, any inflamed condition producing yellow or green pus.

Antimonium Tartaricum: Has a marked action on chest complaints, mainly for loud rattling or whooping coughs.

The Benefits Of Feldenkrais Therapy

Founded by **Dr. Moshe Feldenkrais**, a renowned Israeli physicist.

The Feldenkrais Method is a system of re-educating the body for efficient painfree movement and graceful posture.

To rehabilitate himself after series of crippling knee injuries, Dr. Feldenkrais developed over 1,000 unique exercises designed to retrain the movement learning centers of the brain and relieve pain and stiffness. The Feldenkrais therapy he developed has provided long term relief for thousands of people around the world.

What

~Two parts to therapy.

~**Awareness Through Movement:** Group lessons in which participants are guided through slow gentle movements designed to replace old movements with easier and more efficient ones. Through this sensory motor learning, new neuromuscular patterns are formed in the brain.

~**Structural Integration:** Individual therapy with hands on touch and movement coaching and re-education.

Practitioners

800 to 1,000 hours of training over 3 to 4 years required for certification. Feldenkrais Guild of North America at 1-800-775-2218 will provide list of practitioners in your area.

Useful For

Chronic back, shoulder pain, neck pain, hip joint pain, foot/ankle pain, headache, chronic musculoskeletal pain, injuries, whiplash, jaw tension, eyestrain, muscle stiffness, repetitive strain injury, sciatica and stroke.

Research

Some research showed benefit in fibromyalgia, multiple sclerosis, rheumatoid arthritis, low back pain.

Reference

Relaxercise, The Easy New Way To Health And Fitness by **David and Kaethe Zemach-Bersin**, and **Mark Reese** (Harper and Rowe, 1990).

The Feldenkrais Method For Dynamic Health by **Steve Sharfman**. Website: www.feldenkrais.com

Trager Therapy
Moving Medicine

Trager Psychophysical Integration is the innovative learning approach to movement re-education founded by **Dr. Milton Trager** after overcoming a congenital spinal deformity. In the process of healing himself and others who sought his help, he developed a series of light, gentle, non-intrusive and highly beneficial movements. Trager therapy helps alleviate pain and immobility in a wide variety of chronic and painful musculoskeletal and neuromuscular conditions.

How To Find A Practitioner

Practitioner certification by the **Trager Institute**, a non-profit educational foundation established by Trager, takes one to two years to complete. It includes beginning, intermediate, and advanced training, documented field work with clients, and continuing education. The Institute has a listing of practitioners worldwide at 415-388-2688 fax 415-388-2710.

Trager Session

A session takes from 1 to 2 hours while the client lies on a table fully or partially dressed. The practitioner uses gentle rhythmical touching, rocking, pulling, and rotation of the neck, torso, legs and arms. Thus deep seated physical and mental patterns are released and the client experiences greater mobility and relief from muscle stiffness, tension and spasm.

Mentastics

Mental gymnastics or mindfulness in motion is a system of simple effortless and enjoyable movements that encourage feelings of freedom and lightness in the body. A short period of instruction in mentastics is offered after each individual session. as well as in groups.

Uses

~Any chronic muscular or joint problem.

~Fibromyalgia, rheumatoid arthritis, osteoarthritis, muscular dystrophy, multiple sclerosis.

~Traumatic injuries, muscular injures, stroke, polio, nerve injuries, Parkinson's disease, asthma and emphysema.

Further Info

~Trager Mentastics: Movement as a Way to Agelessness by Milton Trager (Station Hill Press, 1987).

~**Moving Medicine: The Life and Work of Milton Trager, M.D.** by **Jack Liskin**. Website: site www.trager.com

Natural Treatments For Fibromyalgia

People who suffer from fibromyalgia often say they wake up in the morning feeling like they've been run over by a truck. This is typical of the condition known as fibromyalgia (**FM**).

FM affects mainly women in their late 30's and 40's, with symptoms of generalized pain and aching throughout the body, morning stiffness, fatigue, disturbed sleep, and multiple tender spots on the body. The cause of FM is unknown but it may be part of chronic fatigue syndrome (**CFS**).

Diagnosis

~Widespread muscle pain, aching or stiffness.

~Eleven out of eighteen trigger points located on body tender when pressed on.

~Absence of other conditions that would account for the pain.

~Non-refreshing sleep, frequent headaches, numbness, tingling, pain in the neck and shoulders, irritable bowel syndrome.

Treatment

~Gentle exercise and massage.

~Stress reduction and relaxation exercises.

~Acupuncture stimulation of trigger points and tender points.

~Nutritional supplements including magnesium, Vitamin-B-1, Vitamin-B-3, Vitamin-B-12, essential fatty acids, antioxidants.

~Trial of co-enzyme-Q-10 90 to 300mg daily for six weeks.

~Trial of vitamin-B-12 injections 1,000 micrograms three times a week.

~Elimination diet to identify food allergies.

~Cut out sugar, junk food, excessive animal products.

~Tryptophan or 5-HTP helpful for sleep and pain.

~Amino acid phenylalanine 500 to 1,000mg in the morning.

~Small doses of antidepressant drugs at bedtime may help.

~Niacinamide 500 to 1,500mg a day helpful for pain.

~A new supplement called S-Adenosylmethionine (SAM) 800mg helps reduce symptoms.

~Magnetic therapy often helpful either localized or sleeping on magnetic mattress (**Magnetico** at 1-800-265-1119).

~MSM or methylsulfonylmethane is an exciting new supplement which relieves pain in 50 percent of the cases. The dosage of MSM must be increased until pain relief is achieved. The usual dosage is 5gm to 30gm divided in three doses, with each meal.

Natural Remedies For Cold And Flu

Antibiotics work well for infections caused by bacteria. But colds and flus are caused by viruses, which are not killed by antibiotics. Natural remedies help relieve the symptoms, shorten the duration of viral illnesses, and boost the immune system.

Oscillococcinum

~Most popular flu remedy in France.

~A homeopathic remedy that heightens the immune response to viral illnesses.

~Can be taken with other remedies.

~Research in the British Journal of Clinical Pharmacology (Mar/89) showed faster flu recovery compared to a placebo.

Herbal Immune Boosters

Echinacea Or Purple Coneflower: Most popular herbal antibiotic, reduces the severity and duration of cold and flus, and stimulates the immune system. Usual dose of the tincture (herb preserved in alcohol) is 40 drops 4 to 6 times a day.

Garlic Raw Or In Odourless Capsules: Fights viral, bacterial and yeast infections. Take two to four capsules with each meal. Garlic and Mullein oil ear drops are very helpful for earaches.

Propolis: Known as the Russian penicillin, it is collected by bees to protect the hives from infection. It fights infection and boosts the immune system.

Supplements

Vitamin-C: As soon as cold starts, take vitamin-C in doses of 500 to 1,000mg every hour until stool loosens. Stay at that high dose until your cold is over. Gradually reduce down to 500mg a day. If pregnant stick to daily doses of no more than 500 to 2,000mg a day.

Vitamin-A: In the 1920's and 30's, it was called the anti-infection vitamin. It cuts down the recurrent infection rate. Usual doses are 20,000IU up to 100,000IU a day during infections only.

Zinc: 30 to 50mg per day is an immune booster. Zinc lozenges sucked throughout day reduce the duration of sore throats.

Slippery Elm Lozenges: Slippery elm is a soothing herb that coats inflamed mucous membranes, and provides immediate relief for the pain of sore throats.

Dietary Measures: Go off food for a day or two, and stick to clear broths or miso soup. Fruit juices bring on more mucous.

Cautions: All doses are for non-pregnant adults. Children may take all these remedies, but at reduced dosages. If your symptoms worsen or persist, see your family doctor.

Natural Help For Osteoarthritis

Osteoarthritis is the most common form of arthritis, and is usually progressive, resulting in severe pain and disability. The joints commonly involved are the knees, neck, back, hips and fingers. Symptoms include pain, inflammation and decreased range of motion.

Helpful Supplements

MSM or Methylsulfonylmethane is a natural sulfur based supplement that relieves pain and also contributes to the maintenance and repair of cartilage and joints. The dosage must be gradually increased until pain relief is achieved. The usual dose is 5 to 30gm daily in divided doses with meals. The pain killing effect may develop in days, weeks or months, depending on the severity of the problem.

Glucosamine Sulphate is a naturally occurring component of joint cartilage. Studies to date indicate an effect similar to non-steroidal anti-inflammatories (NSAID's like motrin). It may also help rebuild cartilage. Takes 4 to 6 weeks to work. Dosage 1,500 to 3,000mg daily in three divided doses with meals.

Cod Liver Oil containing 10,000IU's Vitamin-A and 400IU Vitamin-D and flax seed oil 1 to 2 TBS daily.

Niacinamide in dose of 900mg to 3,000mg is excellent for pain. For doses of over 1,500mg seek doctor's supervision.

Buffered Vitamin-C in high doses has an anti-inflammatory effect. Vitamin-E has antioxidant characteristics and is synergistic with Vitamin-C.

Bromelain (sulphur containing proteolytic enzymes from the stem of the pineapple plant) 125mg to 450mg three times daily on an empty stomach can reduce joint swelling and increase mobility.

Diet

~Avoid nightshade foods for four to six weeks (tomatoes, eggplants, potatoes, peppers).

~Elimination diet to find food allergies.

~Cold water fish such as mackerel, herring, salmon and sardines.

~Drink plenty of pure water.

~Eat red and blue berries like cherries, blueberries or drink 4 ounces of black cherry juice daily.

Herbs

~**Devil's Claw**, conflicting study results, may be useful.

~**Yucca** an extract from the desert yucca plant reduces swelling, pain and stiffness in one double blind study.

~**Topical Cayenne Pepper** applied to joints relieves pain.

~**Sea Cucumber** extract as homeopathic or capsules approved in Australia for arthritis.

Physical Therapies

~**Swimming** and **Isometrics**.

~**Heat Treatments** including hot castor oil packs.

~**Hydrotherapy**, hot and cold alternating packs.

~**Acupuncture** very useful for pain and swelling.

Natural Help For Insomnia

Over the past century we have reduced our average hours of sleep by more than 20 percent. The **United States National Commission On Sleep Disorders** reported widespread sleep deprivation with disastrous consequences. The cost of sleep disorders and sleep-related accidents adds up to billions of dollars in the both the U.S. and Canada.

Getting a good night's sleep may be the single most important thing you can do for your health.

Easy Things To Do

~Take a hot bath with epsom salts at bedtime.

~Avoid eating later than 6 pm.

~Listen to a relaxation tape or calming music at bedtime.

~No caffeine after noon.

~Exercise vigorously in the evening.

~Avoid taking B-vitamins in the evening.

Supplements You Can Take At Bedtime

~Calcium 1,000 to 1,200mg and magnesium 300 to 600mg.

~Niacinamide 500mg.

~Melatonin 1 to 6mg or Tryptophan 2 to 4gm.

Herbal Helpers

Valerian: This "herbal valium" has been well studied. One placebo controlled study of 128 patients showed that taking 400mg to 900mg of valerian root at bedtime resulted in decreased time required to fall asleep at night, a reduction in night awakenings as well as an increase in dream recall, with no hang over effect.

St John's Wort: This herb is officially licensed in Germany for the treatment of anxiety, depressive disorders and sleep disorders. It can be taken at night and helps sleep as well as reducing anxiety and depression.

Combinations: Combinations of valerian and other sedative herbs like passion flower, hops and skullcap are also helpful.

Natural Treatments For Ulcers

More than four billion dollars each year are spent on anti-ulcer drugs in North America. Peptic ulcers affect 10 to 15 percent of men and 4 to 15 percent of women at least once in their lives.

A peptic ulcer is a raw area in the stomach or duodenum resulting from erosion by stomach acid. Most ulcers are caused by infection by a bacteria known as heliobacter pylori.

Ulcer Medications

Antacids: Neutralize excess acidity (example Malox).

Acid blockers: Drugs which block acid secretion (Tagamet, Zantac, Losec, Prevacid).

Sulcrafates: Form a protective layer over the ulcer crater (Sulcrate).

Antibiotic Combinations: Success rate is over 80 percent. **Triple Therapy:** 1 week course of 2 antibiotics plus a special acid blocker. **Quadruple Therapy:** 2 week course of bismuth (pepto-bismal) plus 2 antibiotics and an acid blocker.

Licorice Root (Glycyrrhiza Glabra)

~Fourteen double blind studies show favourable results of licorice root vs placebo or ulcer drugs.

~Widely used in Europe.

~Stimulates normal defence mechanisms of gut lining.

~Helps prevent ulcer formation.

~Inhibits growth of heliobacter pylori.

Deglycyrrhinated Licorice

~One major component of licorice root is glycyrrhetinic acid, which is 50 to 100 times sweeter than sugar.

~Long term ingestion of high doses of glycyrrhetinic acid can cause high blood pressure, low potassium and water retention.

~DGL (Deglycyrrhinated Licorice) retains all positive benefits of licorice root without negative side effects.

~Dosage is two 380mg tablets chewed well twenty minutes before each meal.

Other Natural Treatments

~Raw green cabbage juice for stomach ulcers.

~Raw potato juice for duodenal ulcers.

~Amino acid glutamine strengthens gut lining.

~Extra vitamin-C, vitamin-E and vitamin-B-6; extra zinc supplement.

~Eliminate allergic foods from diet.

~Avoid smoking, caffeine, alcohol.

Natural Trauma Remedy

Arnica montana is a perennial herb that grows on mountain slopes around the world. It has bright yellow flowers and looks like a daisy. For hundreds of years, this plant has been used externally for falls sprains and bruises. In its special homeopathic form, it is one of the great trauma remedies.

Homeopathic Arnica

~Remedy of choice for falls, sprains, blows, wounds, fractures, soft tissue injury.

~Useful before and after surgery, dental work and childbirth.

Also Helps Heal

~Muscular soreness, strains, and charley horse.

~Eye injuries, head injuries and concussions.

~Mental and physical shock from injury, loss, grief.

~Effects of past trauma, especially if person has never been well since injury or fall.

~Not effective for chronic pain.

How To Take

~Pellets, or liquid by mouth every 5 to 10 minutes until stable, then hourly, then four times daily.

~Safe for children.

~No harmful side effects.

What It Does

~Decreases and prevents further pain.

~Reduces bruising, swelling and bleeding.

~Prevents secondary infection.

~Accelerates healing.

Herbal Arnica

~Gels, creams, ointments, poultices applied to affected area.

~Not for use when skin is broken i.e. open cut, wound, or abrasion.

~Do not take internally (except homeopathic).

~For best results, combine oral homeopathic arnica with external preparations.

Reference

Homeopathy For Musculoskeletal Healing, by **Asa Hershoff** (North Atlantic, 1996).

Kava Kava
For Anxiety

Kava Kava (Piper Methysticum) is a robust and attractive perennial shrub with smooth-shaped heart leaves that is native to many South Pacific Islands. It is harvested when it is 6 to 8 feet in height.

The part used is the root, where the active ingredients, known as the kavalactones, are concentrated.

Actions

~Induces tranquility and sociability.

~Promotes deep and restful sleep.

~Muscle relaxing and anti-convulsing effects.

~No drowsiness or sedation.

~No addictive properties.

~Acts on certain area of brain to modulate fear and anxiety.

Dosage

~Quality extract contains 30 to 70 percent of kavalactones.

~100mg two or three times a day.

Research

~Kava compares favourably to tranquilizers.

~Kava compares favourably to placebo.

~Kava helpful for anxiety associated with menopause.

~Possible future use in treatment of epilepsy.

Side Effects

~Mild gastrointestinal disturbances.

~Dry scaly skin rash, dizziness, muscle weakens only with excess prolonged consumption.

~Side effects disappear after stopping herb.

Cautions

~Do not use if pregnant or lactating.

~Do not use for young children and infants.

~Do not use with antidepressants or other sedatives.

Coping With Lupus Naturally

Lupus erythematosus is an auto-immune disease, in which the body's immune system attacks the connective tissue of the body as if it were foreign, causing inflammation. Connective tissue surrounds all body structures and holds them together.

Lupus affects nine times as many women as men. The incidence is higher in certain ethnic groups, particularly blacks and Chinese. Over one million Americans and 50,000 Canadians have lupus.

The most common type, discoid lupus erythematosus, affects only exposed areas of skin. The more serious form is systemic lupus erythematosus or SLE which can affect the skin, eyes, blood, nervous system, heart, joints and kidneys.

Triggers Of SLE

~Anticonvulsants, beta blockers, penicillins, sulfa drugs, birth control pills, and estrogen hormone replacement.

~Physical and mental stress, exposure to sun, immunization, viral infections and pregnancy.

~Chronic yeast or parasite infections.

~Delayed food and chemical allergies.

~Common allergies include dairy, red meat, caffeine, sugar, corn, wheat.

~Possible heavy metal hypersensitivity, including mercury fillings.

Natural Treatments

~Test for and eliminate food allergies through an elimination diet.

~Improve digestion since 80 percent have severe deficiencies of stomach hydrochloric acid (HCL) Take HCL, enzymes or Swedish bitters.

~Take plant sterols and sterolins (plant fats) which decrease both the inflammatory response and the antibody formation to the body's own tissues.

~Treat candida and parasites if present.

Supplements

~Antioxidant vitamins to protect against tissue damage including mixed carotenes, grape seed extract, bioflavonoids, vitamins C and E, and co-enzyme-Q-10.

~Vitamin-B-12 injections 1,000 to 2,000 micrograms twice weekly helpful.

~Over 50 percent of women have low levels of DHEA and testosterone and benefit from replacement with natural hormones.

~High quality multi-mineral vitamin, supergreen drink, B complex, flaxseed oil, and fish oil.

~The minerals zinc, selenium, calcium, magnesium.

Chronic Fatigue Syndrome

Chronic fatigue syndrome is a disabling physical illness affecting 1 to 2 percent of the population. Seventy percent of the sufferers are women, and 10 percent are teens and children.

Likely precipitated by viral illness, CFS is caused by numerous predisposing factors that weaken the immune system. These include the overuse of antibiotics and steroids, environmental toxins, nutritional deficiencies, poor digestion and absorption, chronic yeast and parasite infections, physical traumas like surgery and car accidents, major psychological traumas, and chronic stress.

Definition

~Debilitating fatigue for six or more months.

~No previous history of similar symptoms.

~No other serious illness to account for the fatigue.

~No improvement with rest.

~60 percent or greater reduction in ability to perform daily activities.

Other Symptoms: Sleep disturbances, depression, brain fog, muscle pain, low grade fever, sore throat, painful swollen lymph glands, prolonged muscle fatigue after exercise lasting more than 24 hours; impairment in short term memory or concentration; multi-joint pain without joint swelling or redness; headaches of a new type, pattern or severity; and unrefreshing sleep.

Diagnosis

~Blood tests usually normal.

~Immune defects seen in two thirds of patients i.e.decrease in natural killer cells, increase in helper cells or increase in the ratio of helper cells to suppressor cells.

~Abnormal specialized brain scans.

Treatment

~Note that there are two optimal recovery opportunities at 2 to 3 years and at 4 to 5 years after onset of illness.

~Use an elimination diet to identify food allergies.

~Digestive enzymes with meals three times a day.

~A high quality diet emphasizing fresh fruits and vegetables, whole grains and beans, supplemented with chicken and fish.

~Balance rest and activity, graduated exercise programme, gentle massage.

~Counselling and St. John's Wort for depression, antidepressants if necessary.

~Cognitive Therapy to change belief systems about self and illness.

~Tryptophan by prescription in doses of 2,000 to 4,000mg for insomnia. In the U.S. use 5-hydroxy-tryptophan (50mg of 5-hydroxy-tryptophan equals 500mg of tryptophan).

Supplements

~Multivitamin and multi-mineral in capsules four to six daily, plus a supergreen drink twice daily.

~Four capsules of evening of primrose plus two cod liver oil capsules twice daily at breakfast and lunch.

~Trial of daily vitamin-B-12 injections 1,000 micrograms daily for one month.

~Magnesium 300mg to 500mg daily at bedtime or throughout the day.

~Other important supplements include zinc, vitamin-E, mega-B-50, betacarotene, and vitamin-C.

~Six week trial of co-enzyme-Q-10 90 to 200mg daily.

~Treat chronic yeast and parasite infections.

~Support adrenal glands with extra vitamin-C, pantothenic acid, and adrenal glandulars 2 to 3 times a day.

~Support liver function through supplements and herbs.

~A course of immune stimulating herbs like echinacea, astralagus etc.

MSM Great Help For Chronic Pain And Arthritis

Methylsulfonylmethane or MSM is a natural sulphur compound, which is the major breakdown product of dimethylsulfoxide or DMSO. DMSO is an effective anti-inflammatory liquid with a strong garlic like odour. More than 55,000 studies worldwide have proven the efficacy of DMSO for painful inflammatory conditions of the muscles and joints.

MSM has the advantage of having no odour, being easy to take by mouth and it also stays in the body longer than DMSO. Like DMSO, MSM is very safe and non-toxic. It can do everything DMSO did as well as helping for many types of diseases for which Western medicine offers only limited help.

Actions Of MSM

~Relieves pain.

~Reduces inflammation.

~Dilates blood vessels and increases blood flow.

~Reduces inflammation.

~Reduces scar tissue.

~Immune normalizing effect in autoimmune disease.

Dosage

~Most economical to take in powdered form.

~Best taken with meals, can be taken with hot water or tea.

~Main side effect is diarrhea and stomach upset.

~Work up gradually to dosage that eliminates pain.

~Don't take at bedtime, as it may keep you awake.

~For painful inflammatory conditions take both orally and topically.

~Benefits may occur in days, weeks or months.

~The more severe the condition, the higher the dose required.

~Noticeable improvement may take months.

~Does not interfere with any prescription drug.

~Do not take with blood thinners or high dose aspirin.

~No toxic effects even at doses with up to 40 to 60 grams daily.

~Safe for children.

Uses

~Rheumatoid arthritis.

~Osteoarthritis.

~Fibromyalgia.

~Chronic back pain.

~Tension headaches.

~Carpal tunnel syndrome.

~TMJ syndrome.

~Tendinitis, bursitis.

~Inflammatory bowel disorders.

~Lupus and scleroderma.

~Interstitial cystitis.

~Seasonal allergies.

~Chronic sinusitis.

~Asthma.

References

The Miracle Of MSM, The Natural Solution For Pain by **S. Jacobs, R. Lawrence**, and **M. Zucker** (Putman, 1999).

Plant Steroids Aid The Immune System

Plant fats are present in every single plant. Known as sterols and sterolins, these were first identified in 1922. These fats are chemically very similar to those of animal fat, but are totally different in their biological functions. In nature, these plant fats are tightly bound to the fibers of the plants, and for this reason they are difficult to digest and absorb. Raw seeds and cold pressed nut oils are moderate sources of these plant fats.

Dr. Patrick Bouic at the University of Stellenbosch in South Africa has done extensive research on plant sterols and sterolins. Bouic found that these substances decrease the inflammatory response in autoimmune diseases, while at the same time inhibiting the antibody reaction against the body's own tissues.

How Sterolins And Sterols Work

~Help correct the imbalance causing autoimmune disease at the source.

~Inhibit the damaging effects of antibodies attacking the body.

~Enhance natural killer T-cell activity which fight viruses, fungi and bacteria.

~Decrease the T2-helper cells that cause inflammation and tell body when to increase antibody production.

~Increase T1-helper cells that attack viruses, bacteria and cancer cells and tell the body when to stop producing antibodies.

~Balance the ratio between T1-helper cells and T2-helper cells.

Useful In

~Autoimmune diseases like lupus and rheumatoid arthritis.

~Hepatitis-C.

~Type I diabetes.

~Tuberculosis.

~Fibromyalgia.

~Chronic fatigue syndrome.

~Benign prostatic hyperplasia.

~To offset side effects of cancer treatments such as chemotherapy and radiation.

How To Take

~60mg of a blend of sterols and sterolins one or twice a day.

~Called Moducare in English speaking countries and Harzol in Germany.

~May take two capsules three times a day for loading dose first week only.

~Best taken on an empty stomach.

~One or two capsules twice daily.

~No side effects.

~Safe for pregnant and nursing moms.

~Safe for infants and children.

~Children under 5 one capsule per day.

~Children 5 to 12 can take 2 capsules daily.

~Four to six weeks to develop full effect.

Further Information

The Immune System Cure by **Lorna Vanderhaeghe** and **Patrick Bouic** (Prentice Hall, 1999).

Lorenzo's Oil And The Myelin Project

Lorenzo, the only son of **Agosto** and **Michaela Odone**, and the hero of the film Lorenzo's Oil, has the rare genetic disorder known as adrenoleukodystropy (ALD) In this disorder, there is progressive breakdown (dystrophy) of the white (leuko) covering of the nerves (myelin) in the brain and spinal chord, associated with an underactive adrenal gland (adreno). Pre-natal diagnosis is made through amniocentesis.

ALD is due to the lack of enzymes that break down very long chain fatty acids (VLCFA) which results in an accumulation of VLCFA in the blood and tissues of the body, with subsequent harmful effects.

In Boys: Average age of onset is 5 to 10 years. The usual progression is loss of speech, blindness, deafness, progressive paralysis, and death within two years after onset.

In Adults: symptoms develop slowly and resemble multiple sclerosis.

Treatment

The Odones discovered a mixture of edible oils that can prevent ALD as well as halt its progression, when combined with a special diet. Although it is too late for Lorenzo, many children are benefiting from this programme.

The Vital Role Of Myelin

Specialized cells wrap myelin around the nerve in a spiralling motion. Myelin is made up of 60 percent fat and 40 percent protein. It insulates every nerve, assuring proper conduction of nerves from one part of the body to another.

Eight other inherited diseases involve the breakdown of myelin as well as the most well known of the demyelinizing diseases, multiple sclerosis.

The Myelin Frontier

The **Myelin Project**, a non-profit foundation, aims to discover ways to regenerate the myelin sheath around the nerves. The project has created a world wide network of 12 top research labs, financed many studies, and encouraged a cooperative approach to research. (www.myelin.org or call 1-202-452-8994).

Researchers have been able to successfully implant myelin generating cells into animals. In 1999, **Dr. Timothy Vollmer** of Yale University Medical School started a trial where myelin generating cells will be transplanted into 5 MS patients.

The Sun Heals As Well As Harms

Despite the well-publicized harmful effects of the sun, there is a wonderfully positive side to sun exposure. The best approach is to avoid the sun during peak hours, and rely more on shade and physical barriers than chemical barriers.

The Healing Sun

~Up to 75 percent of Vitamin-D comes from sun exposure, which is necessary to prevent rickets and osteoporosis.

~Sunshine is a more reliable source of Vitamin-D than milk.

~Spend 10 to 15 minutes in the sun without sunscreen before 11am or after 4pm.

~Fresh air and sunshine are still healthful, in off peak hours, with suitable protection.

~Sun exposure may reduce the risk of breast cancer.

The Harmful Sun

One million Americans and about 60,000 Canadians will get skin cancer every year from sun exposure. A child born today has a 1 in 7 chance of developing skin cancer during her lifetime.

UVB (B for Burning): UVB affects the outer layers of the skin and causes sunburn, delayed tanning, wrinkling, and skin cancer. It is strongest between 11am and 4pm from early spring to early fall.

UVA (A for Aging): UVA do not burn but penetrate the skin deeply causing aging skin, sagging and skin cancer. They are present all year round and throughout the day.

High Risk Factors for Skin Cancer

~Red or blond hair.

~Blue, green or grey eyes.

~Freckles easily or has many moles.

~Always burns before tanning.

~Two or more blistering sunburns before age 18.

~Works or spends a lot of time outdoors.

Don't Rely On Sunscreen Alone, Remember The Eight S's

~Seek shade.

~Slip on a shirt.

~Slap on a sombrero.

~Slop on some sunscreen.

How To Protect Yourself

Stay out of the direct sun from 11 am to 4 pm; seek out shade or carry a large umbrella. If you must be out in the sun during that time do the following:

~Put on sunglasses with 100 percent UV filter.

~Wear a wide brimmed hat, a long sleeved shirt, long pants.

~Apply a broad spectrum sunscreen that contains **PABA** and **NON-PABA** with a SPF (sun protection factor) of at least 8 for dark skinned people and 15 for fair skinned people.

Other Tips

~The newest sunscreens contain the antioxidant vitamins: Vitamin-E, Vitamin-C and betacarotene, which provide protection against UV damage.

~If you want a tanned look, eat excessive amounts of foods high in beta-carotene, eg. carrot juice, and/or take betacarotene supplements.

Cautions

~Avoid indoor tanning devices which emit 2 to 5 times more UVA than the sun.

~Sunscreens have never been proven to prevent skin cancer, only sunburn.

~Some researchers have postulated a link between the heavy use of chemical sunscreens and the rise in skin cancer rate.

Sick Men Afraid To Be Wimpy

Fearful of being considered weak or wimpy, many men ignore serious health symptoms like chest pain, fatigue, depression, insomnia, urinary problems, chronic cough and change in bowel habits. The result is delayed diagnosis, needless suffering, and decreased life span.

Facts About Men's Health

~Men in their 40's and 50's have more serious diseases than women the same age.

~Men do not live as long after cancer is diagnosed, due to late diagnosis.

~Men's inability to handle stress, express feelings and seek support puts them at higher risk for suicide, heart conditions and problems due to smoking and alcohol abuse.

~Heart disease, lung and colon cancer are strongly linked to unhealthy living.

What Kills Men

~Heart Disease, 37 percent.

~Cancer, 28 percent.

~Lung Disease, 9 percent.

~Accidents, 8.7 percent.

In an Ottawa study of 200 men, 30 percent reported depression, 10 percent considered suicide. Marriage breakdown is the major cause of suicide in men.

What You Can Do

~Improve your diet with more fibre, less fat, less alcohol and less caffeine.

~Pay attention to your symptoms and check with doctor promptly.

~If you are age 50-70, have your doctor check your prostate every year.

~Depression and anxiety are real illnesses for which you can get support and treatment.

~Take stress reduction courses or urge your employer to sponsor courses at your workplace.

~Take antioxidant vitamin-C and vitamin-E with betacarotene for extra insurance against heart disease and cancer.

~Take a good multivitamin as well as a supergreen drink.

The Red Meat Debate

Health experts disagree as to whether a meat based diet is an optimally healthy one. People who consume a diet mainly based on fruits, vegetables, whole grains and beans have lower rates of cancer, heart disease and bone loss.

Hormone implants in beef artificially raise hormone levels in cattle. Further concerns are high concentrations of pesticides in the fat of meat and dairy (like dioxin and other pesticides that are estrogen mimickers).

According to one theory, type O blood types need more protein usually animal protein, to thrive. Some claim that type O people tend to feel unhealthy and low energy on strictly vegetarian diets.

Several of the popular diets depend on high protein consumption usually from meat and dairy. Finally, many people have cultural traditions around meat consumption.

Beef

~High amounts of complete protein.

~Contains B vitamins including vitamin-B-12.

~Contains potassium and phosphorus.

~Contains moderate amounts of vitamin-A.

~Beef liver rich in nutrients especially vitamin-A, vitamin-B, and iron but also concentrates toxic chemicals unless organic.

Pork

~High protein content and other qualities similar to beef.

~Ham and bacon have high sodium and additive levels.

~Must be well cooked because pork more easily infected with bacteria and parasites.

Lamb

~High protein content.

~Moderate fat content.

~Usually antibiotics and hormones not used in raising lamb.

Organic Meat

~Always preferable as no hormones antibiotics or other chemicals used; preferably free range.

~Wild game like deer, rabbit, mouse free of hormones and antibiotics, usually less fat.

Ethical Considerations

~Twenty vegetarians can be fed on the amount of land required to feed one meat eater.

~Sixty million people could be fed on the amount of land, water and energy freed from growing grains and soybeans to feed livestock if Canadians reduced their intake of meat by only 10 percent.

~Crowded and cruel conditions in which livestock are often raised.

Rules For Meat Eaters

~Eat only lean meats.

~Trim away all fat.

~Avoid cured or smoked meats including lunch meat, sausages and hot dogs with their high salt content and cancer causing chemicals.

~Use meat only in moderation, not as main staple.

~Eat more high fibre foods like fruits and vegetables to compensate for low fibre meat.

~Add more fish to your diet.

Lung Cancer And Women

Lung cancer is the most common cause of cancer deaths in North America, responsible for a third of cancer deaths in men and a fifth in women. Lung cancer has now overtaken breast cancer as the leading cause of cancer death in women. Most lung cancer could be prevented by quitting smoking, but second hand smoke can also cause cancer.

Symptoms

~Early stages, none.

~Cough up phlegm in 80 percent.

~Shortness of breath, wheezing, chest pain.

~Coughing up blood.

Causes Of Lung Cancer

Certain: Smoking, second hand smoke, exposure to radiation, asbestos, uranium, radon gas, heavy metals and industrial chemicals.

Probable: Air pollution, genetic predisposition, low levels of antioxidant vitamins.

Dangers Of Second Hand Smoke

~Increases the risk of lung and cervical cancer.

~Increases the risk of heart disease.

~Children of smokers have lower birth weights, more respiratory infections and ear infections.

~Pregnant mothers exposed to second hand smoke had nicotine in their hair equivalent to having smoked four cigarettes a day.

Prevention

~Find a way to stop smoking, use the nicotine patch or chewing gum. A new prescription drug may be much more effective than the patch. Bupropion hydrochloride (Zyban) relieves the psychological cravings and withdrawal symptoms of nicotine withdrawal.

~Use the herb mullein and other respiratory herbs to clear the lungs after you stop.

~Pay attention to air quality.

~Ensure work areas are properly ventilated.

~Take Vitamin-C 500mg four times a day, Vitamin-E 200 to 400IU's a day and betacarotene 100,000IU's a day before and after quitting, as well as a good multivitamin and mineral and supergreen drink.

Conventional Treatment

Usual options are surgery, radiation, and chemotherapy.

Only one in four are candidates for surgery which has a five year survival rate of 25 to 40 percent. Overall only 10 to 15 percent survive for five years or longer.

Alternative Treatment

~A comprehensive programme under the guidance of an experienced practitioner is recommended.

~**The Alternative Medicine Definitive Guide to Cancer**, by **Diamond, Cowden and Goldberg** (Future Medicine, 1997).

~**Cancer Therapy: The Independent Consumer's Guide**, by **Ralph Moss** (Equinox, 1995).

~For $275 U.S., **The Moss Reports** provides a detailed 30 to 50 report specific to your type of cancer including alternative treatments, and how to obtain them (718-636-4433).

Alternative Therapies For Breast Cancer

Many factors contribute to the development of cancer. Natural medicine uses methods that stimulate the body's natural ability to heal, and corrects imbalances and lifestyle factors that led to the disease. Alternative medicine can be used alone, as part of a treatment plan that includes conventional therapy, or to prevent recurrence.

Diet Pointers

~Eliminate chemical and pesticide exposure (concentrated in the fat of meat and dairy).

~Aim at low animal fat, high fibre diet.

~Eat organic when possible.

~Increase fruits and vegetables.

~Soy foods have protective effect.

~Cheat ten percent.

Minimal Daily Supplements

~500 to 1,000mg of Ester-C.

~400IU. of Vitamin E.

~30,000IU's of betacarotene.

~400mg selenium.

~A high quality multi-vitamin and mineral, in capsule form daily.

~Spirulina or other supergreen drink, high in trace minerals, antioxidants and easy to digest protein.

Other: Adrenal glandulars, pantothenic acid, thymus glandulars, herbs to strengthen the liver, and herbs to promote lymphatic drainage.

Specific Remedies

There is no one right remedy. The treatment programme must be individualized, under the supervision of a practitioner.

714-X: An immune booster, developed by a Canadian scientist, can be ordered by your doctor or practitioner.

Essiac: Native herbal remedy developed by a Canadian nurse Rene Caisse, quality varies greatly, so buyer beware.

Iscadora: Fermented preparation of European mistletoe, approved for medical use in Germany and Switzerland. Enhances immune function.

Ozone: A highly active form of oxygen that is usually injected directly into the veins by a medical practitioner. It has been used extensively in Europe for over 50 years.

Maitake Mushroom (Dancing Mushroom): Has been studied extensively in Japan. It has been very effective in stopping the growth of animal tumours. Maitake mushroom is a powerful immune stimulant.

Imagery: Imagery is a powerful tool. It is best to create your own images to see your cells fighting the cancer, to see yourself healed and to marshal inner resources

Self-Nurturing: Sometimes breast cancer patients are **too nice**. Learn to say no to other's demands and do relaxing and soothing things for yourself.

Emotional Support: A fighting attitude is the best for survival. The worst is a helpless or hopeless attitude. But don't despair, if you fall into this later category, you can change your attitude with some work. Just expressing your feelings in a supportive atmosphere can increase survival.

Resources

Breast Cancer, Breast Health, The Wise Woman Way, by **Susun Weed** (Ashtree Publishing, 1995).

A Guide To Unconventional Cancer Therapies, by **The Ontario Breast Cancer Exchange Program. 905-727-3300**.

The Alternative Medicine Definitive Guide To Cancer, by **Diamond, Cowden and Goldberg** (Future Medicine 1997).

Healing Choices Cancer Report System is a detailed 30 to 50 page report on alternatives plus consultation call 718-636-1679.

Treating Cervical Cancer & Abnormal PAPS Naturally

The good news is that early cervical cancer has a cure rate of over 95 percent and can be detected by regular Pap smears.

Early precancerous changes of the cervix (dysplasia) can be prevented and reversed through the use of nutritional supplements and lifestyle changes.

Genital warts and even cancer in situ (cancer confined to the surface of the cervix that has not spread to the deeper tissues) respond favourably to natural treatments.

In 1993, in the United States there were 16,000 new cases of invasive cervical cancer and 7,500 deaths. In Canada, there were 1,300 new cases and 400 deaths. In the third world, cervical cancer is the leading cause of cancer death, with 550,000 new cases of invasive cancer annually.

Over 50 percent of women with invasive cancer have never had a Pap smear and die within 2.5 years of diagnosis. Another 30 percent of women with invasive cancer have had infrequent PAP tests.

How Often Should You Get A PAP Smear?

~Every year for all sexually active women between 18 and 35.

~Every 3 years for women between 35 and 69, then discontinued if all previous smears negative.

~If abnormal, get checked for infections which can cause mild to moderately abnormal smears, which return to normal after treatment.

Risk Factors For Cervical Cancer

~Two to four times increased incidence with smoking.

~May be sexually transmitted: 95 percent of invasive cancers are positive for wart virus.

~HIV positive women have 8 to 11 times higher risk.

~Women who have taken the pill, especially if taken for more than 10 years.

~Condoms, diaphragms and cervical caps have protective effect.

~Risk increases with number of sexual partners and earlier age of first sexual encounter.

Natural Treatments For Abnormal PAPS

~Can be prevented and reversed.

~Folic acid alone can reverse mildly abnormal Paps.

~Vitamin-A applied to the cervix using a cervical cup four days in a row, then 2 to 4 days a month for 3 to 6 months reverses mild or moderate cervical dysplasia.

Suggested Supplements: folic acid 10mg per day for three months than 2.5mg daily, Vitamin-B-6 50mg three times a day, Vitamin-B-12 1mg a day; betacarotene 20,000IU's per day; Vitamin-C 1,000mg per day, Vitamin-E 200 to 400IU's per day; selenium 400mcg per day; zinc pincolate 30mg per day.

Treatment

With moderate and severe dysplasia, and cancer in situ, cryosurgery, cone biopsy or **LEEP** (loop electrode excision procedure) to remove abnormal cells. These procedures result in a 95 percent curative. Invasive cancer requires a hysterectomy and other more aggressive treatment.

Naturopathic doctor, **Dr. Tori Hudson**, has devised a diet, vitamin and herb protocol that includes a herbal pack and vitamin-A applied to the cervix. This programme has reversed cancer in situ and genital warts. To find a naturopath close to you call **The American Association of Naturopathic Physicians** 206-323-7610 or **The Canadian Naturopathic Association** 416-233-1043.

How To Prevent Cancer

Eighty percent of all cancers are related to environmental factors. This includes second hand smoke, contaminated food, water and air, heavy metals, industrial chemicals, pesticides, and radiation.

Nothing is known about the toxic side effects of 80 percent of the 50,000 industrial chemicals introduced in the last 50 years.

Organochlorines are persistent toxic chemicals produced by the industries that make PVC plastics and bleached white paper products. These chemicals are concentrated in the fat of meat and dairy.

The good news is that there is much you can do to reduce your toxic load and accumulative total exposure. In addition, you can prevent the free radical damage caused by these potentially cancer causing agents through taking nutritional supplements.

Diet

~Trim fat from meat, eat only low fat dairy.

~Reduce or eliminate red meat.

~Choose deep sea fish (like arctic char, halibut, orange roughy, red snapper, sea bass and tuna).

~Eat plenty of fruits and vegetables.

~Eat organic food as much as possible.

~Filter your water.

~Avoid binge drinking or heavy alcohol use.

Lifestyle

~Refuse to use bleached paper products, including sanitary napkins and tampons (unbleached sanitary products are found in health food stores).

~Avoid dark permanent and semi-permanent hair dyes.

~Use meditation, prayer or other stress relieving strategies.

~Get help for depression.

Home And Work

~Avoid using chemicals and pesticides for home, lawn and garden.

~Take off shoes at door to reduce tracking lead and other contaminants into the house.

~Use alternatives to PVC building materials.

~Eliminate soft PVC children's toys.

~Move electric clock to the foot of the bed.

~Keep your water bed heater turned off at night.

~Sit three feet from your computer screen and four feet from others' computers.

~Improve air quality at home and at work.

Supplements

~Take a good multi-mineral and vitamin daily.

~Take antioxidants vitamin-C, vitamin-E and betacarotene daily.

~Take supergreen drinks containing wheat sprouts and sea algae for antioxidants and trace minerals.

Reference

~**The Breast Cancer Prevention Program**, by **Samuel Epstein** and **David Steinman** (Macmillan, 1997).

~**The Safe Shopper's Bible** by David Steinman (Macmillan, 1995).

~**Greenpeace Websites** (www.greenpeace.org and www.greenpeacecanada.org).

Mammograms

Introduction

A mammogram or X-ray picture of the breast is used to both to diagnose and screen for breast cancer. Twenty five percent of women have predictable risk factors, but the main risk is age. Hormone replacement therapy for six or more years is thought to increase the risk of breast cancer by as much as forty percent.

Why

~You or your doctor find a suspicious lump in your breast and you want to find out if it is cancer.

~Your breasts are normal but you want to see if a tiny cancer has started to grow.

Usefulness Of Routine Screening

~Must be performed well and read well. Best done in centers that do at least 20 to 30 mammograms a day.

~For women 50 and older, there is a 30 to 40 percent reduction in yearly breast cancer death rate.

~For women under 50, there is no proven reduction in death rate.

Drawbacks Of Screening Mammograms

False Positives: If suspicious mammogram and biopsy done, only 10 to 20 percent turn out to be cancer.

False Negatives: About 1 to 5 percent of mammograms read as normal but cancer present, more often in women under 50.

In younger women, breasts are more dense, and mammograms harder to read. In addition, cancer can appear in the interval between screenings.

Other Aids

Thorough exam of breasts by trained doctor or nurse every year alone may reduce death rate as much as exam plus mammogram in women 50 or older.

Self exam of the breasts is effective only if well taught. An educational tool can teach women accurate self exam using an instructional video and breast model. Contact **Mammacare 1-800-MAM-CARE** or 1-800-626-2273 or 352-375-0607 or 352-375-6111 fax. Website is at www.mammacare.com

How To Avoid Caesarean Sections

One in five women in Canada and the United States will have major abdominal surgery to deliver their babies. These surgical births or Caesarean sections are the most common operation performed in the United States and Canada. About one million women in the U.S. and up to 66,000 in Canada get C-Sections every year.

Up to fifty percent of sections are unnecessary. Forty percent are repeat sections two to four times riskier for the mother compared to vaginal births.

The United States has the highest C-section rate in the world followed by Canada and Australia. European countries have half the C-section rate, but the same good results for baby and mom.

First Time Sections

~20 to 30 percent of first sections due to the catch all diagnosis of "dystocia".

~Dystocia refers to a difficult or prolonged labour; failure of cervix to open up fast enough; or pelvis too small.

~Incorrect diagnosis if made in the latent or slow part of labour.

~Labour is faster if mother is moving and walking throughout labour.

~Optimal position for pushing is squatting or sitting semi-upright which increases pelvic diameter.

Why The High C-section Rate?

~False belief that once a Caesarean, always a Caesarean.

~Depends on the doctor's philosophy, training, convenience, fear of lawsuits and economic incentives.

~Some say,"once a cutter, always a cutter."

~Overuse of fetal monitors, inductions, early rupture of membranes.

~Mother lying flat or immobile.

~Lack of skilled labour support.

~Lack of informed choice, find out what your doctor's C-section rate is. If it's over 15 percent, be wary.

When They're Recommended

~Severe complications during pregnancy or delivery.

~Severe diabetes.

~Baby lying horizontally.

~Sudden fall in the baby's heart rate during labour or delivery.

~Baby much too large.

~Active herpes, premature baby.

Do Not Repeat Section If

~Reason for first section does not reoccur (most reasons do not).

~Healthy uncomplicated pregnancy.

~Horizontal and not a vertical cut into uterus with previous section.

~Single baby in the normal head down position.

~No new reason for a cesarean develops during pregnancy or labour.

~No more than one to two previous sections.

Advantages Of Vaginal Births Over Caesareans

~Same risks for the baby.

~2 to 4 times lower maternal death rate.

~More pain and weakness, longer recovery following section.

~Six times lower risk of getting a chronic and disabling pelvic infection.

~Women feels empowered vs negative emotional impact of C-section.

Resources

C/SEC (Cesarean/Support/Education & Concern), **508-877-8266**. C/Sec serves parents and professionals who want information and support in relation to Cesarean childbirth, prevention and vaginal birth after Cesarean.

International Cesarean Awareness Network at 310-542-6400 fax 310-542-5368. www.childbirth.org/section/ICAN.html Its purpose is to support and inform women and their doctors, while actively lobbying for changes in birth practices.

Optimal Birth Positions

Lying on your back is probably the worst position for a normal birth. It tends to lengthen the time of pushing, and increases the chance of a Caesarean section or forceps delivery. This position is also harder on the baby, with an increased incidence of abnormal fetal heart rate patterns, and higher acidity in the umbilical chord blood which reduces oxygen to the baby.

The Options

~Lying on the left or right side with the leg supported.

~Squatting.

~Sitting semi-upright.

~Kneeling or standing (supported by attendants).

~Using special birthing chair.

Advantages

~Working with gravity.

~Shorter pushing stage.

~Less strain on the mother's tissues.

~Less need for an episiotomy.

~Squatting increases the pelvic diameter by 20 to 30 percent, moves the base of the spine back, helps the baby's head come down.

~Research also showed a shorter second stage, less pain and less forceps and sections for squatting moms.

Birth Tips, There Is No Need For Military Style Pushing

~After the cervix is fully opened up, there may be no urge to push for up to an hour. Rest and be thankful.

~Push only when the urge is overwhelming.

~Do not hold breath, but use quick pushes for four to six seconds, with mouth open and relaxed.

~Strenuous bearing down with long periods of breath holding may predispose to irregular fetal heart rhythms and interfere with oxygen getting to the baby.

~The baby's head and shoulders should ideally emerge between contractions. To stop pushing use short panting breaths like blowing on hot soup to cool it off.

Preparation

Find sympathetic midwife or doctor, work out your birthing preferences

Find good prenatal classes that teach breathing and relaxation techniques.

Some midwives suggest gentle massage of perineum (area between vagina and rectum) with olive oil daily for two to four weeks before birth.

New Hope For Painful Lumpy Breasts

Painful lumpy breasts are not normal and cause women a great deal of discomfort and anxiety. Up to 50 to 80 percent of women have some form of cystic breast disease, which is not associated with a greater risk of breast cancer.

What Is Cystic Breast Disease

~A vague term that covers a whole range of breast lumpiness and pain from mild to severe.

~Breast tenderness and enlargement for a few days before the period is normal.

~Some women with lumpy breasts have daily pain and discomfort, with an occasional larger, clearly defined cyst, which can be drained in the office under local anesthetic. If the cyst remains, have a mammogram and possible breast biopsy.

~About 30 percent of women with lumpy breasts have severe incapacitating pain that interferes with sleep and normal daily activities with frequent formation of cysts and scar tissue.

What Can Be Done

~Daily: Vitamin-B-6 50 to 100mg; Evening of primrose oil capsules two to six; Vitamin-E 400IU; Magnesium 200 to 400mg.

~Caffeine avoidance (not proven) has helped some.

~A high fibre low fat diet high may help. A three month trial off dairy may be worthwhile.

~Natural progesterone gel or cream rubbed into the breasts during last two weeks of cycle. A six percent natural progesterone cream can be ordered by your doctor through the **Women's International Pharmacy (1-800-279-5708)** or any compounding pharmacy. (to find the one closest to you, call 713-933-8400 or 1-800-927-4227).

~Hot castor oil packs.

~Iodine replacement.

Iodine Replacement

Canadian surgeon **Dr. William Ghent** found cystic breasts were caused by deficiency of one specific type of iodine in breast tissue. He treated this iodine deficiency with a special form of iodine, not yet on the market. Treatment resulted in 95 percent of women having their breast tissue return to normal. (see October 1993 **Canadian Journal of Surgery**).

Until the product comes on the market, increase consumption of seaweeds like kelp and dulse and ocean fish like cod, sea bass, haddock, and perch. Some have found liquid dulse available in health food stores helpful. A prescription iodine known as Lugol's solution (1 drop equals 30mg iodine) 1 to 10 drops daily should be added for persistent or severe problems.

Electronic Fetal Monitoring

The electronic fetal monitor (EFM) tracks the baby's heartbeat and records the pressure of the uterus during labour contractions. Introduced in the 1970's, EFM was first used only for high risk pregnancies. Before proper studies were completed, EFM became routine in most Canadian and American hospitals. Eighty percent of women having babies are now hooked up to an EFM.

What Is EFM

The external EFM consists of two straps which go around your abdomen. One strap holds a pressure gauge to record contractions, and the other strap an ultrasound transmitter to detect the baby's heartbeat. This information provides a continuous printed record of heartbeat and contractions.

With the internal fetal monitor, an electrode is inserted into the baby's scalp and linked to a recording device by a wire inserted though the mother's vagina.

The baby's heart rate usually speeds up during contractions. A heart rate which slows down during or after contractions may mean that the baby is having some difficulty.

Is It Useful?

~Recent research has shown that EFM during labour does not improve the outcome for the baby.

~Intermittent heart beat checks by a nurse or midwife using a hand held stethoscope are as effective as EFM.

~This was true for high risk as well as low risk women.

~Routine use of EFM increases the C-section rate.

Other Disadvantages

~Mother confined to bed during labour.

~Annoying beeping alarm if mom changes position.

~EFM machines frequently break down and malfunction.

~Wide variation in EFM interpretation from one doctor or nurse to another.

~False alarms can only be sorted out through taking a sample of blood from the baby's scalp veins to measure the oxygen level and PH, which is traumatic for the baby.

~Can take the place of regular checking by the caregiver.

Other Options

~Find out whether your doctor uses EFM routinely.

~If you have no major risk factors, request your baby be monitored without EFM.

~Doppler stethoscopes may improve reliability of fetal monitoring during labour compared to the ordinary fetal stethoscope.

~Soothing presence, touch, words of caregiver or labour coach (doula) decrease complications.

A **hysteroscope** is a small lighted instrument (scope) used to look inside a woman's uterus (hyster). A video camera attached to the hysteroscope allows greater accuracy, as the doctor can see the inside of the uterus on a TV screen.

The uses of hysteroscopy range from a 10 to 15 minute office procedure for diagnosis to long complex operations under general anesthetic for treatment of various conditions.

How It's Done

The hysteroscope is inserted into the vagina, then through the cervical opening into the womb. A side connection to the hysteroscope allows a salt or sugar solution or carbon dioxide gas to flow into the uterus, to expand it and make it easier to see inside.

Useful For

~Identifying the cause of excessive or irregular bleeding.

~Diagnosing uterine fibroids (benign tumours).

~Diagnosing uterine and cervical polyps (benign tube-like protrusions).

~Diagnosing and treating uterine cancer.

~Surgically removing small fibroids and polyps.

~Removing larger fibroids after they've been shrunk with medication.

~Examining the uterus in infertility investigations.

~Finding and removing a misplaced IUD.

~Destroying the uterine lining (endometrial ablation) for women with severe bleeding, as an alternative to hysterectomy.

Complications

~Office procedure is very safe.

~With general anesthetic, 3 percent complication rate.

~Complications include uterine perforation; reaction to the liquid or gas used to expand the uterine cavity; small risk of gas embolism (blocked blood vessel caused by gas in the blood) fluid overload and heart failure; rarely pelvic infection.

The New View Of Endometriosis

Endometriosis (endo) means normal tissue in an abnormal location. It occurs when tissue like that which lines the inside of the uterus, (the endometrium) grows in parts of the body where it doesn't normally grow such as the bottom of the pelvis, uterine ligaments, tubes, ovaries, bowel, and bladder.

For five to ten million women in the U.S, and half a million women in Canada, (teenage years right through to menopause) it is a frustrating, chronic, painful and unpredictable disease, which is challenging to treat.

Symptoms

~Severe abdominal, pelvic or back pain.

~Increasingly painful periods and painful sex.

~Many types and timing of pain, which can occur at any time of cycle.

~Location and depth significant; small implant on uterine ligaments can be very painful and widespread involvement of the ovaries painless.

~Up to 75 percent of women with endo have been dismissed by their doctors as neurotic.

~Infertility common, but not proven to be caused by endo. except when organs distorted out of shape.

~Common symptoms reported: 68 percent painful periods; 52 percent bowel changes; infertility 40 percent; painful sex 32 percent and back/thigh pain 20 percent.

Diagnosing Endo

~Tentative diagnosis through pelvic exam if there are tender or lumpy ligaments or ovarian cysts.

~Laparoscope (a slender light-containing telescope to look at the pelvic organs) necessary for definitive diagnosis.

~All suspicious areas must be biopsied and sent to the lab.

~Usual blue or black spots or dark brown cysts not always seen.

~Doctor must search for atypical implants, which are clear, white, red and yellow.

Medical Treatment

~Can help pain but not infertility.

~Pain killers.

~Hormones like progesterone or danazol.

~The newest hormone blockers cause instant menopause, with many side effects.

Surgical Treatment

~Endo tissue removed with scissors, laser, or electric cautery.

~Can help pain or infertility caused by organ distortion.

Alternative Treatments

~Natural progesterone pills, suppositories or cream.

~Series of at least 12 acupuncture treatments.

~Nutritional therapies, herbs and homeopathy supervised by naturopath.

~Treat chronic yeast infection if present.

For info and support call the **Endometriosis Association** at 1-800-426-2END.

PMS
And Premenstrual Strength

Ninety percent of women in their reproductive years have symptoms before their periods. Half have mild symptoms a few days before their periods. The other 50 percent have symptoms that are more severe and last longer. Of this group, 5 to 12 percent will experience incapacitating premenstrual syndrome or PMS.

Reasons

~Exposure to pollutants (pesticides, dioxins) which mimic the action of estrogen.

~High stress levels, especially from dual pressure of work and family.

~Woman have many more periods in their lifetimes and less pregnancies.

Definition

Physical and emotional symptoms 1 to 14 days before period that go away at or during period and that interfere with relationships and daily activities.

Symptoms

Physical: Breast swelling and tenderness, weight gain, abdominal bloating, constipation or diarrhea, headaches, sugar and salt cravings, clumsiness, insomnia, changes in sex drive.

Emotional: Mood swings, anxiety, irritability, weeping, anger, rage, depression, suicidal thoughts, physical or verbal aggression.

Diagnosing PMS?

Write down your symptoms every day, rating severity on a scale from 1 to 10 for three months.

If symptoms clustered in two weeks before period, probable PMS.

Treatment

Diet: Reduce sugar, salt, caffeine, alcohol. Small frequent meals. Avoid processed and junk food. Reduce dairy and meat.

Supplements: Vitamin-B-6, 50 to 200mg daily. Evening of primrose oil 2 to 6 capsules a day. Vitamin-E 200 to 400 IU daily. Magnesium 300 to 500mg daily.

Other: Natural progesterone pills, suppositories or cream. Tryptophan 2,000 to 6,000mg a day helpful for insomnia, depression, irritability and mood swings

~Treat yeast infections and food allergies.

~Check for low thyroid function.

~Take herbs to improve liver function.

Stress Reduction: Counselling and support. Consult with a sympathetic doctor. Drugs as last resort.

Positive PMS

~Enjoy increased energy levels, sex drive and creativity.

~Be more assertive, have the courage to tell the truth.

~Examine the causes of anger such as marital problems and get help.

~Take time out for yourself.

~Specify how others can help you.

~Insist others pull their weight in the household.

Coping With Pelvic Infection

Pelvic inflammatory disease (**PID**) affects 100,000 Canadian women, and over one million women in the United States. It is the leading cause of preventable infertility and tubal pregnancy. Other long-term complications such as chronic pain, scarring of pelvic organs, and chronic infection, are common after only one episode.

What Is PID?

PID is an infection or inflammation of a woman's uterus, tubes, and ovaries. PID is usually caused by sexually transmitted diseases like chlamydia and gonorrhea. Chlamydia is the main cause of new PID in women age 15 to 29. If left untreated, these infections can travel up into the uterus and tubes.

Women who have procedures that open the cervix like D-and-C's, abortions, and insertion of IUD's are also vulnerable to infection.

How Can A Woman Tell If She Has PID?

~Symptoms include lower abdominal pain, low back pain, fatigue, fever, vaginal discharge, vaginal bleeding, abdominal swelling, painful sex and painful periods. Often there are no symptoms present or just one or two.

~The diagnosis is suspected if the doctor finds uterine and tubal tenderness or swelling, and pain on moving the cervix during pelvic exam.

~Cervical cultures and blood tests may be negative.

~Definitive diagnosis only through laparoscopic exam with cultures being taken for confirmation.

Three Part Treatment Of PID

~Multiple antibiotics to kill the infection.

~Sexual partners treated with antibiotics.

~Complete bed rest and abstinence from sex to help the pelvic organs heal.

Hysterectomy is **NOT** recommended although one in every ten women hospitalised with PID in Canada receives a hysterectomy. Even with severe infections, treatment with intravenous antibiotics and surgical drainage has been found to be more successful than hysterectomy.

Prevention

~Yearly chlamydia cultures, especially for those under 24 and between 15 and 19, and for each new sexual partner. Also check for common vaginal infection known as bacterial vaginosis.

~Condom use offers the best protection against chlamydia, gonorrhea, herpes, venereal warts and AIDS.

Canadian PID Society, PO Box 33804, Stn D, Vancouver, BC. V6J 4L6. Phone: **604-684-5704**.

The Sexes Aren't Equal When It Comes To Booze

A woman's body handles alcohol very differently from a man's. The female body breaks down alcohol more slowly. A woman's body also contains less water, thus less dilution factor. During PMS, alcohol absorption is accelerated.

When a woman goes for help, her doctor might not recognize her problem and prescribe tranquilizers. Women drinkers are usually secretive and drink mostly in private. Between 30 and 50 percent of women alcoholics have been sexually abused as children or adults.

Health Effects

~Women drinkers have a death rate 3 to 7 times those of women who don't drink.

~Cirrhosis of the liver and mental deterioration at half the alcohol consumption of men.

~Nerve inflammation caused by lack of Vitamin-B-1.

~Menstrual irregularities.

~During pregnancy, serious and irreversible damage to the baby.

~Anemias due to deficiencies of iron and folic acid.

~Higher risk of osteoporosis and breast cancer.

Safe Drinking Guidelines: The New 0-3-4-12 Rule

On some days, no drinks, on any day, a woman should have no more than 3 drinks and a man no more than 4 drinks; with no one consuming more than 12 drinks a week. Problem drinkers outnumber alcoholic drinkers four to one and would benefit greatly from cutting down on drinking.

Getting Help

Alcoholics Anonymous has a well known twelve step programme and support system, which is widely available. Check your phone book for the group nearest you.

As an adjunct to AA, **Women For Sobriety** is geared specifically to women to help them develop a stronger sense of self and take charge of their recovery. To find the group nearest you, call **1-800-333-1606**.

Nutritional Support

All heavy and moderate drinkers should be taking the B vitamins, Vitamin-C and a good multi-mineral and Vitamin daily. Coming off alcohol, it is important to avoid caffeine, sugar, and refined food and to continue the vitamins. Acupuncture and massage may also help.

Cage Test

Two or more positive replies suggest problem drinking.

~Did you ever try to **Cut Down** on your drinking?.

~Did you ever fell **Angry** or annoyed when someone commented on your drinking or your behaviour while drinking?.

~Did you ever feel **Guilty** about your drinking?.

~Did you ever have a drink or "Eye-Opener" in the morning to get rid of the hangover or to face the day?

Miscarriage
The Need For Support

Between 10 and 30 percent of all pregnancies end in miscarriage. Afterwards, a woman may be surprised by her intense emotional reaction, and her urgent need for support. At the same time, friends and family may feel uncomfortable discussing the death of a baby so early in pregnancy.

Even for a short-lived pregnancy, research shows that women go through a grieving process similar in every way to women whose babies died much later in pregnancy or after birth. However, the grieving period is shorter, lasting 3 to 12 months.

Common Causes

Genetic: About half of early miscarriages involve a missing or extra chromosome in the fetus.

Structural: Twenty percent of aborted embryos are malformed

Hormonal: Low progesterone, thyroid dysfunction

Infection: Ureaplasma, chlamydia or any infection causing a high fever

Other: Heavy smoking or alcohol use; incompetent cervix, malformed uterus

Rules for Grieving

~Tell loved ones and friends how you feel.

~Don't be embarrassed to ask for help; specify what you need.

~Get answers to all your questions re the miscarriage, including all possible causes.

~Remember your baby in any way that seems right to you, including naming the baby. Pay attention to what your body needs to recover.

~Wait at least 3 to 6 months before trying to conceive again.

For Support Persons

~Listen to her feelings, and make her feel understood.

~Avoid advising, judging, evaluating or interpreting.

~Avoid comments like, "Keep your chin up," "That's life," or "It's nature's way of getting rid of defective fetuses," or "you can try again."

~Validate her right to grieve.

Resources

Surviving Pregnancy Loss, by **Rachelle Freidman** and **Bonnie Gradstein** (revised 1996, Citadel Press), **Preventing Miscarriage: The Good News**, by **Jonathan Scher** (Harper and Collins, 1991), **How To Prevent Miscarriage And Other Crises Of Pregnancy**, by **Stefan Semchyshyn** and **Carol Colman** (Macmillan, 1990).

Natural Progesterone

Natural progesterone (NP) is one of the two main female hormones made by the ovaries, and has many beneficial roles in the body.

Natural progesterone has few side effects and can be used as part of a treatment programme for endometriosis, fibroids, PMS, cystic breasts, infertility, and irregular bleeding. It can also be used alone or with estrogen to treat menopausal symptoms and to prevent bone loss.

Prolonged stress and chemicals that mimic the action of estrogen may combine to create a progesterone deficient state by the time women are in their mid-thirties.

What It Does

~Rises to highest levels during pregnancy.

~Predominates during the second half of the menstrual cycle.

~Acts as a "mother hormone".

~Converts into cortisone, estrogen or testosterone.

~Acts as a natural diuretic and antidepressant.

~Promotes the action of thyroid hormones.

~Normalizes blood sugar levels.

~Stimulates the building of bone.

~Protects against uterine and breast cancer.

~Increases the good cholesterol (HDL cholesterol).

Synthetic Progesterones

Synthetic progesterones or progestins (often mistakenly called progesterones) do not resemble the body's own progesterone, and have very different side effects. These include mood swings, irritability, depression, weight gain, and bloating. After menopause, the progestin part of hormone therapy can cause bleeding or spotting. Women can easily switch from the synthetics (ex. provera) to natural progesterone.

How To Take Natural Progesterone

Since it is destroyed by stomach acid, natural progesterone has to taken in the form of a skin cream, vaginal suppository or specially made oral capsule. These preparations can be made up by any compounding pharmacy. Prometrium, a natural progesterone oral capsule used in Europe for many years, is now available by prescription in both Canada and the U.S.

Natural progesterone is usually taken for 12 to 14 days in the second half of the menstrual cycle. After menopause it can be taken for 21 to 25 days a month.

The main side effect of NP is drowsiness, which can be offset by taking the main dose at night.

Resources

International Academy of Compounding Pharmacists at 713-933-8400 or 1-800-927-4227; **Transitions for Health** 1-800-888-6814 or 503-226-1010 natural progesterone cream (available without a prescription, except in Canada).

Natural Help For The Nausea And Vomiting Of Pregnancy

Nausea and vomiting in the first three months of pregnancy is normal. The cause is unknown, but it does not indicate unconscious rejection of the baby. By 16 to 20 weeks of pregnancy, the nausea usually begins to taper off.

Women often worry about possible effects on their baby. Research shows that healthy women have enough reserves to supply the growing fetus, even if they eat little in the first three months. Another study showed that the presence of nausea and vomiting rather than their absence was more likely associated with a favourable outcome of the pregnancy.

What To Do

Diet: Eat small frequent meals high in protein or complex carbohydrates. Avoid sugar or artificial sweeteners. Carry raw almonds, rice cakes or whole wheat crackers to keep blood sugar constant.

Powdered Ginger Root: Three or four capsules a day followed with water, first thing in the morning. Repeat as necessary during the day.

Slippery Elm: Soothing and strengthening herb for the stomach. It possesses as much nutrition as oatmeal yet so gentle it can be retained by the most sensitive stomachs. Take in powdered form in capsules or make into a gruel by mixing it with honey and hot water.

Vitamin-B: 50 to 100mg a day, is a very effective anti-nauseant. It should be taken as part of a mega Vitamin-B-50 capsule containing the rest of the B-vitamins.

Blue Green Algae: Such as spirulina, is very high in protein and other nutrients and easy to digest. Mixed with mashed bananas or other fruit.

Acupuncture: Treatments by an experienced practitioner can eliminate nausea.

For severe nausea and vomiting; If your nausea does not respond to any of the above measures, or is very severe, ask your doctor about diclectin (doxylamine 10mg and Vitamin-B-6 10mg), which has been proven to be safe during pregnancy.

Natural Relief For Menopausal Symptoms

Hot Flashes

Vitamin-E: 400IU up to 800IUs a day. Maximum of 100IU if you have high blood pressure, or take drugs that decrease blood clotting. One study showed 100IU or more of vitamin-E daily reduced heart disease risk by 60 percent.

Vitamin-C And Bioflavonoids: A controlled study of 94 women showed that 200mg of vitamin-C combined with 200mg of bioflavonoids six times a day, offered complete relief from hot flashes in two-thirds of the women, and partial relief in one fifth.

Evening Of Primrose Oil: Take two capsules after meals up to six or eight a day. If you get diarrhea, cut back on the dose, or take the capsules with meals.

Bee Pollen: Start with two capsules or chewable tablets a day. Work up to as many as 12 or more until the hot flashes stop. Make sure you aren't allergic to bee pollen.

Black Cohosh Extract: Research has been carried out in thousands of patients in Europe. One study of 639 patients showed that as early as 4 weeks after the onset of therapy, there was clear improvement in menopausal symptoms in as many as 80 percent of patients without side effects. Other studies have shown results comparable to prescription estrogens.

Mood Swings, Irritability And Insomnia

Mega B-50 Capsules: Take one or two with breakfast and one or two more with lunch, depending on how stressed you feel. Avoid bedtime use, as it may keep you awake.

Vitamin-C: 500 to 1,000mg of a natural vitamin-C capsule containing bioflavonoids.

Calcium-Magnesium Capsules: Take 800 to 1,200mg calcium and 300 to 600mg magnesium at bedtime on an empty stomach. The capsules have a calming effect and will help you sleep.

Tryptophan: Tryptophan is an amino acid, one of the building blocks of protein and is available only by prescription. In doses of 2,000mg to 4,000mg it helps you to sleep without a hangover effect.

Depression and Anxiety

St. John's Wort has been studied extensively in Europe and shown to be highly effective for the treatment of mild to moderate depression with few side effects. The herb can take up to three weeks to develop its mood elevating effects.

Kava is a shrub in the pepper family that grows in the South Seas. It has an anti-anxiety effect roughly equivalent to the effect of valium. One study of menopausal women showed the kava group had a marked reduction in anxiety, menopausal symptoms and an increased sense of well being. Kava is safe for long term use.

Vaginal Dryness

Vitamin-E: Use the same dose as suggested for hot flashes (don't double the dose for the two symptoms).

Vitamin-C: as above.

Vitamin-E Oil: Insert into the vagina with an eye dropper or cotton tip applicator or rub into the area by hand.

Regular Sex Or Masturbation: Regular sexual activity increases the tone and lubrication of the vaginal tissues.

Estrogen Vaginal Creams Or Ring: in low doses applied locally very effective and safe. Also very useful for urinary problems.

Vitex Agnus Castus: Also known as chaste tree, this slow acting tonic for the female system reduces hot flashes and dizziness, strengthens vaginal tissues, and decreases nervousness. The usual dosage is twenty drops of the tincture twice a day for three to six months at time.

Black Cohosh Extract: is another alternative which reverses vaginal dryness.

Natural Alternatives To Hormones

In spite of considerable pressure, only 15 percent of Canadian women, and 40 to 50 percent of American women take hormones. The bottom line is that healthy women do not want to take lifelong medication, with troublesome side effects and unknown long term risks. Natural medicine offers many safe and effective choices.

Natural Hormones

Natural Progesterone: In capsules, vaginal suppositories and skin cream. The oral capsule form, used widely in Europe for many years, is now widely available by prescription as Prometrium. Natural progesterone can replace synthetic progesterone, with less side effects and a better effect on cholesterol.

Natural Estrogen: In oral capsules, vaginal cream and skin cream through compounding pharmacies, derived from plant sources. Some contain a higher ratio of estriol, an estrogen thought to be protective of breast cancer.

General Remedies for the Whole System

Acupuncture And Chinese Medicine: They give excellent relief of menopausal symptoms, and can play a preventative role as well.

Homeopathy: There are many excellent homeopathic remedies- either single or in combination- for menopause available at pharmacies and health food stores. If possible, obtain specific individualized remedies from a homeopathic doctor.

Aromatherapy Pure clary sage oil, and sage oil are hormone balancers- they balance estrogen, progesterone and testosterone. The oils can be applied to the wrists, inner thighs, armpits, and bottom of the feet two or three times daily, four days on, four days off.

Vitex Agnus Castus: (Chaste Tree) slow acting tonic reduces hot flashes and dizziness, strengthens vaginal tissues, and decreases nervousness. Twenty drops of the tincture twice a day for three to six months.

Dong Quai: Root famed in Chinese medicine for the female constitution, balances estrogen in the body. Take two capsules two or three times a day with meals. Herbalist Susun Weed suggests taking dong quai for 4 weeks, followed by ginseng for 2 weeks, repeat cycle for as long as necessary.

Ginseng: Panax ginseng, either Oriental or North American, will increase energy levels and metabolic rate, stimulate the immune system, and help normalize body functions. Not recommended for those who are anxious, or have insomnia or high blood pressure.

Black Cohosh Extract: This herb has been well researched in Europe. One study of 639 patients showed clear improvement in menopausal symptoms in 80 percent of the patients with few side effects. Other studies have compared the herbal extract to premarin and shown comparable results in terms of alleviating menopausal symptoms.

Ipriflavone: Over 60 clinical trials in Europe and Japan have shown that this soy derivative prevents and reverses osteoporosis. The same studies have shown that ipriflavone is safe and has few side effects.

Glandulars: Adrenal glandular extracts, vitamin-C, pantothenic acid, licorice root tea very helpful for most women for 3 to 6 months at a time.

Lifestyle Aids

~Smoking and alcohol worsen symptoms, accelerate aging.

~Cut out excess sugar, sugar substitutes, junk food (worsen irritability, moodiness, and depression).

~Do weight-bearing exercise at least three times a week to prevent osteoporosis.

~Lift weights twice a week.

~Take more time for yourself.

~Meditation or relaxation exercises 10 to 20 minutes daily.

Natural Remedies For The Discomforts of Pregnancy

Pregnancy is a good time to get out of the habit of taking a pill for every ache, pain, cold or flu. Many drugs, even an aspirin or cold remedy, are not safe for use during pregnancy. If in doubt, check first with your doctor. Many discomforts of pregnancy can be handled through simple natural means, without resort to drugs that can harm the growing fetus.

Constipation

~Drink six to eight glasses of pure water a day.

Eat high fibre food such as fresh fruit, vegetables and whole grains.

~Take one to two tablespoons of unsulphured blackstrap molasses in warm water once or twice a day (Be sure to brush your teeth well afterwards).

~Ground flax seed, two tablespoons in water twice a day or metamucil (psyllium seed powder) without sugar are safe natural laxatives.

~Walk or do aerobic exercises to promote regular bowel movements.

~Take magnesium with your calcium to help as a muscle relaxant and laxative.

Heartburn

~Eat slowly and chew your food thoroughly to enable salivary enzymes to work.

~Drink fluids between meals instead of with meals.

~Avoid aluminum or sodium bicarbonate antacids. Calcium is a natural antacid used in doses of up to 1,200mg per day. Magnesium should always be taken with calcium at about half the dosage of the calcium.

~One teaspoon of slippery elm bark powder mixed with honey or hot water neutralizes stomach acidity and soothes the stomach. Or take slippery elm capsules or lozenges.

Morning Sickness

~Eat small frequent meals high in protein or complex carbohydrates.

~Take 3 to 4 powdered ginger root capsules with a glass of water, first thing in the morning and repeat as necessary three to four times a day.

~Slippery elm powder or capsules.

~Vitamin-B-6, 50 to 100mg a day, is a very effective anti-nauseant.

Backache And Hip Pain

~Stretch daily and do regular aerobic exercise.

~Pay attention to your posture and avoid high heeled shoes.

~See a chiropractor on a regular basis throughout pregnancy.

~Do gentle abdominal strengthening exercises.

Chlamydia, The Greatest Threat To Reproductive Health

Chlamydia (pronounced kluh mid-DEE-uh) is the most common sexually transmitted disease in the U.S. and Canada. The good news is that chlamydia is simple to test for and easy to cure. The bad news is that many high risk teenagers and women in their 20's are being neither tested nor treated.

Five million women in the United States and half a million in Canada will become infected with chlamydia every year, yet 60 percent of them will have no symptoms. Chlamydia can also complicate pregnancy, and be transmitted to the baby during birth.

Chlamydia can travel up into the womb and tubes, causing scarring and infertility. Chlamydia causes an estimated 50 percent of pelvic infections and 25 percent of tubal pregnancies.

Who Is At Risk For Chlamydia?

~Highest risk if under 24, new sex partner within 6 months, using no birth control or using pill.

~Pill makes you more susceptible to chlamydial infection.

How To Protect Yourself

~Condoms afford the best protection against chlamydia as well as gonorrhea, herpes, venereal warts and AIDS.

~Diaphragm and cervical cap provide more protection than the pill.

~Chlamydia testing essential before IUD fitting, abortion, D-and-C and at first prenatal visit.

~Get tested once a year if sexually active and again for every new sexual partner.

Signs And Symptoms

~Increased or abnormal vaginal discharge.

~Upper or lower abdominal pain.

~Pain on urination.

~Irregular vaginal bleeding.

Treatment

~Tetracycline or erythromycin, given for 7 to 10 days, for yourself and your sexual partner.

~If chronic yeast problem, add acidophilus and anti-yeast medication.

~Repeat chlamydia test four to six weeks after treatment finished.

Permanent Birth Control

When a woman or a couple becomes certain they want no more children, or no children at all, permanent birth control or sterilization is an option. The next question is who should get sterilized, the man or the woman?

Option One: Vasectomy

The vas deferens, which carries the sperm from the testicle to the penis is cut on each side.

~Simple 30 minute operation.

~Performed under local anesthetic.

~Very safe, complications rare.

~Reversal easier: 40 to 90 percent of the time, the vas can be sewn back together.

~Subsequent pregnancy rate is 18 to 60 percent.

~No long-term side effects.

Option Two: Tubal Ligation

The fallopian tubes connecting the ovaries to the uterus are cut, burned or blocked so that the egg cannot travel to meet the sperm in the vagina.

~Requires operating room, specialised equipment, anaesthetist and gynecologist.

~Five times more major complications than vasectomy.

~Reversal is a lengthy costly operation involving major abdominal surgery.

~Reversal more difficult: in 30 to 60 percent of cases, tubes can be sewn back together.

~Subsequent pregnancy rate is 40 percent.

Important Considerations Before Tubal Ligation

~Your feelings if one of your children died; or if your partner died and you remarried.

~Your financial resources; your support network; your work goals.

~Partner's co-operation in birth control and his feelings about vasectomy.

~Your energy level, major health problems, age.

~Your feelings as a woman and the role of children in your life.

~Your goals for work, schooling or training.

~Your beliefs about birth control and abortion.

Long-Term Complications And Possible Side Effects Reported

~Heavier menstrual periods.

~Increased menstrual pain.

~Increased risk of hysterectomy.

~Scar tissue in the pelvic area.

~Premature menopause.

Important Vaginal Infection Overlooked

Bacterial Vaginosis (BV) causes 45 percent of all vaginal infections and affects 30 percent of pregnant women. In 50 percent of women, the condition is harmless and causes no symptoms. However, when there are symptoms, it can easily be mistaken for yeast infection and treated incorrectly at home.

During pregnancy, BV may result in serious complications, and should be screened for at the first prenatal or pre-abortion visit, and treated promptly.

What Is It

The healthy vagina is acidic and has lots of helpful bacteria called lactobacillus which protect against infection. In BV these good bacteria in the vagina are replaced by a variety of other bacteria which can be harmful and the vagina becomes alkaline.

Symptoms when present are increased whitish vaginal discharge and an unusual fishy kind of odour and alkaline PH of the vagina. It can be easily diagnosed after a sample of discharge is examined.

Complications In Pregnant Women With BV

~Five times more uterine infections after C-section.

~Four times more vaginal infections after hysterectomy.

~Three times more pelvic infections after abortion.

~Two to three times more late miscarriage and premature delivery.

Treatment

~If no symptoms no treatment necessary.

~No need to treat the sexual partners.

~If symptoms, oral or vaginal medicines used.

~Vaginal metronidazole or clindamycin are as effective as the pills, with much fewer side effects.

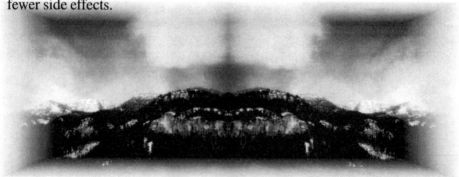

New Ways Of Dealing With Fibroids

Fibroids are benign tumours or growths of the uterus, which are two to three times more common in Afro-American women. Fibroids are the main reason for one third of all hysterectomies. However, fibroids can be removed surgically by themselves, and the uterus saved. In some cases, a comprehensive natural approach can be used to shrink fibroids or bring bleeding under control.

Fibroids are made of smooth muscle and fibrous tissue. They can vary from the size of a pea to a size of a melon. They are made of hard white grisly tissue that has a whorl-like pattern. Fibroids can be easily diagnosed through a pelvic ultrasound.

Fibroid Symptoms

~No symptoms.

~Heavy bleeding.

~Pelvic pressure.

~Urinary frequency.

~Pain is unusual.

Complications

~Degeneration.

~Twisting of fibroid on stalk.

~Infertility, miscarriage.

~Enlarged ureter, possible kidney damage.

Fibroid Treatments

Wait And See: If no symptoms or close to menopause.

Hysterectomy: Many possible side effects.

Surgical Removal: Through the hysteroscope, laparoscope or abdominal surgery.

Embolization: New technique, tiny pellets block off blood supply to fibroid.

Natural Medicine: Multi-pronged approach.

Natural Rx For Fibroids

~Decrease estrogen overload.

~Support liver function.

~Increase pelvic and general circulation.

~Cleanse and detoxify.

~Deal with emotional conflicts.

~Visualization.

Diet To Decrease Estrogen Exposure

~Most dioxins concentrated in the fat of beef and dairy.

~Eat organic, fresh, local, seasonal food.

~High fibre low fat diet.

~Avoid sugar, sugar substitutes, additives, refined and fried foods, caffeine, nicotine, alcohol.

Liver Support

~To improve the breakdown of estrogen in the liver.

~Fresh lemon juice daily.

~Liver herbs (dandelion root, milk thistle, burdock, artichoke, turmeric) support and detoxify liver.

~Bitter greens (endive, dandelion, escarole, radicchio).

~Swedish bitters help digestion and improve liver function.

General Support

~Correct low thyroid function if present.

~Extra vitamin-C, pantothenic acid, and adrenal glandulars to support adrenal function.

~Use natural progesterone cream or capsules, day 12 to 26 of cycle to overcome estrogen dominance.

~Take daily: B-Complex 50 to 100mg, 1,000mg bioflavonoids, 1,000mg each of methionine, choline and inositol to improve liver function and finally flax seed oil one to two tablespoons.

Reducing Pelvic Congestion

~Castor oil or green clay packs.

~Hydrotherapy.

~Osteopathy.

~Visceral manipulation.

~Yoga.

Is Episiotomy Necessary?

Episiotomy is a surgical incision into the area between vagina and rectum to enlarge the opening through which the baby will be born. After the birth, the edges of the cut are frozen and sewn back together.

It is routinely performed in 40 to 80 percent of births, especially first births. Many women feel that this cut is the most disabling part of childbirth.

Why Is It Done?

Many doctors perform episiotomies without being aware that their routine use has no scientific basis.

Valid reasons for episiotomy include forceps delivery, breach baby, premature delivery, and finally to speed delivery if baby's heart rate drops or baby shows signs of distress.

Side Effects

~Episiotomy may extend into rectum.

~Pain and bleeding.

~Stitches can breakdown; delayed healing.

~Painful sex, may last up to 6 months.

What It Does Not Do

~Prevent later bladder or bowel problems.

~Make vagina tighter.

~Heal faster or with less scarring. In fact, small to medium tears heal more easily and with less pain.

Prevention Before Birth

~Practise relaxation, toning and relaxation of pelvic floor muscles i.e. do Kegel's exercises 25 to 50 times a day.

~Practice breathing that stops pushing, a pant and blow-type of breath like blowing on hot soup in rapid short breaths.

~Find a good midwife or sympathetic physician.

Prevention During Birth

~Choose semi-upright or squatting position to allow gravity to help you.

~Push for shorter time periods, only when urge overwhelming.

~Keep mouth loose and relaxed while pushing.

~Let baby's head and shoulders come out as slowly as possible, between contractions, with coaching from doctor or midwife.

~Use the pant and blow type of breathing to stop pushing.

Is Ultrasound Overused In Pregnancy?

Originally used only in high risk pregnancies, ultrasound is now offered routinely many times throughout pregnancy. Routine use is now officially recommended one time only at 16 to 18 weeks. Diagnostic ultrasound is useful for high risk or complicated pregnancies.

During an ultrasound examination, high frequency sound waves scan the mother's abdomen and then reflect the fetus and placenta on a video screen. Ultrasound technology has advanced to the point where it can show genetic as well as structural fetal abnormalities.

Research shows that routine ultrasound does not improve the outcome for the baby. Long term risks for the baby are unknown and have not been adequately studied. As with other technologies like electronic fetal monitoring, ultrasound was in widespread use before its risk versus benefit ratio could be studied.

Routine Ultrasound

~Performed on healthy low risk women.

~Identifies structural abnormalities of baby.

~Predicts delivery date within two weeks 89 percent of the time.

~Shows placental position but 90 percent of low lying placentas on first ultrasound move into normal position by birth.

~Down's syndrome can now be detected with about 75 percent accuracy, especially when combined with blood tests.

Diagnostic Ultrasound

~Takes longer and answers specific questions.

~Useful for high risk pregnancies in women with diabetes, high blood pressure and other complications.

~Required for amniocentesis (taking sample of amniotic fluid to test for genetic testing).

~Necessary when complications of pregnancy develop such as tubal pregnancy, suspected twins, abnormal bleeding, too much or too little waters, and baby small or growing too slowly.

~To check for abnormal placental position.

How To Avoid Unnecessary Ultrasounds

~Keep records of periods before pregnancy to get accurate birth date.

~Have doctor or midwife check baby's position manually and baby's heart with fetal stethoscope.

~Decide how important it is to know fetal abnormalities in advance.

~Ask your doctor what information is expected from ultrasound and will that information change my care. Could other tests find out the same information?.

~No need for more than one ultrasound in a normal low risk pregnancy.

Dr. DeMarco's Christmas Gift List 1995

Books

Encyclopedia Of Natural Medicine, by **Michael Murray** and **Joseph Pizzorno** (revised, 1998). A bible for natural medicine, this book details nutritional and herbal remedies for every ailment, complete with scientific references.

Staying Healthy With Nutrition, by **Dr. Elson Haas** (Celestial Arts, 1992) a detailed and comprehensive guide to diet and nutritional medicine, including cleansing diets and fasting.

Return To The Joy Of Health, by **Dr. Zoltan Rona** (Alive Books, 1995). Dr. Zoltan Rona's 408 page book outlines the complementary medical approach to a large number of illnesses.

A Guide To Unconventional Cancer Therapies, by the **Ontario Breast Cancer Information Exchange Project**. A tabbed manual with information on alternative therapies. **1-905-727-3300**.

What Your Doctor Won't Tell You, by **Jane Heimlich** (Harper, 1990). A well researched book on alternatives for the treatment of hypertension, cancer, cataracts, etc, including chelation therapy.

Breaking The Vicious Cycle, by **Elaine Gotschall** (Kirkton Press, 1998). An effective specific carbohydrate diet that can provide lasting relief for ulcerative colitis, Crohn's disease, chronic diarrhea, and irritable bowel syndrome.

Audiovisual

Cynthia's Workout I to IV, Holistic TV fitness instructor does gentle low impact aerobics. 1-800-265-9891.

Eat For Energy videos by **Sophia Jesswein**. A lively video that emphasizes sprouting and live foods as well as how to prepare grains and beans (604-922-0285).

The Herbalist CD-ROM, by **Dr. David Hoffman**. Includes basic principles, actions, herbal pharmacopoeia, 171 colour photos and natural herbal walk.

New Books

Encyclopedia Of Nutritional Supplements, by **Michael Murray** is a comprehensive review of uses of vitamins and minerals (Prima, revised 1998).

Childhood Illnesses And Allergy Connection, by **Dr. Zoltan Rona** (Prima, 1996) is a nutritional approach to overcoming and preventing childhood illness.

Complete Candida Yeast Guidebook, by **Jeanne Marie Martin** and **Dr. Zoltan Rona** is everything you need to know for recovery plus sumptuous recipes (Prima, 1996).

Optimal Wellness, by **Ralph Golan**, is a thorough reference book on alternatives for major health problems (Ballantine, 1995).

Natural Alternatives To Prozac, by **Michael Murray** is a well researched guide for mild to moderate depression (Morrow, 1996).

What You Doctor May Not Tell You About Menopause by **John Lee**. The definitive book on natural progesterone (Warner, 1996).

Breast Cancer Breast Health, by **Susun Weed** America's well known herbalist and wise woman has written a well researched and thoughtful book on diagnosis, prevention and treatment. (Ash Tree, 1996).

Audio-Visual

Greer Childer's Body Flex's Video, is a dynamic exercise program for weight loss and improved lung capacity (1-800-263-2911).

Sounds True Catalogue, is a comprehensive catalogue of learning and healing audiotapes (1-800-333-9185).

Honouring Women's Wisdom, by **Christiane Northrup** is a six tape set covering all aspects of women's health. (1-800-525-9000).

Other

Flax Seed Eye Pillows are soothing for the eyes.

Aromatic Bath Oils for relaxing or energizing.

Mini-Trampoline is a great indoor aerobic workout that promotes lymphatic drainage.

Dr. DeMarco's Christmas Gift List 1997

Books

The Power of Superfoods, by **Sam Graci** (Prentice Hall, 1997) is a practical enthusiastic overview of nutrition and timeless rules for healthy living, $29.95.

Dr. Susan Love's Hormone Book (Random House, 1997) is an excellent review of the pros and cons of hormones for the undecided including alternatives to hormones, $35.00.

Estrogen The Natural Way, Over 250 Easy And Delicious Recipes For Menopause by **Nina Chandler** (Villard, 1997) provides new ways to add soy and flax seed to your diet.

Close To The Bone, Life Threatening Illness And The Search For Meaning, by **Jean Shinoda Bolen** (Scribner, 1996) is a helpful book for both patients, their families and loved ones.

Cancer As A Turning Point A Handbook For People With Cancer, Their Families And Health Professionals, by **Lawrence LeShan** (Plume, revised 1994).

An Alternative Medicine Definitive Guide To Cancer, by **W. John Diamond**, **W. Lee Cowden** with **Burton Goldberg** (Future Medicine 1997). This 1,116 page book is an exhaustive review of natural treatments for cancer with protocols from 37 doctors, extensively referenced, $69.95.

Stocking Stuffers

~Energizing super green products.

~Rescue remedy flower remedy for panic or stress.

~Flu kit: echinacea, zinc lozenges, vitamin-A and vitamin-C.

~Slippery elm lozenges for sore throat.

~The Essential Seven: high quality essential oils: lavender, lemon, peppermint, peace and calming, panaway, joy, purification. These oils are indispensable for first aid and household use.

Young Living Essential Oils These oils are of the highest quality. Call 1-800-763-9963 and use the live prompt for easier and faster service. Your first order requires the member number of whomever has educated you about the oils.(#124899) To become a distributor, (the most economic way to purchase the oils), there is a minimum first order of $50. In addition, you are required to purchase a Policies and Procedure Manual for $5. The Essential 7 kit can he ordered from them.

Audiovisual

Listen To Your Body, by **Carola Barczak** a series of five ninety minute videos that discuss 55 nutritional factors in depth (705-746-7839).

The Herbal Prescriber, by **Christopher Hobbs** (1995) is disc based software that provides quick access to over 2,000 remedies and 30 therapeutic diets for 450 common ailments (1-800-373-7105).

Other

~Shower head that removes chlorine from the water.

~The kefir maker, (kefir is a unique healthful cultured milk food with similar health benefits as yogurt) 1-800-663-2212.

~Ecosave laundry discs (set of 3 last for 700 loads) eliminate the use of harsh detergents, available at health food stores.

Dr. DeMarco's Christmas Gift List 1998

Books

Making The Best Of The Basics, Family Preparedness Guidebook, by **James Stevens** (Old Leaf Press, 1997). The bible on how to store food water and essentials for any emergency, whether natural disaster or getting laid off (www.get ready.net).

The Breast Cancer Prevention Program, by **Samuel Epstein** and **David Steinman** (Macmillan, 1997). Comprehensive guide to environmental, lifestyle, and occupational risk factors for breast cancer, and how to avoid them, with detailed references.

What Your Doctor May Not Tell You About Premenopause, by **Dr. Jesse Hanley**, **Virginia Hopkins** and **Dr. John Lee**. (Warner, 1999) is an excellent guide on how to balance your hormones and your life naturally in the tumultuous years leading up to menopause.

The Tea Tree Oil Bible, by **Ali, Grant, Nakla, Patel, Vegotsky** (Ages, 1998). An excellent guide to the first aid and household use of this powerful disinfectant anti-inflammatory and immune stimulant,

St. John's Wort, A Common Sense Guide To Understanding And Using St. John's Wort, by **Hyla Cass** (Avery, 1998). This psychiatrist provides a practical guide, including how to make the switch from drug treatments

Stocking Stuffers

~Small homeopathic first aid kit.

~Aromatherapy samplers.

~Beeswax candles.

~Echinacea herbal candies.

Audio-Visual

African Healing Dance Video, by **Wyoma And The Dancers** and **Drummers of Damballa**, (Sounds True, 1997). step by step course on healing African dance.

Rhythms Of The Chakras, Drumming For The Body's Energy Centers, by **Glen Velez** (Sounds True).

Synchronicity Tapes, Meditative Music That Can Induce A Relaxed Theta Wave State, Sounds True Catalogue (1-800-333-9185).

A-Z Word Index

electro-acupuncture* 123, 138, 179, 193
electro-magnetic fields, ELF* 145
electro-magnetic fields* 145, 146
electro-magnetic radiation* 146, 160
electro-magnetic waves, ELF* 145
electro-muscle stimulation* 157
electrode excision, loop* 235
electrolysis* 153
electromagnetic fields* 156
electromagnetic radiation* 93
electronic fetal monitoring* 245, 275
electrotherapy* 195
ELF electro-magnetic fields* 145
ELF electro-magnetic waves* 145
elimination diet, food* 142
elm, slippery* 46, 150, 159, 190, 207, 260, 265, 279
elmiron* 106
embolism, gas* 247
embryos, aborted* 256
emotional reaction* 256
emotional stress* 103
emphysema* 202
Encephalitis* 118
endocrinologist* 24, 42, 174
endometrial ablation* 54, 55, 197
endometrial-like tissue, abnormal* 99
endometriosis, mild* 184
endometriosis pain* 100
endometriosis patients* 99
endometriosis, severe* 184
endometriosis, symptoms of* 100
endometriosis* 17, 99, 100, 101, 102, 178, 184, 185, 248, 249, 258
endometrium* 99, 248
enema, barium* 149
enteroviruses* 118
environmental allergies* 42, 48, 64, 109, 142
environmental contaminants* 99
environmental medicine* 20, 91, 93, 189
environmental pollution* 93, 178
environmental toxins* 94, 183, 218
environments, polluted* 192
enzymes, cellulase* 129
enzymes, digestive* 138, 141, 219
enzymes, liver* 96
enzymes, pancreatic* 124
enzymes, plant* 150, 161
enzymes, proteolytic* 208
enzymes, salivary* 265
epilepsy* 33, 215
episiotomy* 241, 273
epsom salt* 158
erythematosus, discoid lupus* 147, 216
erythematosus, systemic lupus* 147, 216
erythromycin* 267
escarole* 272
essential oils* 54, 55, 56, 189, 197, 198, 279
essiac* 89, 90, 233
Ester-C* 232
estradiol* 178
estriol* 178, 263
estrogen, action of* 95, 162, 166, 177, 178, 250, 258
estrogen, amount of* 104, 174

estrogen, benefits of* 95
estrogen, breakdown of* 272
estrogen designer drug* 95
estrogen dominance* 94, 272
estrogen, effect of* 95, 104, 173
estrogen hormone replacement* 216
estrogen, levels of* 153, 177
estrogen, natural* 95, 263
estrogen overload* 272
estrogen pills* 111
estrogen, plant* 163
estrogen receptor modulators* 95
estrogen receptor* 93, 95
estrogen rich foods* 162
estrogen* 25, 26, 83, 93, 94, 95, 103, 104, 110, 111, 153, 157, 162, 163, 166, 173, 174, 177, 178, 183, 216, 228, 250, 258, 262, 263, 264, 272, 279
estrogen-like compounds* 95
estrogens, natural plant* 174
estrone* 178
ethylene diamine tetracyclic* 30
ethylene* 30
eucalyptus* 56, 198
evening primrose oil* 29, 48, 81, 104
exercise, aerobic* 25, 100, 266
exercise, fatigue after* 218
exercise, weight-bearing* 264
exercises, abdominal strengthening* 266
exercises, breathing* 139
exercises, relaxation* 205, 264
exposure, pesticide* 232
exposure, radiation* 101
exposure, sun* 225
extract, adrenal glandular* 133, 264
extract, black cohosh* 104, 171, 173, 261, 262, 264
extract, ginkgo biloba* 158
extract, grape seed* 148, 158, 217
extract, grapefruit seed* 48, 125, 179
extract, licorice root* 45
extracts, cola vera* 158
eye disease, diabetic* 133
eye diseases, serious* 132
eye doctor* 131
eye drops* 132, 133, 135
eye exams* 132
eye muscles* 131
eye pressure, elevated* 132
eye problems* 131, 163
eye specialist* 133, 135
Eye-Opener* 255
eyelids, twitching* 131
eyes, irritated* 131
eyesight* 131
eyestrain, computer related* 131
eyestrain* 39, 131, 201
eyewear, protective* 133

Letter-F

facial hair* 153
fair skinned people* 226
fallopian tubes* 268

Books, People & Orgs Index